Treasures

A Reading/Language Arts Program

 Macmillan/McGraw-Hill

Contributors

Time Magazine

Students with print disabilities may be eligible to obtain an accessible, audio version of the pupil edition of this textbook. Please call Recording for the Blind & Dyslexic at 1-800-221-4792 for complete information.

A

The *McGraw·Hill* Companies

 Macmillan/McGraw-Hill

Published by Macmillan/McGraw-Hill, of McGraw-Hill Education, a division of The McGraw-Hill Companies, Inc., Two Penn Plaza, New York, New York 10121.

Printed in the United States of America

1 2 3 4 5 6 7 8 9 006/055 13 12 11 10 09

Treasures

A Reading/Language Arts Program

Program Authors

Dr. Diane August
Senior Research Scientist, Center for
 Applied Linguistics
Washington, D.C.

Dr. Donald R. Bear
University of Nevada, Reno
Reno, Nevada

Dr. Janice A. Dole
University of Utah
Salt Lake City, Utah

Dr. Jana Echevarria
California State University, Long Beach
Long Beach, California

Dr. Douglas Fisher
San Diego State University
San Diego, California

Dr. David J. Francis
University of Houston
Houston, Texas

Dr. Vicki L. Gibson
Educational Consultant, Gibson Hasbrouck
 and Associates, Massachusetts

Dr. Jan E. Hasbrouck
Educational Consultant – J.H. Consulting
Los Angeles, California

Dr. Scott G. Paris
Center for Research and Practice,
National Institute of Education
Singapore

Dr. Timothy Shanahan
University of Illinois at Chicago
Chicago, Illinois

Dr. Josefina V. Tinajero
University of Texas at El Paso
El Paso, Texas

Mc Graw Hill **Macmillan/McGraw-Hill**

Program Authors

Dr. Diane August

Center for Applied Linguistics, Washington, D.C.

- Principal Investigator, Developing Literacy in Second-Language Learners: Report of the National Literacy Panel on Language-Minority Children and Youth
- Member of the New Standards Literacy Project, Grades 4–5

Dr. Donald R. Bear

University of Nevada, Reno

- Author of *Words Their Way* and *Words Their Way with English Learners*
- Director, E.L. Cord Foundation Center for Learning and Literacy

Dr. Janice A. Dole

University of Utah

- Investigator, IES Study on Reading Interventions
- National Academy of Sciences, Committee Member: Teacher Preparation Programs, 2005–2007

Dr. Jana Echevarria

California State University, Long Beach

- Author of *Making Content Comprehensible for English Learners: The SIOP Model*
- Principal Researcher, Center for Research on the Educational Achievement and Teaching of English Language Learners

Dr. Douglas Fisher

San Diego State University

- Co-Director, Center for the Advancement of Reading, California State University
- Author of *Language Arts Workshop: Purposeful Reading and Writing Instruction* and *Reading for Information in Elementary School*

Dr. David J. Francis

University of Houston

- Director of the Center for Research on Educational Achievement and Teaching of English Language Learners (CREATE)
- Director, Texas Institute for Measurement, Evaluation, and Statistics

Dr. Vicki Gibson

Educational Consultant Gibson Hasbrouck and Associates, Massachusetts

- Author of *Differentiated Instruction: Grouping for Success*

Dr. Jan E. Hasbrouck

Educational Consultant JH Consulting, Los Angeles

- Developed Oral Reading Fluency Norms for Grades 1–8
- Author of *The Reading Coach: A How-to Manual for Success*

Dr. Scott G. Paris

Center for Research and Practice, National Institute of Education, Singapore

- Principal Investigator, CIERA, 1997–2004

Dr. Timothy Shanahan

University of Illinois at Chicago

- Member, National Reading Panel
- President, International Reading Association, 2006
- Chair, National Literacy Panel and National Early Literacy Panel

Dr. Josefina V. Tinajero

University of Texas at El Paso

- Past President, NABE and TABE
- Co-Editor of *Teaching All the Children: Strategies for Developing Literacy in an Urban Setting* and *Literacy Assessment of Second Language Learners*

Consulting and Contributing Authors

Dr. Adria F. Klein
Professor Emeritus,
California State University,
San Bernardino

- President, California Reading Association, 1995
- Co-Author of *Interactive Writing* and *Interactive Editing*

Dolores B. Malcolm
St. Louis Public Schools
St. Louis, MO

- Past President, International Reading Association
- Member, IRA Urban Diversity Initiatives Commission
- Member, RIF Advisory Board

Dr. Doris Walker-Dalhouse
Minnesota State University,
Moorhead

- Author of articles on multicultural literature and reading instruction in urban schools
- Co-Chair of the Ethnicity, Race, and Multilingualism Committee, NRC

Dinah Zike
Educational Consultant

- Dinah-Might Activities, Inc. San Antonio, TX

Program Consultants

Kathy R. Bumgardner
Language Arts Instructional
Specialist
Gaston County Schools, NC

Elizabeth Jimenez
CEO, GEMAS Consulting
Pomona, CA

Dr. Sharon F. O'Neal
Associate Professor
College of Education
Texas State University
San Marcos, TX

Program Reviewers

Mable Alfred
Reading/Language Arts Administrator
Chicago Public Schools, IL

Suzie Bean
Teacher, Kindergarten
Mary W. French Academy
Decatur, IL

Linda Burch
Teacher, Kindergarten
Public School 184
Brooklyn, NY

Robert J. Dandorph
Principal
John F. Kennedy Elementary School
North Bergen, NJ

Suzanne Delacruz
Principal, Washington Elementary
Evanston, IL

Carol Dockery
Teacher, Grade 3
Mulberry Elementary
Milford, OH

Karryl Ellis
Teacher, Grade 1
Durfee School, Decatur, IL

Christina Fong
Teacher, Grade 3
William Moore Elementary School
Las Vegas, NV

Lenore Furman
Teacher, Kindergarten
Abington Avenue School
Newark, NJ

Sister Miriam Kaeser
Assistant Superintendent
Archdiocese of Cincinnati
Cincinnati, OH

LaVonne Lee
Principal, Rozet Elementary School
Gillette, WY

SuEllen Mackey
Teacher, Grade 5
Washington Elementary School
Decatur, IL

Jan Mayes
Curriculum Coordinator
Kent School District
Kent, WA

Bonnie Nelson
Teacher, Grade 1
Solano School, Phoenix, AZ

Cyndi Nichols
Teacher, Grade K/1
North Ridge Elementary School
Commack, NY

Sharron Norman
Curriculum Director
Lansing School District
Lansing, MI

Renee Ottinger
Literacy Leader, Grades K–5
Coronado Hills Elementary School
Denver, CO

Michael Pragman
Principal, Woodland Elementary School
Lee's Summit, MO

Carol Rose
Teacher, Grade 2
Churchill Elementary School
Muskegon, MI

Laura R. Schmidt-Watson
Director of Academic Services
Parma City School District, OH

Dianne L. Skoy
Literacy Coordinator, Grades K–5
Minneapolis Public Schools
Minneapolis, MN

Charles Staszewski
ESL Teacher, Grades 3–5
John H. William School, No. 5
Rochester, NY

Patricia Synan
New York City Department
of Education

Stephanie Yearian
Teacher, Grade 2
W. J. Zahnow Elementary
Waterloo, IL

Unit 7   The Big Question

What is the weather like today?

Enuring Understanding and Essential Questions

In this unit, children will read and write about the weather. As they progress through the unit, they will also develop and apply key comprehension skills that good readers use as they read.

Big Idea	**Enduring Understanding**	**Essential Questions**
Theme: Weather	Changes in weather affect our lives.	What is the weather like today?

Comprehension	**Enduring Understanding**	**Essential Questions**
Identify Main Idea and Details Week 1	Good readers understand the main idea of what they read and the details that support it.	Which details from the text help you understand the main idea?
Identify Setting Week 2	Good readers think about where the story takes place.	What important details can you remember about the setting of the story?
Distinguish Between Fantasy and Reality Week 3	Good readers understand if the story they are reading is about something real.	What details of the story help you to know if it is fantasy or reality?

Theme: Weather

Planning the Unit

Unit Theme Opener

Teaching the Unit

Literature Selections

Wrapping Up the Unit

Additional Resources

Unit Assessment

Theme: **Weather**

Unit Theme Opener, page xvi

Big Book

Big Book

ORAL LANGUAGE	WEEK 1	WEEK 2
• **Oral Vocabulary** • **Phonemic Awareness**	**Theme** Kinds of Weather ✔ **Phonemic Awareness** Phoneme Isolation Phoneme Segmentation Phoneme Blending	**Theme** Seasons ✔ **Phonemic Awareness** Phoneme Isolation Phoneme Blending Phoneme Segmentation
WORD STUDY		
• **Phonics** • **High-Frequency Words**	✔ **Phonics** Introduce /e/e (Initial and Medial) ✔ **High-Frequency Words** *this*, *do*	✔ **Phonics** Introduce /b/b (Initial and Final) /i/i (Initial) ✔ **High-Frequency Words** *and*, *what*
READING		
• **Listening Comprehension** • **Fluency** • **Leveled Readers**	✔ **Comprehension** **Strategy:** Visualize **Skill:** Identify Main Idea and Details **Fluency** Build Fluency: Word Automaticity Echo-Read, Read for Fluency Approaching *Do You Like Rain?* On Level *What Can You Do?* Beyond *Look at the Weather* ELL *You Can Do This*	✔ **Comprehension** **Strategy:** Visualize **Skill:** Identify Setting **Fluency** Build Fluency: Word Automaticity Echo-Read, Choral-Read, Read for Fluency Approaching *What Can Len Do?* On Level *Go and Play* Beyond *How the Bear Lost His Tail* ELL *You Can Play*
LANGUAGE ARTS		
• **Grammar** • **Writing**	**Grammar** Describing Words **Writing** Weather Report	**Grammar** Describing Words **Writing** A Sentence

Read-Aloud Trade Book

WEEK 3

Theme
How Weather Affects Us

Phonemic Awareness
Phoneme Isolation
Phoneme Blending
Phoneme Segmentation

Phonics
Review Initial: /b/b, /l/l, /e/e; Medial /e/e;
Final: /b/b
-it, -ip, -ib, -id Word Families

High-Frequency Words
this, *do*, *and*, *what*

Comprehension
Strategy: Visualize
Skill: Distinguish Between Fantasy and
Reality

Fluency
Build Fluency: Word Automaticity Echo-
Read, Choral-Read, Read for Fluency
Approaching *What Can We Do?*
On Level *In the Snow*
Beyond *The Woodpecker*
ELL *Snow*

Grammar and Writing
Describing Words, Sentences

Half-Day Kindergarten

Use the chart below to help plan your half-day kindergarten schedule. Choose Small Group and Workstation Activities as your time allows during the day.

ORAL LANGUAGE

- **Phonemic Awareness**
- **Build Background**
- **Oral Vocabulary**

WORD STUDY

- **Phonics:** /b/b, /l/l, /e/e
- **High-Frequency Words:** *this, do, and, what*

READING

- **Share the Big Books:** *A Rainy Day; In the Yard*
- **Read-Aloud Trade Book:** *Bear Snores On*
- **Read-Aloud Anthology**
- **Big Book of Explorations**
- **Fluency Practice**

LANGUAGE ARTS

- **Shared Writing**
- **Interactive Writing**
- **Independent Writing**

INDEPENDENT PRACTICE

- **Activity Book Pages**
- **Practice Book Pages**
- **Handwriting Practice**

Unit 7 Resources

Literature

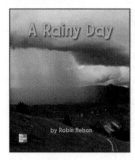

Big Book

Big Book

Read-Aloud Trade Book

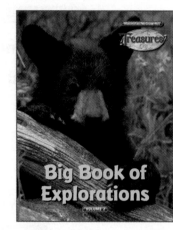

Big Book of Explorations (2)

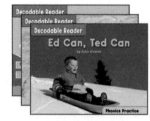

Decodable Readers

Approaching Level

On Level

Beyond Level

ELL

Leveled Readers

Read-Aloud Anthology
Includes Plays for Readers Theater

Oral Vocabulary Cards
(30 sets)

Retelling Cards

Teaching Support

Teacher's Edition

Teacher's Resource Book

Home-School Connection

High-Frequency Word Cards

Word-Building Cards

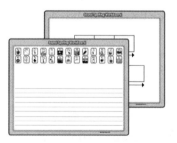

Sound-Spelling WorkBoards

Puppet

Sound-Spelling Cards

Photo Cards

Student Practice

Activity Book

Practice Book

Handwriting
- Ball and Stick
- Slant

Literacy Workstation Flip Charts

Differentiated Resources

English Language Learners

ELL Resource and Practice Books

Visual Vocabulary Resources

Response to Intervention

Tier 2   **Tier 3**

- Phonemic Awareness
- Phonics
- Vocabulary
- Comprehension
- Fluency

Class Management Tools

How-to Guide

Rotation Chart

Weekly Contracts

Assessment

Assess Unit Skills
- Phonemic Awareness
- Phonics
- High-Frequency Words
- Listening Comprehension

Unit Assessment

Teaching Chart

Digital Solutions

Go to **ConnectED** http://connected.mcgraw-hill.com
Online Center

☑ Prepare/Plan

ONLINE www.macmillanmh.com

Teacher's Edition Online

TeacherWorks Plus
All-In-One Planner and Resource Center

Available on CD-ROM
* Interactive Teacher's Edition
* Printable Weekly Resources

Implementation Modules

* Support on how to implement the reading program

Balanced Literacy Planner

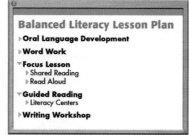

Balanced Literacy Lesson Plan
▸ Oral Language Development
▸ Word Work
▾ Focus Lesson
   ▸ Shared Reading
   ▸ Read Aloud
▾ Guided Reading
   ▸ Literacy Centers
▸ Writing Workshop

* Create customized weekly balanced literacy planners

ELL Strategies

* Teaching strategies for English Language Learners

Reading Video Library

* Video clips of instructional routines

Leadership Handbook

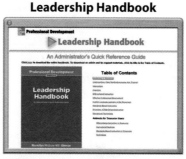

* Professional development for school principals

☑ Teach/Learn

ONLINE www.macmillanmh.com

Animated Activities

* Animated comprehension activities

Classroom Presentation Toolkit

* Weekly transparencies, graphic organizers, and guided instruction and practice

Additional Professional Development

* **Instructional Routine Handbook**
* **Writing Professional Development Guide**
* **Managing Small Groups**
* **Leadership Handbook:**
  An Administrator's Quick Reference Guide

Also available
Reading Yes!
Video Workshops
on CD-ROM

LOG ON ▶ VIEW IT   READ IT   LEARN IT   FIND OUT

☑ **Assess**

Leveled Reader Database

- Search and print Leveled Reader titles

Weekly Activities

- Oral Language
- Research Roadmap
- Research and Inquiry
- Vocabulary and Spelling
- Author and Illustrator

ONLINE   www.macmillanmh.com

Progress Monitoring

- Prescriptions for Reteaching
- Student Profile System

Online and
CD-ROM materials are
Interactive White Board Ready!

IWB

Available on CD

- **Listening Library**
- **Sound Pronunciation**

- **New Adventures with Buggles and Beezy**

Theme: Weather

Diagnostic Assessment

Screening, Diagnosis, and Placement

Use your state or district screener to identify children at risk. In addition, see tests in the **Diagnostic Assessment** book for information on determining the proficiency of children according to specific skills. Use the results to place children in the program.

- Diagnostics should be given at the beginning of the school year after you have had time to observe children and they become familiar with classroom routines. Use the diagnostics to determine children in need of intervention or to identify specific prerequisite skill deficiencies that you need to teach during Small Group differentiated instruction time.

Progress Monitoring Assessment

Meeting Grade-Level Expectations

Use these tests at the end of each unit (every 3 weeks). Multiple questions and next-steps information are provided.

Ongoing Informal Assessments
- Daily Quick Check Observations

Formal Assessments
- **Unit Assessment**

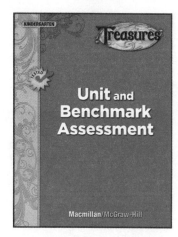

Benchmark Assessment

Give once a year to determine whether children have mastered the grade-level content standards and to document long-term academic growth.

Test Alignment

GRADE K UNIT 7 ASSESSED SKILLS	TerraNova/CAT 6	SESAT	TPRI	DIBELS*
COMPREHENSION STRATEGIES AND SKILLS				
• Strategy: Visualize	◆	◆	◆	◆
• Skills: Identify main idea and details, Identify setting, Distinguish between fantasy and reality	◆	◆	◆	◆
VOCABULARY/HIGH-FREQUENCY WORDS				
• Words that compare, Sound words				
• *this, do, and, what*	◆	◆	◆	◆
PHONEMIC AWARENESS				
• Phoneme isolation	◆	◆	◆	◆
• Phoneme blending	◆	◆	◆	◆
• Phoneme segmentation	◆	◆	◆	◆
PHONICS				
• *Ee, Ll, Bb*	◆	◆	◆	◆
• *Hh, Dd, Rr*	◆	◆	◆	◆
TEXT FEATURES				
• Photographs				
GRAMMAR				
• Describing words (adjectives)				

*Data from DIBELS serve as indicators of overall reading comprehension performance, not specific skills.

KEY

TerraNova/CAT 6	TerraNova, The Second Edition
SESAT	Stanford Early School Achievement Test
TPRI	Texas Primary Reading Inventory
DIBELS*	Dynamics Indicators of Basic Early Literacy Skills

Theme Project: Wild, Wonderful Weather

Introduce the Theme

Sing the theme song. Then Guide children to generate questions related to the theme and topic of class-wide interest. For example: *What is the weather like today? Do you know what meteorologists are and what they do?*

You'll Sing a Song, and I'll Sing a Song

You'll sing a song,

And I'll sing a song,

And we'll sing a song together.

You'll sing a song,

And I'll sing a song

In warm or wintry weather.

Song on Listening Library Audio CD

Research and Inquiry
Self-Selected Theme Project

Step 1 **Planning a Project**

What do I want to learn about weather?

- Use the **Big Books** and **Photo Cards** to show types of weather.
- Ask children to use describing words to discuss the kinds of weather they have experienced.
- Help children determine sources that might supply information about the weather.

Step 2 **Doing the Project**

- Guide children to use information books, encyclopedias, and videos about weather to gather evidence.

Step 3 **Document and Evaluate Research**

How can I share what I have learned?

You might suggest:

- recording the weather on a chart for two weeks
- drawing a picture of themselves outside in each of the four seasons
- making a scrapbook of weather using pictures and words

Help children decide what materials they will need for their presentation. See the Unit Closer on pages 1810–1811

Research Strategy

You can get information about your topic in a book. You can also watch and listen to a video that shows true information about weather. A weather video can show you what weather is like where you live and in faraway places around the world.

Teaching Chart 44A

Introduce Theme Project

WEATHER

Let's look at this photo. It shows two children holding an umbrella in the rain. Point to the children, the umbrella, and the rain falling as you describe the picture. *Does it rain a lot where you live? Are you prepared for rain by wearing a raincoat and carrying an umbrella?* Look at the photo together as you discuss the following:

- Ask: *How do you think the children feel?*

- Ask: *Do you think they are having fun in the rain? How can you tell?*

- Throughout the unit we will be learning about kinds of weather, seasons, and how weather affects us.

Connect to Content

Science

Point out to children that some places in the United States get a lot of rain. For example, Mobile, Alabama, usually gets the most rain of all of the states. Its subtropical weather is influenced by the Gulf of Mexico. Explain that rain is needed to prevent brush fires in places such as Texas.

Connect to Content

What Should I Wear?

Ask: *How do we dress for different kinds of weather?*

■ Ask children to identify pieces of clothing and then sort them by season into four baskets. Label the baskets by season.

■ Have children work in small groups to make a card to represent each season. Have one child pick a season card and dress up in clothing from the appropriate basket. Have other children guess the season.

■ When finished, have children make and record observations about what they learned.

Character Building: Responsibility

Use the What Should I Wear? activity to discuss ways that children can be responsible for their own health. Explain that wearing clothing such as jackets, hats, and rain boots helps to protect our bodies from wind, snow, and rain.

Minilesson

Using the Media: Weather Forecasts

Explain Most daily and weekly newspapers include local or national weather forecast. A **weather forecast** predicts, or guesses, what the weather will be like tomorrow and for the next few days. A weather forecast can help us plan our activities, know what to wear, and know what kind of weather to expect outside.

Discuss Ask: *Why is it helpful to know what the weather will be?* (It will help in choosing what to wear and which activities to do.)

Apply Have children locate the weather forecast in their local newspaper. As a class, discuss the components of a typical weather forecast.

Connect to Content

The Four Seasons

Ask: *Can you hear Spring, Summer, Fall, and Winter?*

- Play a CD of Vivaldi's "The Four Seasons." Ask children to close their eyes as they listen and imagine what season they hear in the music.

- Stop the CD after each piece and ask children to draw and label pictures of what they "see" in their imagination.

- Display children's drawings on a bulletin board titled *We Hear Seasons*.

Communication

Help children

- engage in substantive conversations, building on prior responses and remaining following rules for discussion, including taking turns and speaking one at a time;

- identify techniques used in media and understand the main idea or message.

Minilesson

Using Pictures to Document Research

Explain Sometimes, the best way to record what you have learned is by using pictures. A **meteorologist** is a scientist who studies the weather. Meteorologists use pictures in their job every day. They look at maps and charts to find out what the weather will be like. For a meteorologist, pictures are more useful than words for sharing information.

Discuss Ask: *What are some pictures we could use to tell about weather?* (The sun, clouds, raindrops, lightening bolts)

Apply Have students research the weather in different areas of the world. Students should use pictures with labels to record their data.

LOG ON ▶ **FIND OUT**

Research For technology research and presentation strategies, see the Computer Literacy lesson on pages 1808–1809. For additional research and inquiry, go to **www.macmillanmh.com**.

Week 1 ★ At a Glance

Priority Skills and Concepts

 Comprehension
- **Genre:** Expository, Legend, Poetry
- **Strategy:** Visualize
- **Skill:** Identify Main Idea and Details
 - **Skill:** Classify and Categorize

 High-Frequency Words
- *this*, *do*

Oral Vocabulary
- Build Robust Vocabulary: *blustery*, *chilly*, *cloud*, *drizzle*, *weather*

Fluency
- Echo-Read
- Word Automaticity

 Phonemic Awareness
- Phoneme Isolation
- Phoneme Blending
- Phoneme Segmentation

 Phonics
- *Ee*

Grammar
- Describing Words (Adjectives)

Writing
- Weather Report

Key

 Tested in Program   Review Skill

Digital Learning

Digital solutions to help plan and implement instruction

☑ Teacher Resources

LOG ON ▶

ONLINE
www.macmillanmh.com

▶ **Teacher's Edition**
- Lesson Planner and Resources also on CD-ROM

TeacherWorks^{Plus}

▶ **Professional Development**
- Video Library

Professional Development

☑ Student Resources

LOG ON ▶

ONLINE
www.macmillanmh.com

▶ **Leveled Reader Database**

▶ **Activities**
- Oral Language Activities
- Phonics Activities
- Vocabulary/Spelling Activities

 Listening Library
- Recordings of Literature Big Books, Read-Aloud Trade Books, and Leveled Readers

Weekly Literature

Theme: Kinds of Weather

Student Literature

A mix of fiction and nonfiction

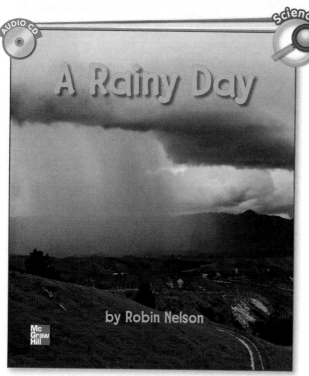

Big Book

Genre | Expository

Big Book of Explorations

Genre | Poetry

Support Literature

Interactive Read-Aloud Anthology

Genre | Legend

Oral Vocabulary Cards
- Listening Comprehension
- Build Robust Vocabulary

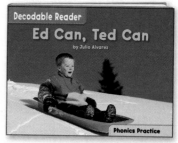

Decodable Reader

Resources for Differentiated Instruction

Leveled Readers: Science

GR Levels A–G

Genre	Expository

- Same Theme
- Same Vocabulary/Phonics
- Same Comprehension Skills

A

Approaching Level

B

On Level

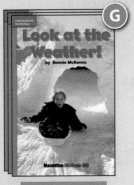

G

Beyond Level

A

ELL

LOG ON ▶ **Leveled Reader Database**
Go to www.macmillanmh.com.

Practice

Activity Book

Practice Book

ELL Practice Book

Response to Intervention

Tier 2

- Phonemic Awareness
- Phonics
- Vocabulary
- Comprehension
- Fluency

Tier 3

Unit Assessment

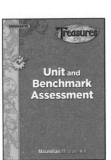

Assess Unit Skills

- Phonemic Awareness
- Phonics
- High-Frequency Words
- Listening Comprehension

HOME-SCHOOL CONNECTION

- Family letters in English and Spanish
- Take-home stories and activities

Go to **www.macmillanmh.com** for Online Lesson Planner

 **TeacherWorks** *Plus*
All-In-One Planner and Resource Center

Professional Development
Video Library

Big Book
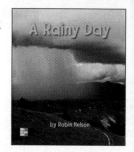

WHOLE GROUP

ORAL LANGUAGE

DAY 1

DAY 2

• **Oral Vocabulary**

❓ Focus Question What is the weather like today?
Build Background, 1566
Oral Vocabulary *blustery, chilly, cloud, drizzle, weather,* 1566

❓ Focus Question What do you see outside this school when it rains?

Oral Vocabulary *blustery, chilly, cloud, drizzle, weather,* 1574
Sound Words, 1581

• **Phonemic Awareness**

Phonemic Awareness
Phoneme Isolation, 1569

Phonemic Awareness
Phoneme Blending, 1582

WORD STUDY

• **Phonics**

Phonics
Introduce /e/e, 1570
Handwriting: Write Ee, 1571
Activity Book, 4
Practice Book, 141

Phonics
Review /e/e, /d/d, /r/r, 1582
Blend with /e/e, 1583

• **High-Frequency Words**

High-Frequency Words
this, *do*, 1568

Review High-Frequency Words, 1584

READING

• **Listening Comprehension**

• **Apply Phonics and High-Frequency Words**

Share the Big Book
A Rainy Day
Strategy: Visualize, 1567
Skill: Identify Main Idea and Details, 1567

Big Book

Reread the Big Book
A Rainy Day
Strategy: Visualize, 1576
Skill: Identify Main Idea and Details, 1576
Retell, 1580
Decodable Reader:
Ed Can, Ted Can, 1584
Activity Book, 5–6
Practice Book, 142
Fluency Echo-Read, 1580

Big Book

• **Fluency**

LANGUAGE ARTS

• **Writing**

• **Grammar**

Shared Writing
Lists, 1573
Grammar
Describing Words (Adjectives), 1572

Interactive Writing
Sentences, 1585

ASSESSMENT

• **Informal/Formal**

Quick Check Phonemic Awareness, 1569

Quick Check Comprehension, 1580

SMALL GROUP Lesson Plan ⟩ **Differentiated Instruction 1560–156**

Half-Day Kindergarten

Teach Core Skills
Focus on tested skill lessons, other lessons, and small group options as your time allows.

Priority Skills

Phonemic Awareness/Phonics	High-Frequency Words	Oral Vocabulary	Comprehension
Phonics /e/*e*	*this, do*	Sound Words	**Strategy:** Visualize **Skill:** Identify Main Idea and Details

---

DAY 3

❓ Focus Question What do you like about rainy weather?

Oral Vocabulary *blustery, chilly, cloud, drizzle, weather,* 1586

Oral Vocabulary Cards: "How Thunder and Lightning Came to Be"

✔ **Phonemic Awareness**
Phoneme Isolation, 1591

✔ **Phonics**
Review /e/*e*, 1592
Blend with /e/*e*, 1593
Read Words, 1593

✔ **High-Frequency Words**
this, *do*, 1590
Activity Book, 7–8
Practice Book, 143–144
Read for Fluency, 1590

Read the Big Book of Explorations:
"The Wind," 13
"Slip on Your Raincoat," 13
"Four Seasons," 14
"Rain on the Rooftops," 14
Literary Element:
Onomatopoeia, 1588

Big Book of Explorations

Independent Writing
Prewrite and Draft a Weather Report, 1595
Grammar
Describing Words (Adjectives), 1594

Quick Check **High-Frequency Words**, 1590

DAY 4

❓ Focus Question Do you know what the weather will be tomorrow?

Oral Vocabulary *blustery, chilly, cloud, drizzle, weather,* 1596

Sound Words, 1599

✔ **Phonemic Awareness**
Phoneme Blending, 1600

✔ **Phonics**
Word Sort, 1600
Blend with /e/*e*, 1601
Activity Book, 9
Practice Book, 145
✔ **Review High-Frequency Words**, 1602

Interactive Read Aloud
Listening Comprehension, 1598

Read Aloud: "Frog and Locust"

Decodable Reader:
Ed Can, Ted Can, 1602

Read Aloud

Independent Writing
Revise and Edit a Weather Report, 1603

Quick Check **Phonics**, 1601

DAY 5
Review and Assess

❓ Focus Question This week we read about kinds of weather. Which do you like best?

Oral Vocabulary *blustery, chilly, cloud, drizzle, weather,* 1604

Sound Words, 1606

✔ **Phonemic Awareness**
Phoneme Segmentation, 1607

✔ **Phonics**
Read Words, 1608
Dictation, 1608
Activity Book, 12

✔ **High-Frequency Words**
this, *do*, *are*, *for*, *you*, *play*, 1606

Read Across Texts
Strategy: Visualize, 1605
✔ **Skill:** Identify Main Idea and Details, 1605
Activity Book, 11

Fluency Word Automaticity, 1606

Independent Writing
Publish and Present a Weather Report, 1609

✔ **Weekly Assessment, 1636–1637**

Differentiated Instruction

What do I do in small groups?

Teacher-Led Small Groups

Independent Activities

IF... children need additional instruction, practice, or extension based on your **Quick Check** observations for the following priority skills

 Phonemic Awareness
Phoneme Isolation, Blending, Segmentation

 Phonics
Ee

High-Frequency Words
this, *do*

 Comprehension
Strategy: Visualize
Skill: Identify Main Idea and Details

THEN...

Approaching	Preteach and
ELL	Reteach Skills
On Level	Practice
Beyond	Enrich and Accelerate Learning

 Suggested Small Group Lesson Plan

	DAY 1	DAY 2
Approaching Level **Tier 2** • **Preteach/Reteach** **Tier 2 Instruction**	• Oral Language, 1610 • High-Frequency Words, 1610 **ELL** High-Frequency Words Review, 1610 • Phonemic Awareness, 1611 • Phonics, 1611 **ELL** Sound-Spellings Review, 1611	• Oral Language, 1616 • High-Frequency Words, 1616 **ELL** • Phonemic Awareness, 1617 • Phonics, 1617
On Level • **Practice**	• High-Frequency Words, 1612 • Phonemic Awareness/Phonics, 1612 **ELL**	• Phonics, 1618
Beyond Level • **Extend/Accelerate** **Gifted and Talented**	• High-Frequency Words/Vocabulary, 1613 **ELL** Expand Oral Vocabulary, 1613 • Phonics, 1613	• Phonics, 1618
ELL • **Build English Language Proficiency** • See **ELL** in other levels.	• Oral Language Warm-Up, 1614 • Academic Language, 1614 • Vocabulary, 1615	• Access to Core Content, 1619

Small Group

Focus on Leveled Readers

Levels A–G

Approaching

On Level

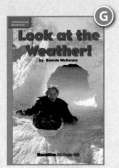
Beyond

ELL

Additional Leveled Readers

LOG ON **Leveled Reader Database**
www.macmillanmh.com

Search by

- Comprehension Skill
- Content Area
- Genre
- Text Feature
- Guided Reading Level
- Reading Recovery Level
- Lexile Score
- Benchmark Level

Subscription also available

Manipulatives

Sound-Spelling WorkBoards

Sound-Spelling Cards

Photo Cards

High-Frequency Word Cards

Visual Vocabulary Resources

DAY 3

- High-Frequency Words, 1620 **ELL**
- Phonemic Awareness, 1620
- Phonics, 1621
- Decodable Reader, 1621

- Decodable Reader, 1622

- Decodable Reader, 1622

- Access to Core Content, 1623
- Grammar, 1623

DAY 4

- Phonemic Awareness, 1624
- Phonics, 1624 **ELL**
- Leveled Reader Lesson 1, 1625

- Leveled Reader Lesson 1, 1626 **ELL**

- Leveled Reader Lesson 1, 1627
  Synthesize, 1627

- Leveled Reader, 1628–1629

DAY 5

- Phonemic Awareness, 1630
- Phonics, 1630 **ELL**
- Leveled Reader Lesson 2, 1631
- High-Frequency Words, 1631

- Leveled Reader Lesson 2, 1632

- Leveled Reader Lesson 2, 1633
- Expand Vocabulary, 1633 **ELL**

- Fluency, 1634
- High-Frequency Words, 1635
- Writing, 1635

Managing the Class

What do I do with the rest of my class?

Teacher-Led Small Groups

Independent Activities

- Activity Book
- Practice Book
- ELL Practice Book
- Leveled Reader Activities
- Literacy Workstations
- Online Activities
- Buggles and Beezy

Classroom Management Tools

Weekly Contract

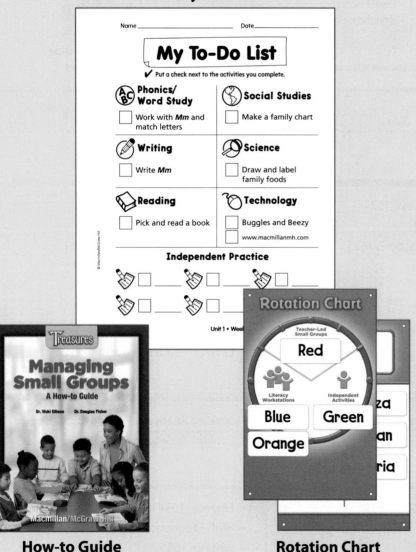

Name _____ Date _____

My To-Do List
✓ Put a check next to the activities you complete.

Phonics/ Word Study
☐ Work with *Mm* and match letters

Social Studies
☐ Make a family chart

Writing
☐ Write *Mm*

Science
☐ Draw and label family foods

Reading
☐ Pick and read a book

Technology
☐ Buggles and Beezy
☐ www.macmillanmh.com

Independent Practice

Unit 1 • Week

How-to Guide

Treasures
Managing Small Groups
A How-to Guide
Dr. Vicki Gibson Dr. Douglas Fisher
Macmillan/McGraw-Hill

Rotation Chart

Rotation Chart
Teacher-Led Small Groups
Red
Literacy Workstations
Independent Activities
Blue   Green
Orange

Phonics Activities

- Match Letters
- Match Letters to Sounds
- Blend Words

Meet the Author/Illustrator

Karma Wilson
- Karma grew up an only child in Idaho.
- Reading was Karma's first love. By the age of 11, she read about one novel a day.
- Karma's books have been translated into dozens of languages.

Other books by Karma Wilson
- Wilson, Karma, and Jane Chapman. *Bear Snores On.* New York: Margaret K. McElderry, 2002.
- Wilson, Karma, and Douglas Cushman. *Never Ever Shout in a Zoo.* New York: Little, Brown Young Readers, 2004.

- Read Other Books by the Author or Illustrator

Practice

Activity Book

Practice Book

ELL Practice Book

Independent Activities

ONLINE INSTRUCTION www.macmillanmh.com

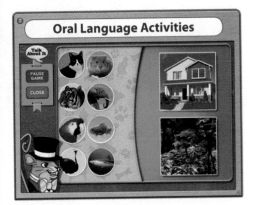

Oral Language Activities

- Focus on Unit Vocabulary and Concepts
- English Language Learner Support

Vocabulary/Spelling Activities

- Differentiated Lists and Activities

Leveled Reader Database

- Leveled Reader Database
- Search titles by level, skill, content area, and more

Available on CD

LISTENING LIBRARY
Recordings of selections
- Literature Big Books
- Read-Aloud Trade Books
- Leveled Readers
- ELL Readers

NEW ADVENTURES WITH BUGGLES AND BEEZY
Phonemic awareness and phonics activities

Leveled Reader Activities

Approaching

On Level

Beyond

ELL

See inside cover of all Leveled Readers.

Literacy Workstations

Reading

Phonics/ Word Study

Writing

Science/ Social Studies

See lessons on pages 1564–1565.

Managing the Class

What do I do with the rest of my class?

Reading

Objectives

- Read and compare books by the same author
- Read a book; write a response to a book

Phonics/Word Study

Objectives

- Use Word-Building Cards to form and read words
- Put words in order to form sentences

Reading — Read an Illustrator — 20 Minutes

Read books by the same illustrator and compare the characters.

❶ Pick an illustrator. ❷ Read the books. ❸ Talk about them.

Do More
- How are the characters in the books alike?
- Write a story. Make pictures like the ones the illustrator made.

LOG ON For more book titles, go to the Meet the Author/Illustrator page on www.macmillanmh.com
© Macmillan/McGraw-Hill
37

Phonics/Word Study — Make a Word — 20 Minutes

Use the Sound Box to make words.

❶ Pick a letter. ❷ Place the letter. ❸ Make a word.

Do More
- Make more words.
- Write the words.

LOG ON For additional vocabulary games go to www.macmillanmh.com
New Adventures with Buggles and Beezy
© Macmillan/McGraw-Hill
37

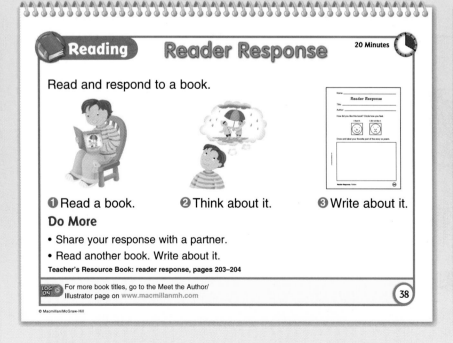

Reading — Reader Response — 20 Minutes

Read and respond to a book.

❶ Read a book. ❷ Think about it. ❸ Write about it.

Do More
- Share your response with a partner.
- Read another book. Write about it.

Teacher's Resource Book: reader response, pages 203–204

LOG ON For more book titles, go to the Meet the Author/Illustrator page on www.macmillanmh.com
© Macmillan/McGraw-Hill
38

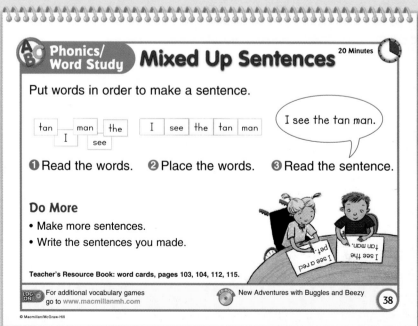

Phonics/Word Study — Mixed Up Sentences — 20 Minutes

Put words in order to make a sentence.

I see the tan man.

❶ Read the words. ❷ Place the words. ❸ Read the sentence.

Do More
- Make more sentences.
- Write the sentences you made.

Teacher's Resource Book: word cards, pages 103, 104, 112, 115.

LOG ON For additional vocabulary games go to www.macmillanmh.com
New Adventures with Buggles and Beezy
© Macmillan/McGraw-Hill
38

Literacy Workstations

Reading · **Phonics/ Word Study** · **Writing** · **Science/ Social Studies**

Literacy Workstation Flip Charts

Writing

Objectives

- Write about a favorite weather activity
- Write sentences using the words *this* and *do*

Content Literacy

Objectives

- Experiment with a variety of materials to find out if they are waterproof
- Sort objects and clothing for different kinds of weather

Writing — Write About Weather
20 Minutes

Write about your favorite weather activity.

I play in puddles in the rain.

I play in puddles in the rain.

❶ Write a sentence. ❷ Draw a picture.

Do More
- Read a partner's sentence speaking in complete sentences.
- Add your sentence to a class book with the title *My Favorite Weather Activity*.

37

© Macmillan/McGraw-Hill

Science — What is Waterproof?
20 Minutes

Find out if water will go through different things.

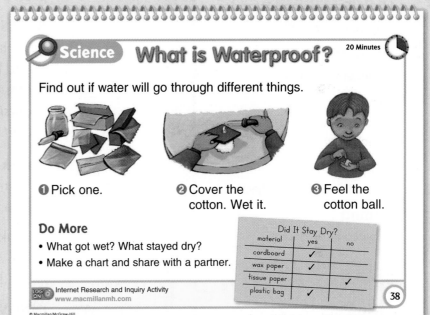

❶ Pick one. ❷ Cover the cotton. Wet it. ❸ Feel the cotton ball.

Do More
- What got wet? What stayed dry?
- Make a chart and share with a partner.

Did It Stay Dry?		
material	yes	no
cardboard	✓	
wax paper	✓	
tissue paper		✓
plastic bag	✓	

Internet Research and Inquiry Activity
www.macmillanmh.com

38

© Macmillan/McGraw-Hill

Writing — What Can You Do?
20 Minutes

Write sentences using **this** and **do**.

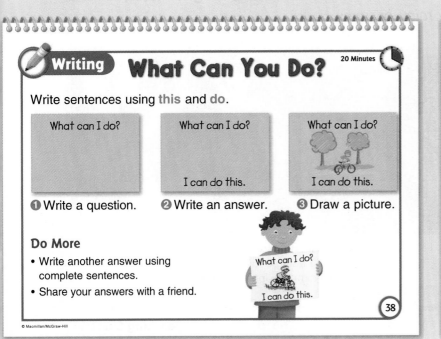

What can I do?

What can I do? / I can do this.

What can I do? / I can do this.

❶ Write a question. ❷ Write an answer. ❸ Draw a picture.

Do More
- Write another answer using complete sentences.
- Share your answers with a friend.

What can I do? / I can do this.

38

© Macmillan/McGraw-Hill

Social Studies — Weather Wear Sort
20 Minutes

Sort objects and clothing for different weather.

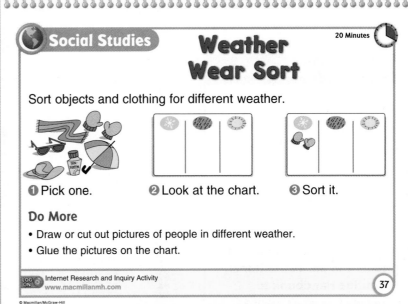

❶ Pick one. ❷ Look at the chart. ❸ Sort it.

Do More
- Draw or cut out pictures of people in different weather.
- Glue the pictures on the chart.

Internet Research and Inquiry Activity
www.macmillanmh.com

37

© Macmillan/McGraw-Hill

DAY 1
At a Glance

WHOLE GROUP

Oral Language
- Build Background

✓ **Comprehension**
- Read *A Rainy Day*
- Strategy: Visualize
- Skill: Identify Main Idea and Details

✓ **High-Frequency Words**
- Introduce *this, do*

✓ **Phonemic Awareness**
- Phoneme Isolation

✓ **Phonics**
- Introduce /e/*e*
- Handwriting: Write *Ee*

Grammar
- Describing Words (Adjectives)

Writing
- Shared Writing: Lists

SMALL GROUP

- Differentiated Instruction, pages 1610–1635

Oral Vocabulary

Week 1

blustery	chilly	cloud
drizzle	weather	

Review

alert	celebration	job
precise	repair	

Use the Define/Example/Ask routine in the **Instructional Routine Handbook** to review last week's words.

Oral Language

 Sing About It **Build Background: *Kinds of Weather***

INTRODUCE THE THEME

Tell children that this week they will be talking and reading about different kinds of **weather**. Discuss what the weather is usually like this time of year.

Write the following question on the board: *What is the weather like today?* Say: *The message has the word* weather *in it. Listen as I break the word into parts: weath-er. Each part is a syllable. How many syllables are in the word* weather? *Repeat with the word* today. Then prompt children to answer the question.

ACCESS PRIOR KNOWLEDGE

- Explain that weather is the condition of the air at a certain place and time. It includes the temperature and the amount of wind, rain, snow, sun, or **clouds**. *What are some things you like to do outside in warm weather? What do you like to do in wintry or very cold weather?*

Think Aloud Let's look at these pictures. It shows two children swimming in a pool. (**Point to the children and pool.**) It shows two children walking in snow. (**Point to the children and snow.**)

- Look at the photographs together and sing the song. Talk about the weather in the photographs. Have children discuss what children are doing and wearing in each kind of weather.

 ### INNOVATE ON THE SONG

Write new verses related to weather, using terms such as *cold, windy, rainy,* or *sunny.*

You'll sing a song,
And I'll sing a song
In warm or wintry weather.

Teaching Chart 44

Share the Big Book

Listening Comprehension

PREVIEW Display the cover. *Now let's read about rainy **weather**.* Read the title and the name of the author. *I see that it is raining. The rain comes from the clouds.* Point to the clouds and rain as you repeat. *What information do you think you will learn from reading this book?*

GENRE: INFORMATIONAL TEXT/EXPOSITORY Tell children this story is **expository** and tells information about real things.

Big Book

STRATEGY Monitor Comprehension: Visualize

EXPLAIN/MODEL Tell children that a good way to understand the words in a book is to picture in your mind what is being described.

Think Aloud On the cover I see rain **clouds** in the distance. I'll try to picture the rain falling on the grass. Can you see it?

SKILL Identify Main Idea and Details

EXPLAIN/MODEL Remind children that sometimes books have a main topic. The details in the book relate to this main idea.

Think Aloud I think this book will be mostly about rain. As I read, I will see if that is the main idea of the book, and I will listen for details about rain.

Read the Big Book

SET PURPOSE Remind children that the purpose of reading nonfiction is to learn facts about real things. Tell them to try to think about the facts they learn and how they relate to the main idea. Use the **Define/Example/Ask** routine to teach the story words on the inside back cover of the **Big Book**.

Respond to Literature

MAKE CONNECTIONS Discuss the book with children. *What did you learn about rain?* Have children draw and label a picture of a rainy day. *What can you do on a rainy day in your community?*

Objectives

- Discuss the theme
- Identify syllables in a word
- Use oral vocabulary words *weather* and *cloud*
- Create song lyrics
- Listen and respond to a story
- Monitor comprehension: visualize/identify main idea and details

Materials

- Teaching Chart 44
- Big Book: *A Rainy Day*

ELL

Use the Interactive Question-Response Guide for *A Rainy Day*, **ELL Resource Book** pages 182–185, to guide children through a reading of the book. As you read *A Rainy Day*, make meaning clear by pointing to the pictures, demonstrating word meanings, paraphrasing text, and asking children questions.

Digital Learning

Song and story on **Listening Library Audio CD**

Objectives

- Read the high-frequency words *this, do*
- Review the high-frequency words *are, for, you, play*
- Identify the words *this* and *do* in speech and text

Materials

- High-Frequency Word Cards: *this, do, are, for, you, play*
- Teaching Chart 45

Reinforce Vocabulary
Review the high-frequency words *this, do, are, for, you, play*. Display the High-Frequency Word Cards for *this, do, are, for, you, play*. Point to or hold classroom objects as you ask questions such as: *What can you do with this pencil? What are some words you can write for me? What game can you and a friend play with this ball?* Guide children to answer in complete sentences using the high-frequency words.

High-Frequency Words

 this, do

this	do

INTRODUCE Display the **High-Frequency Word Card** for **this**. Use the **Read/Spell/Write** routine to teach the word.

- **Read** Point to and say the word *this. This is a book.*

- **Spell** *The word* this *is spelled* t-h-i-s. *What's the first sound in* this? *That's right. The first sound in* this *is /th/. That's why the first letters are* th. *After the* th, *I see* i *and* s. *Let's read and spell* this *together.*

- **Write** *Now let's write the word* this *on our papers. Let's spell aloud the word as we write it:* this, t-h-i-s.

- *Repeat the routine with the word* **do**.

SPIRAL REVIEW **REVIEW *are, for, you, play***
Display each High-Frequency Word Card and have children read the word.

are	for

READ THE RHYME AND CHIME

Ask children to point to *this, do, for,* and *you*. Repeat the rhyme together for fluency. Then add *this* and *do* to the class Word Wall.

Elephant Ed

This is Elephant Ed.
What does this elephant do?
Elephant Ed is an engineer
on Engine Number Two.
Every day Ed rides the line
and toots his horn for you.
Whoo! Whoo!

High-Frequency Words: *this, do*
Phonics: */e/e*

Weather Week I 45

Teaching Chart 45

For Tier 2 instruction, see page 1610.

TIME TO MOVE!

Using the word *this*, have children follow sequential directions by pointing to different body parts as you say the following rhyme: *This is my nose. This is my knee. These are my toes. This is me!*

Phonemic Awareness

Phoneme Isolation

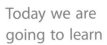

Model

Display the **Photo Card** for *egg*.

Repeat with the Photo Card for *exit*.

Today we are going to learn a new sound. Listen for the sound at the beginning of *egg*: /e/, /e/, *egg*. *Egg* has /e/ at the beginning. Say the sound with me: /e/. What is the sound?

We'll show the thumbs-up sign when we hear /e/ at the beginning of a word.

Read the "Elephant Ed" Rhyme and Chime again. Have children show thumbs up every time they hear /e/.

This is Elephant Ed.
What does this elephant do?
Elephant Ed is an engineer
on Engine Number Two.
Every day Ed rides the line
and toots his horn for you.
Whoo! Whoo!

Review /h/, /d/, /r/

Display the Photo Card for *door*. Repeat with *hammer* and *rock*.

This is a *door*. The beginning sound in *door* is /d/. What is the sound?

Guided Practice/Practice

Display and name each Photo Card.

Children identify the initial sound. Guide practice with the first card.

Say each picture name with me. Tell me the sound at the beginning of the word.

Quick Check

Can children identify the initial sound /e/?

During **Small Group Instruction**

If No → Approaching Level For additional practice isolating sounds, page 1611.

If Yes → On Level Children blend words with /e/, page 1612.

Beyond Level Children read words with /e/, page 1613.

Objectives

- **Isolate initial sound /e/**
- **Review initial /h/, /d/, /r/**

Materials

- **Photo Cards:** *deer, dog, door, egg, elevator, exit, hammer, hat, hen, rabbit, ring, rock*

ELL

Pronunciation Display and have children name Photo Cards from this and prior lessons to reinforce phonemic awareness and word meanings. Point to a card and ask: *What do you see?* (an egg) *What is the sound at the beginning of the word* egg? (/e/) Repeat using Photo Cards with words that begin with the sounds /h/, /d/, and /r/.

Objectives
- Match vowel *e* to the initial sound /e/
- Handwriting: Write *Ee*

Materials
- Sound-Spelling Card: *Egg*
- Teaching Chart 45
- Word-Building Cards
- Handwriting
- Handwriting Teacher's Edition
- Activity Book, p. 4
- Practice Book, p. 141

ELL

Variations in Languages
Speakers of Spanish, Hmong, Cantonese, Haitian Creole, and Korean may have difficulty perceiving and pronouncing /e/. Use the Approaching Level Phonics lessons for additional pronunciation and decoding practice.

Sound Pronunciation

See **Sound Pronunciation CD** for a model of the /e/ sound. Play this for children needing additional models.

Phonics

Ee

✓ Introduce /e/e

Model

Display the *Egg* **Sound-Spelling Card**.

The name of this letter is *e*. The letter *e* stands for the /e/ sound you hear in *egg*. Say the sound with me: /e/. What is the name of this letter? What sound does this letter stand for?

Read the "Elephant Ed" Rhyme and Chime. Reread the title. Point out that the words *Ed* and *Elephant* in the title. Tell children that the words begin with the letter *E*. Model placing a self-stick note below the *E* in *Elephant* and *Ed*.

Elephant Ed

This is Elephant Ed.
What does this elephant do?
Elephant Ed is an engineer
on Engine Number Two.
Every day Ed rides the line
and toots his horn for you.
Whoo! Whoo!

High-Frequency Words: this, do
Phonics: /e/e

Unit 7
Rhyme and Chime

Weather Week I 45

Teaching Chart 45

Guided Practice/Practice

Read the rest of the rhyme. Children place self-stick notes below the *e* in words that begin with *e*. Guide practice with line 1. Repeat with *d* and *h*.

Let's put a sticky note below the word in the line that begins with the letter *e*. The words *Elephant* and *Ed* begin with the letter *e*. Which word in the next line begins with the letter *e*? Yes, the word *elephant* begins with the letter *e*.

Corrective Feedback

Linguistic Differences When the /i/ and /e/ sounds appear before the consonant *m* or *n* in words, such as *pen/pin* and *him/hem*, many speakers of African American Vernacular English won't pronounce or hear the difference. Focus on articulation, such as mouth position for each vowel, during the lesson.

Build Fluency: Sound-Spellings

 Display the following **Word-Building Cards**: *a, c, d, e, f, h, i, m, n, o, p, r, s, t.* Have children chorally say each sound. Repeat and vary the pace.

Handwriting: Write *Ee*

MODEL Model holding up your writing hand. Say the handwriting cues below as you write the capital and lowercase forms of *Ee* on the board. Then trace the letters on the board and in the air as you say /e/. Identify the uppercase and lowercase forms of the letter.

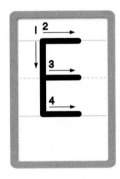

Straight down.
Straight across.
Straight across.
Straight across.

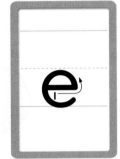

Straight across.
Circle back
and around,
then stop.

PRACTICE Ask children to hold up their writing hand.

- Say the cues together as children trace with their index finger the letters you wrote on the board. Have children identify the uppercase and lowercase forms of the letter.

- Have children write *E* and *e* in the air as they say /e/.

- Distribute handwriting practice pages. Observe children's pencil grip and paper position, and correct as necessary. Have children say /e/ every time they write the letter *e*.

For Tier 2 instruction, see page 1611.

Daily Handwriting
Check that children form letters starting at the top and moving to the bottom. See **Handwriting Teacher's Edition** for ball-and-stick and slant models.

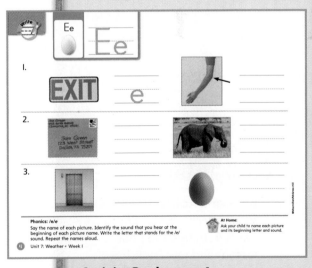

Activity Book, page 4
Practice Book, page 141

Objective

- Recognize describing words (adjectives)

Materials

- Photo Cards: *jewelry, kitten, pizza*
- Big Book: *A Rainy Day*

Grammar
Describing Words (Adjectives)

MODEL Use the **Big Book** *A Rainy Day* to introduce describing words. Point to the photograph on page 2 of the Big Book as you read the sentence: *It is a rainy day!* Ask children what kind of day it is. Explain that the word *rainy* is a describing word. It tells about the day. Explain that describing words tell more about something.

■ Use a describing word in a sentence about the day's **weather**. *What other describing words do we use when we talk about the weather?* (sunny, windy, snowy, **cloudy**)

PRACTICE Show **Photo Cards** for *pizza, jewelry,* and *kitten.*

■ Have children identify each picture. Model using describing words by making up sentences such as:

> *Mary ate* hot *pizza.*
> *This is a* soft *kitten.*

■ Ask children which word tells more about the picture. Then have children make up their own complete sentences about the pictures. Guide them to use describing words in each sentence. Have children identify the descriptive word in each sentence. Dictate a sentence for each child to illustrate. Have partners share their sentences and point out the describing words.

Writing

Shared Writing: Lists

BRAINSTORM

Remind children that in the **Big Book** *A Rainy Day,* they read about all that happens on a rainy day. Point out that there are many different kinds of **weather**. Ask children to name some of them.

WRITE

- Create two lists as shown below. Read each heading together as you track the print.

- Tell children they will write about different kinds of weather.

- Model by reading page 2 of the Big Book. *The boys wear T-shirts, so it must be warm. I will write* warm *on the list about how the weather feels. The sky is gray and cloudy, so I will write* cloudy *on the list about what the sky is like.* Draw a few **clouds** next to the word *cloudy.*

- Have children think of other ways that weather feels. Ask for more words that describe the sky. Add a drawing after each row. Read the completed lists together.

- Call attention to the describing words for weather on the chart, noting that many of the words end in *-y.*

- Save the lists to refer to in other writing activities this week.

The Weather Feels	The Skies Are	
warm	cloudy	☁
hot	sunny	☼
cold	rainy	🌧
very cold	snowy	🌨

Write About It

Tell children to draw a picture of themselves in the rain. *What will protect you from the rain?* Have children write a sentence caption for their picture.

Objective

- Write lists

Materials

- Big Book: *A Rainy Day*

5-Day Writing

Weather Report

DAY 1	Shared: Lists
DAY 2	Interactive: Sentences
DAY 3	Independent: Prewrite and Draft Weather Report
DAY 4	Independent: Revise and Edit Weather Report
DAY 5	Independent: Publish and Present

ELL

Prewriting Planning
Have children find in the Big Book *A Rainy Day* pictures of items that protect from the rain, such as a raincoat, an umbrella, and rain boots. List the words for children to write in sentences or labels to go with their drawings.

Transitions That Teach

While children wait in line, have them talk about the **weather**.

WHOLE GROUP

Oral Language
- Build Robust Vocabulary

✶ **Comprehension**
- Reread *A Rainy Day*
- Strategy: Visualize
- Skill: Identify Main Idea and Details
- Fluency: Echo-Read

Vocabulary
- Sound Words
- Story Words: *gloomy, umbrella*

✓ **Phonemic Awareness**
- Phoneme Blending

✓ **Phonics**
- Review /e/*e*, /d/*d*, /r/*r*
- Blend with /e/*e*
- Decodable Reader: *Ed Can, Ted Can*

Writing
- Interactive Writing: Sentences

SMALL GROUP

- Differentiated Instruction, pages 1610–1635

Oral Vocabulary

Week 1

blustery	chilly	cloud
drizzle	weather	

Review

alert	celebration	job
precise	repair	

Use the **Define/Example/Ask** routine in the **Instructional Routines Handbook** to review last week's words.

Oral Language

Talk About It

Build Robust Vocabulary

INTRODUCE WORDS

Tell children that you are going to talk about the **Big Book** *A Rainy Day*. Read pages 2–15 aloud. *The author tells us that when it is rainy, clouds fill the sky. What words are used at the beginning of the book to tell more about rainy weather?* (wet, gray, gloomy) Have partners take turns asking and responding to questions about the text.

Vocabulary Routine

Use the routine below to discuss the meaning of each word.

Define: **Weather** is the way the outside air is at a certain time and place. Say the word with me.
Example: In Florida the weather is often hot in the summer.
Ask: What is the weather like today? What kind of weather do you like best?

Define: A **cloud** is a white or gray mass floating high in the sky. Say the word with me.
Example: The sun came out from behind a cloud.
Ask: Would you see a fluffy white cloud on a sunny day or a rainy day?

CREATE A WORD WEB

Create a word web, or use **Teaching Chart G1**. Label the circle as shown. *The words* wet, gray, gloomy, *and* dark *can describe a rainy day, so I'll put those words in our word web.*

Guide children to use complete sentences when speaking. Add children's ideas to the word web. Read aloud the text on the completed web with children as you track the print. Add children's suggestions to the web. Read aloud the text as you track the print.

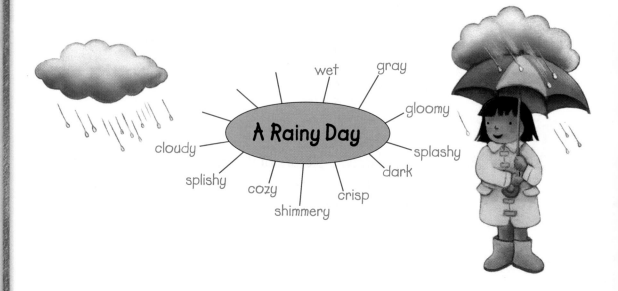

Listen for Rhyme

IDENTIFY RHYME

Remind children that words rhyme when they have the same ending sounds. Have children generate rhyme in response to words from the rhyme. *What rhymes with* snow? *What rhymes with* sky?

RHYME ABOUT WEATHER

Let's sing a fun song about weather, or the condition of the air outside at a certain place and time. Play the fingerplay "A Cloud," using the **Listening Library Audio CD**. Then teach children the words and actions. Then say the rhyme together. Then have children identify the rhyming pairs. (*snow/below; sky/by*)

A Cloud

What brings the rain,

What brings the snow,

Open hands, palm up.

That showers down on us below?

Wiggle fingers, moving downward.

When you look up in the high blue sky,

Look up.

What is the thing you see float by?

A cloud!

Objectives

- Use oral vocabulary words *weather* and *cloud*
- Discuss a rainy day
- Complete a word web
- Generate rhyme

Materials

- **Big Book:** *A Rainy Day*
- **Graphic Organizer; Teaching Chart G1**
- **Listening Library Audio CD**

Digital Learning

Fingerplay on Listening Library Audio CD

ELL   ENGLISH LANGUAGE LEARNERS

Beginning	Intermediate	Advanced
Confirm Understanding Review oral vocabulary using the **Big Book** *A Rainy Day*. Say, for example: *Show me a picture with clouds. Let's say the word* clouds. *Show me a picture with rain. Let's say the word* rain. Continue with other pages.	**Enhance Understanding** Say: *Find a picture that shows something that happens when it is rainy. Tell me what the picture shows.* Guide children to answer in complete sentences.	**Share Opinions** Ask: *What do you like to do on rainy days? How do you feel when it rains? Why is rain important?* Prompt children to elaborate and answer in complete sentences. Write their responses and discuss them.

Objectives

- Monitor comprehension/ visualize
- Identify main idea and details
- Respond to a story
- Retell a story
- Develop fluency

Materials

- Big Book: *A Rainy Day*
- Activity Book, pp. 5–6
- Practice Book, p. 142

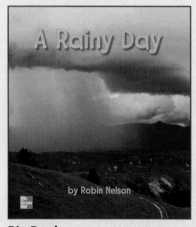

Big Book

Digital Learning

Story on **Listening Library Audio CD**

ELL

pp. 2–3

rainy: Point to the illustration of the rain. Move your fingers like the rain. Have children repeat the word and action.

pp. 4–5

gloomy: Point to the gray sky. Make a sad, *gloomy* face. Have children make a *gloomy* face, while saying the word *gloomy*.

Reread the Big Book
Listening Comprehension

CONCEPTS ABOUT PRINT Display the cover and read the title aloud with children as you track the print. Have children tell what they remember about the book.

 STRATEGY Monitor Comprehension: Visualize

Remind children that creating pictures in their mind as they read and listen to books can help them to understand a story's main idea and details, and other information that is not shown in the photographs.

 SKILL Identify Main Idea and Details

Tell children that they will use the words and photographs to monitor and adjust their understanding by visualizing and learning about the main idea. Display and read pages 2–3.

Think Aloud The main idea of the book is that many things happen when it rains. A detail on these pages is that rain is wet.

Read the **Big Book** and use the prompts on the inside covers.

pages 2–3

PHONICS

- *What is the sound at the beginning of the word rain?* (/r/) *What letter stands for that sound?* (r)

It is a rainy day!
②

The rain is wet.
③

pages 4–5

MAIN IDEA AND DETAILS

- *What is the sky like on a rainy day?* (The sky is gray.)

When it is rainy, the sky is gray.
④

A rainy day is **gloomy.**
⑤

Develop Comprehension

pages 6–7

⭐ **VISUALIZE**

Think Aloud When it rains, the sky is **cloudy**. I can try to picture in my mind what these places will look like when the clouds clear and the sky is blue.

When it is rainy, **clouds** fill the sky.

⑥

Raindrops fall from the clouds.

⑦

pages 8–9

⭐ **MAIN IDEA AND DETAILS**

■ *What are two things that happen because of rain?* (Rain helps flowers grow. After the rain, there are sometimes rainbows.)

When it is rainy, flowers grow.

⑧

We see a **rainbow.**

⑨

pages 10–11

⊘ **CLASSIFY AND**
SPIRAL REVIEW **CATEGORIZE**

■ *Which photograph was taken after it rained?* (the photograph of the flood) *Which one was taken while it was raining?* (the photograph of lightning)

When it is rainy, it can **flood.**

⑩

Lightning can strike.

⑪

Comprehension

Main Idea and Details
● (pages 4–5) On a rainy day, the sky is gray.
● (pages 8–9) The rain helps flowers grow. After the rain, sometimes there are rainbows.

Visualize
● (page 12) This photograph shows the rabbits after they have run out of the rain. I'll try to picture what the rabbits did when the rain started. They felt the raindrops and then ran to a safe hiding place where they would not get wet.

Story Words
(page 5) gloomy   (page 15) umbrella

About the Author: Robin Nelson
Robin Nelson has written many children's books about the wonders of nature, animals, weather, food, and holidays.

Big Book
Inside Back Cover

ELL

pp. 6–7
clouds: Point to the photo of the clouds. Then have children point to and say the word *clouds*.

pp. 8–9
rainbow: Have children touch the rainbow. Point to the colors and say each color word with children.

pp. 10–11
lightning: Point to the lightning and say: *Crash! Lightning!* Ask children to repeat after you.

Main Idea and Details

Explain Remind children that when answering questions about a selection that they often will have to go back to the text to provide evidence.

Discuss Reread pages 12–17. Guide children to use these pages to discuss the main idea and details. *What is the story mainly about? What detail can you find on pages 16–17?*

ELL

pp. 12–13
rabbits, ducks: Point to the animals on these pages and have children repeat their names after you.

pp. 14–15
raincoat, umbrella: Gesture putting on your raincoat and say *raincoat*. Then gesture opening an umbrella as you say *umbrella*. Repeat with children.

pp. 16–17
splash: Point to the child jumping in the puddle and make a splashing sound. *Splash!* Have children repeat after you.

Develop Comprehension

pages 12-13

 VISUALIZE

■ *This photograph shows the rabbits hiding from the rain. Can you picture what the rabbits did when the rain started?* (They felt the raindrops, then ran to a dry place.)

When it is rainy, rabbits hide.

Ducks swim in the rain.

pages 14-15

CONCEPTS ABOUT PRINT
Think Aloud I know that the word *it* is made up of the letters *i* and *t*.

When it is rainy, we put on a raincoat.

We open an umbrella.

pages 16-17

 VISUALIZE

■ *Can you picture in your mind what will happen to the water in the puddle when the boy lands in it?* (The water will splash.)

When it is rainy, we can splash.

A rainy day is fun!

Develop Comprehension

pages 18–19

SELF-QUESTION

Think Aloud Do I understand these pages? Heat changes water into a gas, called vapor. The vapor forms a **cloud** of water droplets. The droplets fall as rain. Yes, I understand.

pages 20–21

AUTHOR'S PURPOSE

■ *Why do you think the author added these pages?* (The author wanted to add more facts about rain and rainy days.)

pages 22–23

PARTS OF A BOOK

Think Aloud The left-hand page is called the glossary. This is a list of words in the book that are related to rain. The right-hand page is called the index. It lists the different topics in the book and on which page to find each topic.

The Water Cycle

The sun warms the water in the oceans. Heat changes the water from a liquid into a gas called water vapor. Water vapor rises into the sky. As the water vapor rises, it cools and forms tiny droplets. These droplets form a cloud. Inside a cloud, the water droplets combine. When the droplets combine, they get heavier and fall to Earth as rain. Rain runs into rivers, lakes, and oceans. Then the water cycle starts again.

(18) (19)

 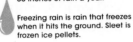

Rainy Day Facts

One of the wettest places on Earth is Mount Wai'ale'ale in Hawaii. An average of 460 inches of rain falls there each year.

Louisiana is the wettest state in the United States. It gets about 56 inches of rain a year.

Freezing rain is rain that freezes when it hits the ground. Sleet is frozen ice pellets.

The heaviest raindrops fall as fast as 18 miles an hour.

Pinecones close up when it is going to rain.

Lightning makes the air so hot that it explodes. The sound it makes is called thunder.

Count the seconds between a flash of lightning and the sound of thunder. If there is a lot of time between the lightning and thunder, the storm is far away. If the lightning and thunder happen almost at the same time, the storm is very close.

(20) (21)

 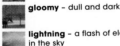

Glossary

clouds – masses of water droplets floating in the air

flood – to overflow with water where it is usually dry

gloomy – dull and dark

lightning – a flash of electricity in the sky

rainbow – an arch of colors that appears in the sky

Index

clouds – 4, 6, 7, 9, 19

flood – 10

flowers – 8

lightning – 11, 21

rainbow – 9

raincoat – 14, 16, 17

raindrops – 7, 19, 20

umbrella – 14, 15, 17

(22) (23)

ELL

pp. 18–19

cycle: Point to the circular graphic and explain the water cycle in simple terms.

pp. 20–21

facts: Point to each fact on the pages and say: *These are facts. They tell things that are true about rain.*

Respond to Literature

TALK ABOUT IT Have children talk about the words and photographs as they revisit the book. Have them refer to the text as they answer the questions.

■ *What was the big idea of the book?* (rain) *What details did you learn about rain?* (where it comes from, what it looks like, etc.) **CONNECT**

Retell

GUIDED RETELLING

Remind children that as they listened to *A Rainy Day,* they used the words and the photographs to understand the book. Now they will retell the story.

- *What does the sky look like when the **weather** is rainy? Is it sunny or **cloudy**?*

- *What are some of the things that happen on rainy days?*

- *When do we see rainbows?*

- *What are some of the things people do on rainy days?*

- *Why do you think the author included a glossary and index?*

- Have children act out their favorite parts of the book.

Fluency: Echo-Read

MODEL Reread page 5, emphasizing the word in boldface, *gloomy.* Then reread pages 6–11 and have children echo-read as you track the print.

Quick Check

Can children identify main idea and details to help understand a story?
Can children begin to retell a story?

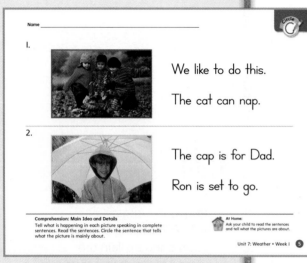

Name _____

1.

We like to do this.

The cat can nap.

2.

The cap is for Dad.

Ron is set to go.

Comprehension: Main Idea and Details
Tell what is happening in each picture speaking in complete sentences. Read the sentences. Circle the sentence that tells what the picture is mainly about.

At Home:
Ask your child to read the sentences and tell what the pictures are about.

Unit 7: Weather • Week 1 5

Activity Book, pages 5–6
Practice Book, page 142

Retelling Rubric

4 Excellent

Retells the selection without prompting, using detailed information, and referring to text structure and features. Clearly describes the main idea.

3 Good

Retells the selection with little guidance, using some details, and occasionally referring to text structure and features. Generally describes the main idea.

2 Fair

Retells the selection with some guidance, using limited details. Partially describes the main idea.

1 Unsatisfactory

Retells the selection only when prompted, using limited details. Does not describe the main idea.

Vocabulary

Sound Words

Chant the following jingle:

> Drip, drop, *down falls the rain.*
>
> Splash, splash, *run through the puddles.*
>
> Crack! Bam! *Lightning and thunder!*
>
> *Time to hurry home!*

- Repeat each line and ask children what words tell a sound.

- Ask children to name other things that make these sounds. *What other **weather** sounds do you know?*

NAME SOUND WORDS Have children talk about the day's weather and suggest sound words.

Story Words: *gloomy, umbrella*

Display page 5 of *A Rainy Day* and point out the word *gloomy* and the picture of the stormy day. *Do you know what* gloomy *means?* Gloomy *means **cloudy** and dark.* Ask how children feel on gloomy days.

Display pages 14–15 and point out the word *umbrella* and the pictures. *When have you used an umbrella?* Point out that umbrellas protect people from rain, snow, and sun.

TIME TO MOVE!

Ask children to gesture getting ready for a rainstorm. Say: *Drip, drop, it's raining! Put on your raincoat. Open your umbrella. Splash through puddles. Crack, bam! Cover your ears. Lightning and thunder! Hurry home.*

Objectives

- **Use sound words**
- **Learn the story words** *gloomy, umbrella*

Materials

- **Big Book:** *A Rainy Day*

Digital Learning

LOG ON For children who need additional language support and oral vocabulary development, use the activities found at **www.macmillanmh.com.**

ELL

Reinforce Meaning Act out a rainstorm. Raise your hands and move your fingers as you say: *Drip, drop, the rain comes down.* Stomp in a puddle and say, *Splash!* Look up to the sky, cover your ears, and say, *Crack! Bam! Here comes the storm.* Repeat and ask children to join you in the rainstorm.

Objectives

- Blend phonemes in words with initial /e/
- Match letters *e, d, r* and initial sounds /e/, /d/, /r/
- Blend sounds to form words with /e/*e*

Materials

- Puppet
- Word-Building Cards
- pocket chart

CCVC: Initial Blends

Explain Display Word-Building Cards *f, r. F* and *r* together stand for the /fr/ sounds as in *frog. What sounds do the letters* fr *stand for together?* Hold up the Word-Building Cards *d, r. D and* r *together stand for the /dr/ sounds as in* drip. Repeat with tr and the word *trap.*

Model Display Word-Building Cards *f, r. F* and *r* together stand for the /fr/ sounds as in *frog. What sounds do the letters* fr *stand for together?* Hold up the Word-Building Cards *d, r. D and* r *together stand for the /dr/ sounds as in* drip. Repeat with *tr* and the word *trap.*

Guided Practice/ Practice Using Word-Building Cards, assist children in blending the word *pram.* Continue with *Fred, trip, trap, trod, drip, drop, drag, prim, prod, crop.*

Phonemic Awareness

✔ Phoneme Blending

Model

Use the **Puppet** to model how to blend the sounds in the word *egg.*

Repeat the routine with *Ed.*

Happy is going to say the sounds in a word. Listen to Happy as he says each sound: /e/ /g/. Happy can blend these sounds together: /eeeg/, *egg.* Say the sounds with Happy: /e/ /g/, /eeeg/. Now say the word: *egg.* What is the word? (*egg*)

Guided Practice/Practice

Say the sounds. Have children blend the sounds to form words. Guide practice with the first word, using the same routine.

Happy is going to say the sounds in a word. Listen to Happy as he says each sound. Blend the sounds to say the word.

/e/ /n/ /d/   /e/ /d/ /j/   /e/ /d/   /ē/ /t/

/e/ /l/ /k/   /ē/ /r/   /e/ /g/   /ē/ /s/ /t/

Phonics

✔ Review

e	d	r

Model

Say the word *egg.* Hold up **Word-Building Card** *e.*

Repeat for *d* and *r.*

Listen as I say a word: *egg.* Say the word with me: *egg. Egg* begins with /e/. I will hold up the *e* card because *e* stands for the /e/ sound at the beginning of *egg.* What is the name of the letter? What sound does it stand for?

Guided Practice/Practice

Children write the letter that stands for the initial sound. Guide practice with the first word, using the routine.

Listen as I say a word. Write the letter that stands for the beginning sound.

deer   rock   elephant   elk   exit

edge   dog   rope   desk   egg

Build Fluency: Sound-Spellings

 Display the following **Word-Building Cards**: *a, c, d, e, f, h, i, m, n, o, p, r, s, t.* Have children chorally say each sound. Repeat and vary the pace.

 ## Blend with /e/e

Model

Place Word-Building Card *E* in the pocket chart.	This letter is capital *E*. Letter *E* stands for the /e/ sound. Say /e/.	
Place the letter *d* next to *E*. Move your hand from left to right. Repeat the routine with *bed*.	This is the letter *d*. The letter *d* stands for the /d/ sound. Listen as I blend the two sounds together: /ed/. Now you say it. (/ed/)	

Guided Practice/Practice

Children blend sounds to form words. Guide practice with the first word.

red	pet	ten	set	met	hen
led	let	men	fed	pen	den

Objectives

- Read decodable words with /e/e
- Read the words *a, do, this, is, to, go, the,* and *play*
- Reread for fluency

Materials

- Decodable Reader: *Ed Can, Ted Can*
- High-Frequency Word Cards: *a, do, this, is, to, go, the, play*
- pocket chart

Decodable Text

For additional decodable passages, see pages 27–28 of the **Teacher's Resource Book**.

Decodable Reader

Read *Ed Can, Ted Can*

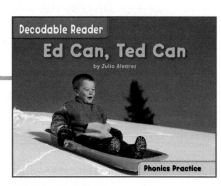
Ed Can, Ted Can

 REVIEW HIGH-FREQUENCY WORDS Display **High-Frequency Word Cards** for **a, do, this, is, to, go, the, play**. Say each word. Review using the **Read/Spell/Write** routine.

MODEL CONCEPTS ABOUT PRINT
Demonstrate book handling. *I hold the book so that the cover is on the front and the words are not upside down. I turn the cover. Then I turn each page as I read it.*

PREDICT Ask children to describe the cover. *Do you think the story will be a made-up story or one that could really happen?*

FIRST READ Children point to each word, sounding out decodable words and saying the high-frequency words quickly. If children have difficulty, provide corrective feedback and guide them page by page.

DEVELOP COMPREHENSION Ask the following:

- *What is this book mainly about?* (activities in different kinds of weather)

- *What kinds of weather are shown?* (warm, sunny, cold, snowy, rainy)

SECOND READ Have partners reread the book together.

Ed is set to go.
Ed can do it!

2

Ted can pet the cat.
Ted can do it!

3

Dan can dip in.
Dan can do it!

4

Nan can hit this net.
Nan can do it!

5

Cam can fit a hat on it.
Cam can do it!

6

Kit can sit in the den.
Kit can do it!

7

Pam can play in it.
Pam can do it!

8

Decodable Reader

Writing

Interactive Writing: Sentences

REVIEW
Display and read aloud the lists that children created for the Shared Writing activity.

WRITE

- *Now we will write sentences about the **weather** we would like for today.*

- Collaborate with children to write the following sentence frames.

> Today the weather is _____.
> It is _____.

- Have children suggest a word for the first frame, using the Shared Writing list. Write the word to complete the sentence. Ask children to help by writing all of the letters they know.

- Continue with the second sentence frame, asking children to select a word for sky conditions from the chart.

- Read the completed sentences aloud and track the print.

- Extend the lesson by working with children to write sentences using more than one descriptive word, in a list. *Today the weather is _____, _____, and _____.*

Write About It
Tell children to draw a picture of the sun in the sky, perhaps at sunrise or sunset. Tell them to write a caption for their drawing, using one of the high-frequency words *are, for,* or *you. Sunsets are in the west.*

Objectives
- **Write sentences**
- **Use letter knowledge to write letters in a word**

Materials
- Shared Writing lists from Day 1

5-Day Writing

Weather Report	
DAY 1	Shared: Lists
DAY 2	Interactive: Sentences
DAY 3	Independent: Prewrite and Draft Weather Report
DAY 4	Independent: Revise and Edit Weather Report
DAY 5	Independent: Publish and Present

ELL

Use New Language Ask children to draw a picture of the kind of weather they like best. Encourage children to use words that describe the weather in their pictures and help them write a caption.

Transitions That Teach
While lining up, have children describe a **cloud** they have seen in the sky.

WHOLE GROUP

Oral Language
- Build Robust Vocabulary
- Oral Vocabulary Cards: "How Thunder and Lightning Came to Be"

✔ **Comprehension**
- Read "The Wind," "Slip On Your Raincoat," "Four Seasons," "Rain on the Rooftops"

✔ **High-Frequency Words**
- Review *this*, *do*

✔ **Phonemic Awareness**
- Phoneme Isolation

✔ **Phonics**
- Review /e/*e*
- Blend with /e/*e*

Grammar
- Describing Words (Adjectives)

Writing
- Independent Writing: Prewrite and Draft a Weather Report

SMALL GROUP

- Differentiated Instruction, pages 1610–1635

Additional Vocabulary

To provide 15–20 minutes of additional vocabulary instruction, see Oral Vocabulary Cards 5-Day Plan. The pre- and posttests can be found in the **Teacher's Resource Book**, pages 226–227.

Oral Language

 Talk About It ## Build Robust Vocabulary

BUILD BACKGROUND

Introduce the story "How Thunder and Lightning Came to Be" using **Oral Vocabulary Card 1** and read the title aloud. *Have you seen a storm with lightning and thunder? Were there clouds in the sky?* Ask children to tell what they think is happening in the picture and to predict what will happen in the story.

- Read the story on the back of the cards. Pause at each oral vocabulary word and read the definition. Check children's understanding using the Use Illustrations, Repeat Modeled Language, and Use Props prompts.

Oral Vocabulary Cards

Vocabulary Routine

Use the routine below to discuss the meaning of each word.

Define: A **drizzle** is a light rain. Say the word with me.
Example: I like to take a walk when it drizzles.
Ask: Do you like to be inside or outside when it drizzles? Why?

Define: When it is **blustery**, there is a strong wind blowing. Say the word with me.
Example: On a blustery day, you can see the trees swaying.
Ask: If you were wearing a hat on a blustery day, what might happen to your hat?

Define: To be **chilly** means to be "a little cold." Say the word with me.
Example: When I'm chilly, I get under a blanket.
Ask: Which would you wear on a chilly day: a bathing suit or a sweater?

- Use the routine on Card 1 to review the words **weather** and **cloud**.

 SPIRAL REVIEW

- Review last week's words: *alert, celebration, job, precise,* and *repair.*

Listen for Rhyme

IDENTIFY RHYME

Tell children that they will sing another song about weather. Play the rhyme and ask children to join in. Have children identify words that rhyme.

Have children listen to the following words and tell which pairs rhyme: *pack/sack, rain/gain, hold/mold, six/sit, ten/five.*

WEATHER TALK

Tell children that people often do different activities when it rains outside. *What do you like to do when the weather is rainy?* (put on boots and raincoat and jump in puddles, stay inside and read, or play board games) Have children discuss today's weather with a partner. Ask them to talk about what they like to do.

Rain, Rain, Go Away

Rain, rain, go away.
Come again some other day.
Sue and Tommy want to play.
Rain, rain, go away!

Objectives

- Discuss the theme
- Use oral vocabulary words *blustery, chilly, cloud, drizzle,* and *weather*
- Recognize and identify rhyming words
- Listen and respond to a folktale

Materials

- Oral Vocabulary Cards: "How Thunder and Lightning Came to Be"

Digital Learning

Song on **Listening Library Audio CD**

Objectives

- Read and respond to a poem
- Identify onomatopoeia

Material

- Big Book of Explorations, Vol. 2: "The Wind," "Slip on Your Raincoat," "Four Seasons," and "Rain on the Rooftops" pp. 13–14

Vocabulary

galoshes rubber shoes that protect your feet from getting wet

autumn another word for the fall season

rooftops tops of houses or buildings

Use a Picture Dictionary
Guide children to use a picture dictionary to look up the word *galoshes*.

Poetry

Genre

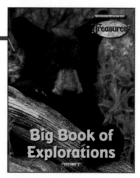

Big Book of Explorations

LITERARY TEXT: POETRY Tell children that today they will read poems about rainy days and other different types of **weather**. *Poets use words in special ways. Some poets place rhyming words at the end of lines; others list rhyming words in a row. We'll see and hear several kinds of words and word patterns in today's poems.*

Remind children of the weather described in *A Rainy Day* and the thunder and lightning in "How Thunder and Lightning Came to Be."

LITERARY ELEMENT: ONOMATOPOEIA
Explain/Model Tell children that poems and songs sometimes use sound words. Explain that sound words, such as *hiss*, *squeak*, *buzz*, and *clang*, actually sound like what they are describing.

- Point to the pictures on page 13.

Think Aloud I see a picture of a duck walking in the rain. When I walk in the rain, I sometimes hear raindrops go *plop* as they hit the ground. The word *plop* is a sound word. It sounds like a raindrop falling into a puddle.

READ THE POEMS
Preview and Predict Turn to "The Wind," "Slip on Your Raincoat," "Four Seasons," and "Rain on the Rooftops" on pages 13 and 14. Read the titles of the four poems. Ask children to predict what kinds of weather the poems might be about.

Vocabulary Introduce and discuss the vocabulary words. Point to each content word in the poems and read the line aloud. Have children repeat each line.

Set Purpose Tell children that as they listen to the poems, they can pay attention to words that describe sounds.

Before reading "Four Seasons," ask children to listen and identify the words that sound the same. After reading, ask children which words sound the same.

Read the poems aloud as you track the print. Emphasize the sound words so that children hear them clearly. After you read each poem, ask children to tell you which sound words they heard.

page 13

page 14

Retell and Respond

Talk About It Have children discuss predictions they made before reading and whether or not they were accurate. Then have them ask and answer their own questions about the poems.

- *What sound words did you hear in "Slip on Your Raincoat"?*

- *What are other sound words that describe the rain and the wind?*

Connect to Content

Science Activity: Patterns in Nature

- Help children identify patterns they see in nature, such as lightning is followed by thunder.

- Have children draw pictures or make an audio tape recording to show one of the patterns discussed.

Write About It

Have children draw their favorite kind of weather. Have them use sound words to describe the weather.

Objective

- Read the high-frequency words *this, do*

Materials

- High-Frequency Word Cards: *This, this, Do, do, you, like, a, is, What, see*
- pocket chart
- Photo Cards: *bear, brown, turtle*
- index card with: question mark
- index card with: period mark
- Activity Book, pp. 7–8
- Practice Book, pp. 143–144

High-Frequency Words

 this, do

SPIRAL REVIEW **REVIEW** Display the **High-Frequency Word Cards** for **this** and **do**. Review the words using the **Read/Spell/Write** routine.

APPLY Build sentences in the pocket chart using High-Frequency Word Cards and **Photo Cards**. Have children point to the high-frequency words. Read each sentence aloud, then have children chorally read it as you track the print with your finger. Use the sentence below and the following: *What do you like? This is a brown bear.*

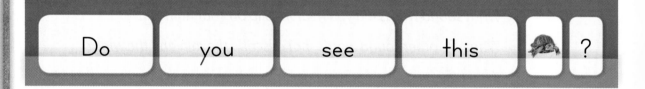

READ FOR FLUENCY Chorally read the Take-Home Book with children. Then have children read the book to review high-frequency words and build fluency.

Activity Book, pages 7–8
Practice Book, pages 143–144

Quick Check

Can children read the words *this* and *do*?

During **Small Group Instruction**

If No → **Approaching Level** Provide additional practice with high-frequency words, page 1620.

If Yes → **On Level** Children can read the Take-Home Book.

Beyond Level Children can read the Take-Home Book.

TIME TO MOVE!

Ask children to copy your movements in order. Touch your toes as you say: *Can you do this?* Bend from side to side and say: *Can you do this?* Continue by jumping and then tapping your head.

Phonemic Awareness

Phoneme Isolation

Model

Display the **Sound Box**. Place a marker in the first box as you say *egg*.

Listen for the beginning sound in *egg*. Say the word with me: *egg*.

Egg has /e/ at the beginning: /e/, /e/, *egg*. I'll place the marker in the first box because I hear /e/ at the beginning of *egg*.

Place a marker in the second box as you say *red*. Repeat with *edge* and *bed*.

Listen for the middle sound in *red*. Say the word with me: *red*. *Red* has /e/ in the middle. **(Say the word as you emphasize and stretch the medial sound.)** I'll place the marker in the middle box because /e/ is in the middle of *red*.

Guided Practice/Practice

Distribute a Sound Box and markers to each child. Children identify the position of /e/ in words. Guide practice with the first word.

Listen to each word I say. Put the marker in the first box or the middle box to show where you hear /e/ in each word.

net   Ed   pen   met   pet   led

egg   end   set   etch   set   exit

Objective

- Identify initial and medial /e/ in words

Materials

- Sound Box
- WorkBoard Sound Boxes; Teacher's Resource Book, p. 136
- markers

Objectives

- Review initial /e/*e*
- Blend letter sounds in words with medial /e/*e*
- Review /r/*r*, /d/*d*
- Read decodable and other one-syllable words

Materials

- Big Book: *A Rainy Day*
- Sound Box
- WorkBoard Sound Boxes; Teacher's Resource Book, p. 136
- Word-Building Cards; Teacher's Resource Book, pp. 95–102
- Word-Building Cards
- pocket chart

Phonics

Review /e/*e*

e

Model

Read aloud pages 2 and 3 of *A Rainy Day*. Stop when you reach the word *wet*.

Repeat with the words *let* and *egg*.

The word *wet* has the sound /e/ in the middle. I will place the Word-Building Card for *e* in the middle box of the Sound Box because I hear /e/ in the middle of *wet* and the letter *e* stands for /e/.

Guided Practice/Practice

Distribute **Word-Building Cards** and **Sound Boxes**. Say each word. Children place the *e* card in a box to show where they hear *e*. Guide practice with the first word.

Listen as I say each word. Place the *e* card in the first or middle box to show where you hear /e/.

edge	let	egg	men	end
exit	red	enjoy	set	pet

Phoneme Addition

Model

Place Word-Building Cards *i* and *t* in the pocket chart.

Add the initial letter *p* to *it* to form the word *pit*.

I will blend these sounds together: /iiit/, *it*.

I will add the letter *p* to *it*. Blend the sounds with me.

Guided Practice/Practice

Children add initial letters to form new words. Guide practice with the first word.

Add the letter *f* to *it*. Blend the sounds. (fit)

sit   hit

Build Fluency: Sound-Spellings

Display the following Word-Building Cards: *a, c, d, e, f, h, l, m, n, o, p, r, s, t*. Have children chorally say each sound. Repeat and vary the pace.

For Tier 2 instruction, see page 1621.

Blend with /e/e

Model

Place **Word-Building Card** *r* in the pocket chart.

This letter is *r*. It stands for the /r/ sound. Say /rrr/.

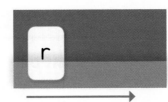

Place Word-Building Card *e* next to *r*. Move your hand from left to right.

This letter is *e*. It stands for the /e/ sound. Listen as I blend the two sounds together: /rrreee/. Now you say it. (/rrreee/)

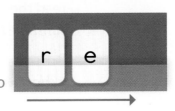

Place Word-Building Card *d* next to *re*. Move your hand from left to right.

This letter is *d*. This letter stands for the sound /d/. Listen as I blend the three sounds together: /rrreeed/. Now you say it. (/rrreeed/)

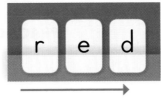

Repeat for *net* and *ten*.

Guided Practice/Practice

Children blend letter sounds to form words. Guide practice with the first word.

men	pet	set	hem	set
hen	pen	met	den	ten

 # Read Words

Apply

Write the words and sentences. Guide practice with the first word, using the blending routine. Read the sentences with children.

men	red
ten	net
Do you see ten men?	
The net is red.	

Corrective Feedback

Blending: Sound Error Model the sound that children missed, then have them repeat the sound. For example, for the word *set*, say: *My turn.* Tap under the letter *e* in the word *set* and say: *Sound? What's the sound?* Then return to the beginning of the word. Say: *Let's start over.* Blend the word with children again.

ELL

Variations in Language Because there is no sound-symbol match for /e/ in Cantonese, Hmong, Korean, or Haitian Creole, some children may need additional practice pronouncing the /e/ sound. Say words with medial /e/ several times for children to repeat.

- Recognize describing words (adjectives)

Materials

- Photo Cards: *banana, bear, penny, snow*
- Oral Vocabulary Cards: "How Thunder and Lightning Came to Be"

ELL

Basic and Academic Vocabulary Display the Photo Cards from the lesson and pair English Language Learners with fluent speakers. Have partners make up sentences that describe the pictured items. Prompt partners to elaborate by using describing words. Write children's sentences, read them chorally, and ask: *What describing words, or adjectives, did you use in your sentence?*

Grammar

Describing Words (Adjectives)

MODEL Use the **Oral Vocabulary Cards** for "How Thunder and Lightning Came to Be" to discuss describing words. Remind children that describing words tell more about something. Turn to Card 1 and read the sentence. *The weather would suddenly turn from beautiful sunshine to wind and rain.* Ask: *Which word describes the sunshine?* (beautiful) *Yes,* beautiful *is the describing word in this sentence.*

- *How would you describe Mrs. Bird in this picture?* (big, striped, silly)

- Turn to Card 2. Ask: *How would you describe the clouds?* (soft, white, fluffy) Tell children that describing words helps us to visualize, or get pictures in the mind of, what is happening in a story.

PRACTICE Show **Photo Cards** for *banana, bear, penny,* and *snow.*

Have children identify each picture. Model using describing words by making up sentences such as:

- *This is a* yellow *banana.*

- *Riki played in the* cold *snow.*

Ask children which word tells more about the picture. Then have them make up their own complete sentences about the pictures. Guide them to use and identify describing words.

Then have children draw a picture to represent one of the words. Have them write or dictate the adjective below their picture.

Writing

Independent Writing: Weather Report

Display the lists from the Shared Writing activity.

BRAINSTORM WRITING TRAIT: WORD CHOICE Explain to children they will write their own **weather** reports as if they were weather forecasters on television. First they will decide which words to use.

Think Aloud Good writers choose their words carefully. To write a weather report, I'll look out the window and think about the weather. It is really cold and gray today, so I'll choose the words *freezing* and **cloudy** to describe the weather.

As children suggest other words to describe today's weather, list them for use as a reference.

PREWRITE
Write the following frame and read it aloud. Complete the sentence by writing the words *freezing* and *cloudy* in the frames. Read the sentence aloud as you track the print.

> Today it is _____ and _____.

- Ask children to pick words to describe today's weather.

DRAFT
Distribute paper, pencils, and crayons.

- Have children write the sentence frame and then complete the sentence by writing two words from the lists. Tell them to add a drawing to their weather report.

- Collect and save children's work to use tomorrow.

Write About It
Tell children to draw a rainy or snowy day and write a caption for it using the words a weather forecaster might use.

Objectives
- Write sentences
- Draw pictures
- Use letter knowledge to write letters in a word
- Understand writing trait: word choice
- Write a caption

Materials
- Shared Writing lists from Day 1

5-Day Writing

Weather Report

DAY 1	Shared: Lists
DAY 2	Interactive: Sentences
DAY 3	Independent: Prewrite and Draft Weather Report
DAY 4	Independent: Revise and Edit Weather Report
DAY 5	Independent: Publish and Present

ELL

Prewriting Planning Before children draw their pictures, guide them in discussing winter clothes and summer clothes. *Do you wear shorts when it snows? When do you wear mittens?* Ask children to draw themselves wearing clothes for summer or winter and label their pictures.

Transitions That Teach
While children pack up, have them describe what they might see outside on a **blustery** day.

WHOLE GROUP

Oral Language
- Build Robust Vocabulary

✔ **Comprehension**
- Read Aloud: "Frog and Locust"

Vocabulary
- Sound Words
- Story Words: *gloomy, umbrella*

✔ **Phonemic Awareness**
- Phoneme Blending

✔ **Phonics**
- Word Sort
- Blend with /e/*e*
- Decodable Reader: *Ed Can, Ted Can*

Writing
- Independent Writing: Revise and Edit Weather Report

SMALL GROUP

- Differentiated Instruction, pages 1610–1635

Oral Language

 Talk About It

Build Robust Vocabulary

DRY AND WET: WEATHER OPPOSITES
Discuss rainy **weather** and dry weather with children.

- *What is it like outside when it rains a lot? Are there a lot of* **clouds***?*

- *What is it like outside when it doesn't rain for a very long time?*

CREATE A CHART
Draw and label a chart as shown below or use **Teaching Chart G3**. Read aloud the headings as you track the print.

Think Aloud When it rains a lot, the ground can get very muddy, so I will put *muddy ground* on our ch art under *Wet Weather*. When it doesn't rain for a long time, the ground can get very dusty, so I'll put *dusty ground* on our chart under *Dry Weather*.

Have children tell what else happens when it rains and when it doesn't rain. Add their ideas to the chart. Then read aloud the chart as you track the print.

Wet Weather	Dry Weather
muddy ground	dusty ground
leafy plants can grow	cactus and some other plants can grow
cloudy skies	clear sky, few clouds
puddles	bright sunshine
	grass is brown

ELL ENGLISH LANGUAGE LEARNERS

Beginning	Intermediate	Advanced
Confirm Understanding Have children go to the window or outside to observe the weather. Describe the weather. Then ask appropriate questions, such as: *Is it dry, or is it rainy? Is the ground muddy or wet? Is it cloudy or is it sunny? Are there clouds in the sky?*	**Enhance Understanding** Have children complete the following sentence frames to express what they like about each type of weather: *I like wet weather because _____. I like dry weather because _____.*	**Express Opinions** Pair children and have partners tell each other what type of weather they like and why. Prompt partners to make up sentences that tell about outdoor activities they like to do in each kind of weather.

Listen for Rhyme

IDENTIFY RHYME

Remind children that words rhyme when they have the same ending sounds. Have children generate rhyme. *What rhymes with* rain? (train, plain, main, brain, cane) *What rhymes with* snow? (glow, slow, throw, mow, tow) Repeat with the word *sky*.

Theme: *Kinds of Weather*

WEATHER SONG

Tell children that they will sing "A Cloud," the song they learned about weather. Play the song and have children join in. Then ask them to name and describe all the forms of weather they have learned.

A Cloud

What brings the rain,

What brings the snow,

Open hands, palm up.

That showers down on us below?

Wiggle fingers, moving downward.

When you look up in the high blue sky,

Look up.

What is the thing you see float by?

A cloud!

Objectives

- **Generate rhyme**
- **Discuss the theme**
- **Point to one word in a sentence**
- **Complete a chart**
- **Use oral vocabulary words** *blustery, chilly, cloud, drizzle,* and *weather*

Materials

- **Graphic Organizer; Teaching Chart G3**

Oral Vocabulary

Have children use each word in a sentence about this week's stories.

blustery	chilly
cloud	drizzle
weather	

Review Work with children to review last week's words.

alert	celebration
job	precise
repair	

Digital Learning

Fingerplay on **Listening Library Audio CD**

DAY 4
WHOLE GROUP

Objectives

- Listen and respond to a legend
- Identify and describe characters
- Retell important events in stories

Materials

- Read-Aloud Anthology: "Frog and Locust," pp. 97–100

ELL

Build Vocabulary Draw a picture of a mountain with a canyon made by a river. Point to the *stream, canyon,* and *mountain* in the picture. Then have children point to and name the parts of the picture.

Readers Theater

BUILDING LISTENING AND SPEAKING SKILLS
Distribute copies of "So Long as There's Weather," Read-Aloud Anthology pages 185–186. Have children practice performing the play throughout the unit. Assign parts. Have children present the play or perform it as a dramatic reading at the end of the unit.

Interactive Read Aloud

Listening Comprehension

GENRE: FICTION/LEGEND
Tell children that a **legend** often explains events that are important to a group of people. Explain that today's legend will be about two characters, a frog and a locust. A locust is a type of grasshopper. *What other stories have we read that were about two animal characters helping each other?* ("The Lion and the Mouse," "Grandfather Bear Is Hungry")

Read Aloud

CULTURAL PERSPECTIVES
"Frog and Locust" is a Pueblo legend. The Pueblo are Native Americans from the southwestern United States, where it is very dry. Rain songs and dances are performed to ask for rain to receive a good food crop.

READ "FROG AND LOCUST"

- **MODEL VISUALIZING** Use the Think Alouds provided at point of use in the legend to guide children to create mental images.

- **MODEL FLUENT READING** Read aloud the legend with fluent expression. Stop occasionally so that children can predict what will happen next and visualize story events.

- **EXPAND VOCABULARY** See page 97 of the **Read-Aloud Anthology** to teach new words using the **Define/Example/Ask** routine.

Respond to Literature

TALK ABOUT IT Have children retell important parts of the story.

- *What did the frog do to get rain? Why didn't his plan work?*

- *How does the story end? What is the message in this legend?*

- Have children dictate or write a new ending to the story.

Write About It
Ask children to draw animals in the rain. Have them write a label or a sentence about their drawing.

Vocabulary

Sound Words

REVIEW SOUND WORDS
Each time you hear a sound word, tap your feet. When you hear another word do nothing. Read the following story:

Jesse awoke to the sound of rain on his window. Drip, drop, drip, drop. *Jesse looked outside. It was* **cloudy**, *gray, and wet. Jesse got dressed and put on a raincoat. He went outside and ran through the puddles,* splash, splash, splash. *Then he heard the sound of thunder,* crack! *Jesse ran inside.* Bam! *went the thunder. Maybe staying inside today wouldn't be so bad after all.*

Story Words: *gloomy, umbrella*

Display pages 4–5 of *A Rainy Day.* Ask children what they like to do inside on *gloomy,* rainy days. *What do you do?*

Display pages 14–15. Ask children what they like to do outside on rainy days. *What do you use or wear outside?*

Objectives
- **Identify and use sound words to describe weather**
- **Review story words** *gloomy, umbrella*

Materials
- **Big Book:** *A Rainy Day*

ELL

Reinforce Understanding
Separate children into three groups to represent falling rain, stomping on puddles, and thunder. Show each group how to move their bodies according to what they are representing and lead them in saying the corresponding sound words: *drip, drop* for falling rain, *splash, splash* for stomping on puddles, and *crack, bam* for thunder. Continue until all groups have had a chance to represent each event.

Minilesson

Lullabies

Explain A lullaby is a soothing song or rhyme used to lull a young child to sleep. Tell children that lullabies usually feature a mother singing to her baby or child. Say that they also contain recurring phrases. Different cultures all around the world have lullabies with these recurring characters. Explain that this lullaby is from Nigeria.

Discuss Ask: *Do you know any lullabies? What characters are in those lullabies?*

Apply Have children listen to the lullaby "Sleep My Baby" from **Read-Aloud Anthology** page 214. Then have them name the characters and the recurring phrases. Finally, recite the lullaby together as a class. Compare this lullaby with the Native American "Chippewa Lullaby."

Objectives

- Blend sounds to form words
- Identify and sort words with /e/*e*, /r/*r*, /d/*d*, /s/*s*, /t/*t*, /p/*p*, /a/*a*, /i/*i*, /n/*n*
- Blend sounds in words with /e/*e*
- Read simple one-syllable words

Materials

- Puppet
- pocket chart
- Word-Building Cards
- Activity Book, p. 9
- Practice Book, p. 145

ELL

Minimal Contrasts
Because there is no direct sound-symbol match for most short vowels in Spanish and other languages, provide additional practice in pronouncing and blending medial /a/ and /i/. List minimal contrast word pairs on the board, such as *pat/pit, sat/sit, tan/tin, ball/bill*. Say the words slowly for children to repeat.

Phonemic Awareness

✓ Phoneme Blending

Model

Use the **Puppet** to model how to blend the sounds in the word *fed*.

Happy is going to say the sounds in a word. Listen to Happy as he says each sound: /f/ /e/ /d/. Happy can blend these sounds together: *fed*. Now you say the sounds with Happy: /f/ /e/ /d/, /fffeeed/. Now say the word with Happy: *fed*.

Repeat the routine with *bat*.

Guided Practice/Practice

Say the sounds. Children blend sounds to form words. Guide practice with the first word, using the same routine.

Happy is going to say the sounds in a word. Listen to Happy as he says each sound. Then blend the sounds together to say the word.

/p/ /e/ /t/	/s/ /e/ /t/	/t/ /e/ /d/
/t/ /e/ /n/	/d/ /e/ /n/	/h/ /e/ /d/

Phonics

✓ Word Sort

Model

Place **Word-Building Card** *e* in the pocket chart.

This is the letter *e*. The letter *e* stands for the /e/ sound. What is the letter? What is the sound that it stands for?

Repeat for *r, p, s, t*.

Write the words on the board.

red	set	pat	tin	rat
pet	sit	ten	sat	pin

Read the words with children. Model sorting the words by medial sound. Group words on the board.

Look at the words. Some of the words can go together. I'll group the words *red* and *pet* because both words have *e* in the middle. The words *set* and *ten* belong in this group because they also have *e* in the middle.

Guided Practice/Practice

Children continue to sort the words by medial sound.

Repeat with initial and final sounds.

Now you will group the rest of the words by middle sound.

Build Fluency: Sound-Spellings

 Display the following **Word-Building Cards**: *a, m, s, p, t*. Have children chorally say each sound. Repeat and vary the pace.

 ## Blend with /e/e

Model

Place Word-Building Card *n* in the pocket chart.

This letter is *n*. It stands for /n/. Say /n/.

Place Word-Building Card *e* next to *n*. Move your hand from left to right.

This letter is *e*. It stands for /e/. Listen as I blend the two sounds together: /nnneee/. Now you say it. (/nnneee/)

Place Word-Building Card *t* next to *ne*. Move your hand from left to right.

Repeat the routine with *set*.

This letter is *t*. It stands for /t/. Listen as I blend the three sounds together: /nnneeet/, *net*. Now you say it.

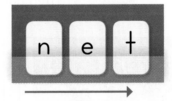

Guided Practice/Practice

Children blend sounds to form words. Guide practice with *fed*.

fed	Ed	Ted	pet
red	Ned	pen	ten

Corrective Feedback

Blending: Sound Error Model the sound that children missed, then have them repeat the sound. For example, for the word *net*, say: *My turn.* Tap under the letter *t* in the word *net* and say: *Sound? What's the sound?* Then return to the beginning of the word. Say: *Let's start over.* Blend the word with children again.

CCVC: Initial Blends

Review Display Word-Building Cards *f, r*. F and r *together stand for the sounds* /fr/ *as in* Fred. *What sounds do the letters* fr *stand for together?* Hold up the Word Building Cards *d, r*. D and r *together stand for the sounds* /dr/ *as in* drip. Repeat with *tr* and the word *trip*.

Model Display Word Building Cards F, r in the pocket chart. *The letters* F *and* r *stand for* /fr/. *Place the* a *to the right of* Fr. *This is the letter* a. *It stands for* /a/. *Let's blend* Fr *and* a, /fraaa/. *This is the letter* n. *It stands for* /n/. *Listen as I blend all four sounds:* /fraaan/, Fran. *Say it with me.* Have children repeat. Continue by modeling the words *Fred, drip, prop, crop, trap*.

Guided Practice/Practice Using Word Building Cards, assist children in blending the word *prim*. Continue with *Fran, trip, trap, prod, drip, drop, drag, prim, pram, crop*.

Phonemic Awareness: /e/
Look at the picture. Say the name of each item. Circle the item if its name begins with the same sound you hear at the beginning of egg.

At Home:
Ask your child to point to and name all the items in the picture that begin with the same sound as egg.

Unit 7: Weather • Week I

Activity Book, page 9
Practice Book, page 145

Objectives

- Read the words *do, this*
- Review the words *a, go, is, play, the, to*
- Read decodable words with /e/*e*
- Reread for fluency

Materials

- Decodable Reader: *Ed Can, Ted Can*
- High-Frequency Word Cards: *do, this, a, go, is, play, the, to*
- Sound-Spelling Card: *Egg*

Decodable Text

For additional decodable passages, see pages 27–28 of the **Teacher's Resource Book**.

Decodable Reader

Read *Ed Can, Ted Can*

 REVIEW Review this week's high-frequency words and phonics skills using the word lists on the inside back cover of *Ed Can, Ted Can*.

Decodable Reader
Ed Can, Ted Can
by Julio Alvarez
Phonics Practice

Ed Can, Ted Can

Review the high-frequency words **do**, **this**, **a**, **go**, **is**, **play**, **the**, and **to** using the **Read/Spell/Write** routine. Then have children chorally read the high-frequency word list.

Review the phonics skill /e/*e* using the *Egg* **Sound-Spelling Card**. Then have children chorally read the decodable word list. Model blending as needed and take note of children who struggle reading these words. Provide additional practice during Small Group time.

MODEL CONCEPTS ABOUT PRINT Demonstrate book handling. *I hold the book so that the cover is on the front and the words are not upside down. I turn the cover. Then I turn each page as I read it.*

 REREAD FOR FLUENCY Have partners reread the book together. Circulate and listen in, providing corrective feedback as needed. Then have children reread the book independently.

Ed is set to go.
Ed can do it!

2

Ted can pet the cat.
Ted can do it!

3

Dan can dip in.
Dan can do it!

4

Nan can hit this net.
Nan can do it!

5

Cam can fit a hat on it.
Cam can do it!

6

Kit can sit in the den.
Kit can do it!

7

Pam can play in it.
Pam can do it!

8

Decodable Reader

Writing

Independent Writing: Weather Report

REVISE AND EDIT

Distribute children's **weather** reports from Day 3. Have children reread them and check for the following:

- Did I write a sentence in my weather report?

- Did I use clear and interesting describing words?

- Did I draw a picture to show the weather?

- Did I begin my sentence with a capital letter and end it with a period?

Circulate and help children as they review and revise their weather reports. Have them check their spelling using their knowledge of letter-sound relationships, the Word Wall, and word lists.

Have children share their writing with a partner.

Magda

Today it is warm and sunny.

Write About It

Tell children to draw a picture of a stormy or **cloudy** day on the ocean. Ask them to write a caption for their drawing.

Objectives

- Revise and edit weather reports
- Use letter knowledge to write letters in a word

Materials

- children's weather reports from Day 3
- Writer's Checklist; Teacher's Resource Book, p. 205

5-Day Writing

Weather Report

DAY 1	Shared: Lists
DAY 2	Interactive: Sentences
DAY 3	Independent: Prewrite and Draft Weather Report
DAY 4	Independent: Revise and Edit Weather Report
DAY 5	Independent: Publish and Present

ELL

Use New Language
Discuss the current weather with children, prompting them to use as many describing words as possible. Then help them complete the sentence frame with appropriate describing words that tell what today's weather is like.

Transitions That Teach

While children are waiting in line, have them tell what they do when they feel **chilly**.

DAY 5
At a Glance

WHOLE GROUP

Oral Language
- Build Robust Vocabulary

✓ **Comprehension**
- Strategy: Visualize
- Skill: Identify Main Idea and Details
- Read Across Texts

✓ **Vocabulary**
- High-Frequency Words
- Build Fluency
- Sound Words

✓ **Phonemic Awareness**
- Phoneme Segmentation

✓ **Phonics**
- Read Words
- Dictation

Writing
- Independent Writing: Publish and Present

SMALL GROUP

- Differentiated Instruction, pages 1610–1635

Review and Assess
Oral Language
Build Robust Vocabulary

REVIEW WORDS

Review this week's oral vocabulary words with children. Explain that all of the words will be used to discuss playing outside. Talk about what it means to play outside. *When you play outside, you can play games in your yard or schoolyard.*

Use the following questions to check children's understanding:

- What type of **weather** is best for playing outside?

- What might a **cloud** look like that is in the sky above as you play outside?

- Would you like to play outside on a **blustery** day?

- What do you wear if it is **chilly** in order to play outside?

- Are you allowed to play outside if there is a **drizzle**? Why or why not?

REVIEW SONGS AND RHYMES ABOUT THE WEATHER

Sing the song "Rain, Rain, Go Away" and have children sing along. Have children describe a rainy day. Then recite the fingerplay "A Cloud" with children. Have them generate words that rhyme with words from the song and rhyme.

Review and Assess
Comprehension

STRATEGY **Monitor Comprehension: Visualize**

REFLECT ON THE STRATEGY Remind children that they can create pictures or sensory images in their mind to help them understand the information in a book. This will help them enjoy and remember the book better. Guide them to adjust comprehension as needed.

Think Aloud I can create a picture in my mind to help me remember the big idea and some of the important details.

SKILL **Identify Main Idea and Details**

Lead children in reviewing the photographs in *A Rainy Day* to help them recall the book. Then use the following questions to review main idea and details:

- *In* A Rainy Day, *what happens in the sky? On the ground?*

- *What do people do when it rains? What do animals do?*

Reading Across Texts

Create a chart to make connections to ideas in the nonfiction selection *A Rainy Day* and the legend "Frog and Locust." You may wish to add columns for "The Wind/Slip on Your Raincoat" and "Four Seasons/Rain on the Rooftops."

A Rainy Day	Frog and Locust
nonfiction	legend
photographs	illustrations
tells about real people, animals, and things	tells about make-believe animals who talk and sing
tells about a rainy day	tells about a day with no rain and a rainy day

Objectives
- Review strategy and skill
- Make connections/compare and contrast genres
- Listen to and share information

Materials
- Big Book: *A Rainy Day*
- Big Book of Explorations, Vol. 2: "The Wind/Slip on Your Raincoat," "Four Seasons/Rain on the Rooftops"
- Read-Aloud Anthology: "Frog and Locust," pp. 97–100
- Activity Book, p. 11

Activity Book, page 11

Objectives

- Review the high-frequency words *this, do, are, for, you, play*
- Review the sound words *drip, drop, splash, crack, bam*
- Build fluency
- Use oral vocabulary words *blustery, chilly, cloud, drizzle,* and *weather*

Materials

- High-Frequency Word Cards; Teacher's Resource Book, pp. 103–110
- High-Frequency Word Cards: *this, do, are, for, you, play*
- index cards with: *drip, drop, splash, crack, bam*
- Big Book: *A Rainy Day*

Fluency

Connected Text Have children reread this week's **Decodable Reader** with a partner. Circulate, listen in, and note those children who need additional instruction and practice reading this week's decodable and sight words.

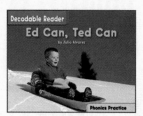

Review and Assess
Vocabulary

High-Frequency Words

Distribute one of the following **High-Frequency Word Cards** to children: **this**, **do**, **are**, **for**, **you**, **play**. *When you hear the word that is on your card, stand and hold up your Word Card.*

- *How* are you *today?*
- This *book is easy to read.*
- *I have a gift* for *my sister.*
- Do you *like cloudy days? Yes, I* do!
- *Can I* play?

Build Fluency: Word Automaticity

Rapid Naming Display the High-Frequency Word Cards *this, do, are, for, you,* and *play*. Point quickly to each card, at random, and have children read the word as fast as they can.

Sound Words

Write the words *drip, drop, splash, crack,* and *bam* on index cards and draw a simple picture to go with each word. Read the words. Have children sort their cards by matching to a picture in the **Big Book** *A Rainy Day*.

TIME TO MOVE!

Have children form a circle and pass around a beanbag to the chant *What will you do with this beanbag for you?* Whoever gets the beanbag on the final *you* does an action, such as making a silly face. Then begin the chant again.

Review and Assess
Phonemic Awareness

 ## Phoneme Segmentation

Objective
- Segment words into phonemes

Materials
- Sound Box
- WorkBoard Sound Boxes; Teacher's Resource Book, p. 136
- markers

Guided Practice

Distribute a **Sound Box** and markers to each child.

Use the Sound Box. Place markers into the boxes as each sound is identified. Children place the markers in their Sound Boxes.

Repeat with *red*.

Listen for the sounds in the word *men*. *Men* has three sounds: /m/ /e/ /n/. Place a marker in each box as you say each sound: /m/ /e/ /n/.

The first sound in *men* is /m/. Point to the first box and say the sound. (/m/) The second sound in *men* is /e/. Point to the middle box and say the sound. (/e/) The third sound in *men* is /n/. Point to the third box and say the sound. (/n/) Now say the word. (*men*)

Practice

Say each word. Children use Sound Boxes to segment words into sounds.

I will say a word. Use your markers and tell me how many sounds you  hear. What are the first, middle, and last sounds?

red	ten	set	Ed	men	pet
net	egg	pen	den	Ted	met

Objectives

- Read simple one-syllable words
- Write simple one-syllable words

Materials

- Word-Building Cards
- 4 index cards with: *This, is, Ned,* period mark
- 6 index cards with: *Do, you, see, the, hen,* question mark
- 7 index cards with: *The, hen, is, in, the, pen,* period mark
- 6 index cards with: *Ned, fed, the, red, hen,* period mark
- WorkBoard Sound Boxes; Teacher's Resource Book, p. 136
- markers
- Activity Book, p. 12

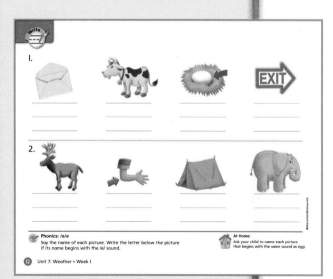

Activity Book, page 12

Review and Assess
Phonics

Build Fluency: Sound-Spellings

Rapid Naming Display the following **Word-Building Cards:** *a, c, d, e, f, h, l, m, n, o, s, p, t.* Have children chorally say each sound as quickly as they can.

Read Words

Apply

Distribute the first set of index cards. Have children stand in sequence.

> Let's read the sentence together.
> *This is Ned.*

Repeat using the other sets of index cards.

> Let's read the sentences together.
> *Do you see the hen?*
> *The hen is in the pen.*
> *Ned fed the red hen.*

Dictation

Dictate sounds for children to spell.

> Listen as I say a sound. Repeat the sound, then write the letter that stands for the sound.
>
> /e/ /d/ /a/ /t/ /i/ /f/
>
> /k/ /o/ /r/ /h/ /n/

Then dictate words for children to spell. Model for children how to use the **Sound Boxes** to segment the sounds in the words. Have them repeat.

Write the letters and words on the board for children to self-correct.

> Now let's write some words. I will say a word. I want you to repeat the word, then think about how many sounds are in the word. Use your Sound Boxes to count the sounds. Then write one letter for each sound you hear.
>
> hip hop pad sad Ed
> dot rot rap hat red
> ram rat fan can hen

Review and Assess
Writing

Independent Writing: Weather Report

PUBLISH
Explain to children that you will gather their **weather** reports to make a class report.

- Brainstorm ideas for a title, such as "Today's Weather."

- Have a few children work on the cover for the book. Write the title on the cover.

- Make holes along the side of the cover and each page of the book.

- Bind the pages together with yarn.

- You may also assist children in using technology to publish their writing.

PRESENT
Ask children to take turns reading their sentences to the class.

LISTENING, SPEAKING, AND VIEWING
- Remind children to speak clearly and to be good listeners when a classmate is speaking.

- Praise children for their hard work and place the finished book in the Reading Workstation for everyone to enjoy. Children may wish to add a copy of their work to their Writing Portfolios.

- You may choose to use this time to review portfolios with children. Have them select favorite samples of their work to share with classmates and family members. Guide children to discuss and dictate sentences about how they have changed as writers.

Write About It
Tell children to draw a sunny day on a mountain or a rainy day on a pond. Have them write a caption for their drawing.

Objective
- Publish and present weather reports

Materials
- children's writing from Day 4

5-Day Writing

Weather Reports

DAY 1	Shared: Lists
DAY 2	Interactive: Sentences
DAY 3	Independent: Prewrite and Draft Weather Report
DAY 4	Independence: Revise and Edit Weather Report
DAY 5	Independent: Publish and Present

Transitions That Teach

While lining up to go to lunch, have children talk about what they like to do when it is **drizzling** outside.

Approaching Level

Oral Language

Objective Preteach oral vocabulary
Materials • none

THEME WORDS: weather, cloud

- Tell children the meanings for **weather** and **cloud**. Weather *is the condition of the air at a certain place and time. It includes the temperature and the amount of wind, rain, snow, sun, or clouds.* Clouds *are fluffy shapes we see in the sky.*

- Discuss the words with children. Ask: *What is the* weather *like today—rainy or sunny? What do the* clouds *look like—white and fluffy or dark and heavy?*

- Have children use the following sentence frames to generate complete oral sentences using the vocabulary words: *Today the* weather *is _____ and I see a* cloud *that looks like a _____.*

High-Frequency Words

Objective Preteach high-frequency words *this, do*
Materials • **High-Frequency Word Cards:** *this, do*

PRETEACH WORDS: this, do

- Display the **High-Frequency Word Cards** for **this** and **do**.

- **Read** Point to and say the word *this. This is the word* this. *It is a word we use when we talk about an object. This is a book.*

- **Spell** *The word* this *is spelled* t-h-i-s. Have children read and spell *this.*

- **Write** Finally, have children write the word *this.* Repeat the routine using the word *do.*

- Have children work with a partner to make up sentences using the words *this* and *do.* Ask them to talk about what they like to do when the weather is bad.

HIGH-FREQUENCY WORDS REVIEW

Display the High-Frequency Word Cards for words previously taught, one card at a time, as children chorally read and spell the word. Mix and repeat. Note words children need to review.

Tier 2

ELL

Partners When pairing children to make up sentences, pair English Language Learners with children who are more proficient. Write their sentences, read them together, and point out the high-frequency words.

Approaching Level

Phonemic Awareness

Objective Identify initial sound /e/
Materials • **Photo Cards:** *egg, elbow, elevator, envelope, exit*

PHONEME ISOLATION

Model

■ Display the **Photo Card** for *egg*. *This is an* egg. *Listen for the beginning sound*: /eeeg/. Egg *begins with* /e/. *Repeat for* exit.

Guided Practice/Practice

■ Display the Photo Cards. Have children take turns selecting a picture, naming it, and saying the initial sound: *This is an _____. _____ begins with* /e/. Guide practice with the first card.

■ Have children note the position of their mouths as they say /e/.

Phonics

Objective Recognize words with initial /e/*e*
Materials • **Sound-Spelling Card:** *Egg* • **Word-Building Cards**
              • **Photo Cards:** *egg, elbow, elevator, envelope, exit*

PRETEACH: RECOGNIZE /e/*e*

Model

■ Display the Photo Card for *egg* and the *Egg* **Sound-Spelling Card**. Say: *The name of this letter is* e. E *stands for the* /e/ *sound you hear at the beginning of* egg. *I will place the* e *card on* egg *because* egg *begins with* /e/. *Repeat with* exit.

■ Say /e/ and trace *e* on your **Word-Building Card**.

Guided Practice/Practice

■ Display the Photo Cards. Point to the Photo Card for *elbow* and have children say the name, repeat the initial sound, and identify the letter. Repeat with remaining Photo Cards for /e/*e*.

■ Guide children to trace the letter *e* on their Word-Building Cards.

■ Identify classroom objects with names that begin with *e*.

SOUND-SPELLINGS REVIEW

Display Word-Building Cards *m, a, s, p, t, i, n, c, o, f, h, d, r,* and *e,* one at a time. Have children chorally say the sounds. Repeat and vary the pace.

Tier 2

Write Weather Sentences

Have children look in old magazines for an example of a type of weather, such as sunny, rainy, snowy, or cloudy. Ask them to cut out the picture, glue it to paper, and then fill in the sentence: *This is a _____ day.*

Puppet

ELL

Relationships Provide additional practice in pronouncing and blending the initial sounds /e/, /p/, /t/, and /n/ and naming the corresponding letters as children point to them.

On Level

High-Frequency Words

Objective Review high-frequency words *this, do, for, you, play, are*

Materials • **High-Frequency Word Cards:** *this, do, for, you, play, are*

REVIEW

- Display the **High-Frequency Word Card** for **this**.

- **Read** Point to and say the word *this. This is the word* this. *It is a word we use when we talk about a person, place, or thing. This is my friend.*

- **Spell** *The word* this *is spelled* t-h-i-s. Have children read and spell *this*.

- **Write** Finally, have children write the word *this*.

- Repeat with **do**, **for**, **you**, **play**, and **are**.

Phonemic Awareness/Phonics

Objective Review recognizing and blending /e/e, /p/p, /t/t, and /n/n

Materials • **Puppet** • **Word-Building Cards** • pocket chart
• **Sound-Spelling WorkBoards**

PHONEME BLENDING

Model

- *Listen as Happy says the sounds for* egg: /e/ /g/. *Now Happy will blend the sounds: /eeeg/,* egg. *Happy blended /e/ /g/ together to say the word* egg. *Repeat the blending with the word* Ed.

Practice

- Have the **Puppet** say /e/ /b/. Ask children to repeat. *Now you blend the sounds and say the word with Happy: /e/ /b/,* ebb. Repeat with the following:

/e/ /l/ /k/	/e/ /l/ /b/ /ō/	/e/ /n/ /d/	/e/ /g/
/h/ /e/ /n/	/e/ /j/	/e/ /l/ /m/	/l/ /e/ /g/

PHONICS: REVIEW /e/e, /d/d, /r/r

Model

- Display **Word-Building Card** *e. The name of this letter is* e. E *stands for the /e/ sound we hear at the beginning of* end. *I'll hold up the* e *card because* end *begins with /e/. Repeat with* d *and* dot, *and* r *and* rod.

Practice

- Write the following words: *elm, elk, dip, Dan, rat, rot.* Have children blend the sounds together to read the word.

Beyond Level

High-Frequency Words/Vocabulary

Objective   Review high-frequency words
Materials   • none

ACCELERATE

- Write *how* and *when* on the board.

- **Read** Point to and say the word *how*. *This is the word* how. *It means "in what way." How do you do that?*

- **Spell** *The word* how *is spelled* h-o-w. *What's the first sound in* how? *That's right. The first sound is /h/. That's why the first letter is* h. Have children read and spell *how*.

- **Write** Finally, have children write the word *how*.

- Repeat the routine with *when*.

- Have children work with a partner to make up oral sentences using the words *how* and *when*.

EXPAND ORAL VOCABULARY

- **Synonyms** Review the meaning of the oral vocabulary word *blustery* with children. Then explain that a *synonym* is a word that means the same thing as another word.

- Say: *A* synonym *for the word* blustery *is* gusty. *When the weather is* gusty, *I feel strong bursts of wind. On a* gusty *fall day, the wind blows leaves off tree branches.*

- Have children take turns using the new word *gusty* in a sentence. Then tell children that they will work with a partner to discuss what might blow away on a gusty day.

Phonics

Objective   Read short *e* words
Materials   • **Sound-Spelling Card:** *Egg*   • **Word-Building Cards**   • pocket chart

ENRICH

- Display the *Egg* **Sound-Spelling Card**. Remind children that the /e/ sound is spelled with the letter *e*. *Egg* begins with the /e/ sound. *Net* has /e/ in the middle.

- Write these words on the board for children to blend and read: *egg, ebb, edge, elf, let, wet, get, when, nest, west, went,* and *help*.

- Display **Word-Building Cards** *e, b, d, g, h, l, m, n, p, s, t, w,* and *x*. Have partners make as many words as they can. Provide time for children to share their lists.

ELL

Partners When pairing children to make up sentences, pair English Language Learners with children who are more proficient. Write their sentences, read them together, and point to the high-frequency words.

ON YOUR OWN

Write Rhyme and Chimes

Have children write and illustrate the Rhyme and Chimes they created in the High-Frequency Words lesson.

ELL ENGLISH LANGUAGE LEARNERS

Oral Language Warm-Up

Content Objective Learn theme vocabulary
Language Objective Sing and act out song to demonstrate understanding
Materials • **Listening Library Audio CD** • **Visual Vocabulary Resources**

✔ BUILD BACKGROUND KNOWLEDGE

All Language Levels

- Introduce the unit theme "Weather" using the song "Rain, Rain, Go Away." Display a picture of rain falling from a cloudy sky, such as a picture from *A Rainy Day* or one of the **Visual Vocabulary Resources**. Teach the word *sky* as you point to the picture. Have children repeat the word three times.

- Play "Rain, Rain, Go Away" on the **Audio CD**. Act out each line as you sing the song. For example, use your fingers to gesture falling rain and use your hands to "push" the rain away.

- Then teach children the song. Emphasize the key word that names a kind of weather: *rain*.

- Play the song several times until children begin to correctly repeat it.

- Ask children to tell about a kind of weather they like. Build on their responses to model speaking in complete sentences. For example: *You like the snow. Snow is cold.*

Academic Language

Language Objective Use academic language in classroom conversations

All Language Levels

- This week's academic words are **boldfaced** throughout the lesson. Define the word in context and provide a clear example from the selection. Then ask children to generate an example or a word with a similar meaning.

Academic Language Used in Whole Group Instruction

Oral Vocabulary Words	Vocabulary and Grammar Concepts	Strategy and Skill Words
blustery	sound words	visualize
chilly	describing words	main idea
cloud		details
drizzle		describing words
weather		

Cognates

Help children identify similarities and differences in pronunciation and spelling between English words and Spanish cognates:

Cognates

visualize   *visualizar*

ELL ENGLISH LANGUAGE LEARNERS

Vocabulary

Language Objective Demonstrate understanding and use of key words by describing weather

Materials • **Visual Vocabulary Resources**

Visual Vocabulary Resources

✓ PRETEACH KEY VOCABULARY

All Language Levels

Use the **Visual Vocabulary Resources** to preteach the weekly oral vocabulary words *blustery*, *chilly*, *cloud*, *drizzle*, and *weather*. Focus on one or two words per day. Use the following routine that appears in detail on the cards.

- Define the word in English and provide the example given.
- Define the word in Spanish, if appropriate, and indicate if the word is a cognate.
- Display the picture and explain how it illustrates or demonstrates the word.
- Then engage children in structured partner-talk about the image, using the key word.
- Ask children to chorally say the word three times.
- Point out any known sound-spellings or focus on a key aspect of phonemic awareness related to the word.

PRETEACH FUNCTION WORDS AND PHRASES

All Language Levels

Use the Visual Vocabulary Resources to preteach the function words and phrases *open (an umbrella)* and *in (the rain)*. Focus on one word per day. Use the detailed routine on the cards.

- Define the word in English and, if appropriate, in Spanish. Point out if the word is a cognate.
- Refer to the picture and engage children in talk about the word. For example, children will partner-talk using sentence frames, or they will listen to sentences and replace a word or phrase with the new function word.
- Ask children to chorally repeat the word three times.

TEACH BASIC WORDS

Beginning/Intermediate

Use the Visual Vocabulary Resources to teach the basic words *raindrops*, *boots*, *umbrella*, *raincoat*, *flood*, and *rainbow*. Teach these "things related to rain" words using the routine provided on the card.

Answer a Question

Have children draw pictures of their favorite type of weather: sunny, rainy, or snowy. Ask children to label their picture.

Snow is fun.

ELL

Partners When pairing children to make up sentences, pair English Language Learners with children who are more proficient. Write their sentences, read them together, and point out the high-frequency words.

Approaching Level

Oral Language

Objectives	Reinforce oral vocabulary; speak in complete sentences
Materials	• none

THEME WORDS: *weather, clouds*

- *We have talked about **weather** and how it changes every day. We look at the temperature and the wind. The **clouds** also give us information about the weather.*

- Have children speak in complete sentences to answer the questions. *What type of weather is best for skiing—snowy or rainy? Explain why. Why is it important to know how the weather is going to be each day?*

- *How do clouds look on a sunny day? How do clouds look on a rainy day?*

- *If the clouds were dark and low, what type of weather would you expect to happen?*

High-Frequency Words

Objective	Reteach high-frequency words
Materials	• **High-Frequency Word Cards:** *this, do*
	• **Sound-Spelling WorkBoards**

RETEACH WORDS: *this, do*

Tier 2

- Distribute a **WorkBoard** to each child. Then display the **High-Frequency Word Card** for **this**.

- Use the **Read/Spell/Write** routine to reteach the word. Point to and say the word. *This is the word* this. *It is a word we use when we talk about an object or place: This is my house.* This *is spelled* t-h-i-s. Have children read and spell *this*. Then have them write the word on their WorkBoards. Repeat the routine with the word **do**.

- Have children work with a partner to make up sentences using the words *this* and *do*. Ask them to talk about what they like to do on sunny days.

CUMULATIVE REVIEW

Display the High-Frequency Word Cards for words previously taught, one card at a time, as children chorally read and spell the word. Mix and repeat. Note words children need to review.

Approaching Level

Phonemic Awareness

Objective Blend sounds to form words
Materials • **Puppet**

PHONEME BLENDING

Tier **2**

Model

■ *Listen as Happy says the sounds for* egg: /e/ /g/. *Now Happy will blend the sounds:* /eeeg/, egg. *Happy blended* /e/ /g/ *together to say the word* egg. *Repeat with* Ed.

Practice

■ Have the **Puppet** say /e/ /b/. Ask children to repeat. *Now you blend the sounds and say the word with Happy:* /e/ /b/, ebb. Repeat with the following:

/e/ /l/ /k/   /e/ /j/   /e/ /d/   /e/ /n/ /d/   /e/ /g/
/b/ /e/ /d/   /l/ /e/ /g/   /r/ /e/ /d/   /l/ /e/ /d/   /f/ /e/ /l/

Phonics

Objective Reinforce letter-sound correspondence for /e/e
Materials • **Sound-Spelling Card:** Egg • **Sound-Spelling WorkBoards**
  • **Word-Building Cards** • **Decodable Reader:** Ed Can, Ted Can

RECOGNIZE /e/e

Model

■ Display the *Egg* **Sound-Spelling Card**. *The letter* e *stands for the* /e/ *sound as in* egg. *What is this letter? What sound does it stand for?* Repeat with *exit*.

■ Trace *e* on a **Word-Building Card**. *I will say a sentence. We will trace* e *on the cards when we hear* /e/. *Edgar exited the elevator.*

Guided Practice/Practice

■ Distribute a **WorkBoard** to each child. Say: *exit, door, egg, elevator, chair, edge, elk, boy, elephant.* Children write *e* on their WorkBoard when they hear a word with /e/. Guide them with the first two words.

■ **Read the Decodable Reader** Read *Ed Can, Ted Can* with children. Have them echo-read each page. Chorally reread the story.

CUMULATIVE REVIEW

Tier **2**

Display Word-Building Cards *m, a, s, p, t, i, n, c, o, f, h, d, r,* and *e,* one at a time. Point to the letters in a random order. Have children chorally say the sound. Repeat and vary the pace.

Puppet

Corrective Feedback

Blending Error If children have difficulty blending sounds, help them note how the position of the mouth changes when they blend /e/ /g/, but the position of the tongue stays the same. *Listen:* /eeeg/, egg. *Now you say it.* /eeeg/, egg. *How does your mouth change? Where is your tongue?*

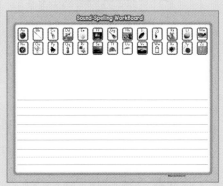
Sound-Spelling WorkBoard

Decodable Reader

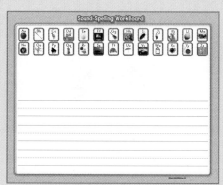

Sound-Spelling WorkBoard

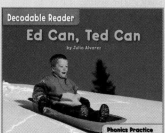

Decodable Reader

On Level

Phonics

Objective	Review recognizing and blending /e/e, /p/p, /t/t, and /n/n
Materials	• **Word-Building Cards** • pocket chart
	• **Sound-Spelling WorkBoards**

✓ CONSOLIDATE LEARNING

- Display **Word-Building Card** e. *The name of this letter is* e. E *stands for the /e/ sound we hear at the beginning of* egg. *I'll hold up the* e *card because* egg *begins with /e/.* Repeat with p and *paper,* t and *table,* and n and *nut.*

- Distribute small Word-Building Cards. Say: *elbow, talk, elk, puppy, nose, edge, top, nine, ebb, test.* Children repeat the initial sound for each word and hold up the appropriate card.

- **Blend Words** Place cards for p, e, and t in the pocket chart. Point to each letter for children to identify. Move your hand from left to right below the letters as you blend the word: /peeet/, *pet. What's the word?* Repeat with *pen, net,* and *ten.*

- Have children write p, e, t several times on their **WorkBoards** as they say /p/, /e/, and /t/. Repeat with p, e, n; n, e, t; and t, e, n.

- **Read the Decodable Reader** Read *Ed Can, Ted Can* with children. Have them reread each page. Then chorally reread the story.

Beyond Level

Phonics

Objective	Read short *e* words
Materials	• **Word-Building Cards** • pocket chart

✓ ACCELERATE

- Display Word-Building Cards s, h, e, l, l in a pocket chart. Blend the sounds to say the word. Point out that the two l's together stand for a single l sound.

- Write these words for children to blend: *shell, smell, step, desk, fresh, twelve, slept, spell,* and *swell.*

ELL ENGLISH LANGUAGE LEARNERS

Access to Core Content

Content Objective Develop listening comprehension
Language Objective Discuss text using key words and sentence frames
Materials • **ELL Resource Book**, pp. 182–185

PRETEACH BIG BOOK

All Language Levels

Use the Interactive Question-Response Guide on **ELL Resource Book** pages 182–185 to introduce children to *A Rainy Day*. Preteach half of the selection on Day 1 and half on Day 2.

- Use the prompts provided in the guide to develop meaning and vocabulary. Use the partner-talk and whole-class responses to engage children and increase student talk.

- When completed, revisit the selection and prompt children to talk about the photos. Provide sentence starters as needed and build on children's responses to develop language.

ELL Resource Book

Big Book

Beginning	Intermediate	Advanced
Use Visuals During the Interactive Reading, select several pictures. Describe them and have children summarize what you said.	**Summarize** During the Interactive Reading, select a few lines of text. After you read them and explain them, have children summarize the text.	**Expand** During the Interactive Reading, select a larger portion of text. After you read it and explain it, have children summarize the text.

Approaching Level

High-Frequency Words

Objective Recognize high-frequency words *this, do, you, for*

Materials • **High-Frequency Word Cards:** *this, do, you, for*
• **Word-Building Cards**

✔ REVIEW WORDS: *this, do, for, you*

- Display the **High-Frequency Word Card** for **do**. Say the word and have children repeat it. Point to each letter and have children name it.

- Distribute small **Word-Building Cards** *d* and *o*. Model putting the letters together to form the word *do*. Then have children form *do*.

- Repeat the above routines with the words **this**, **for**, and **you**.

- Have children take turns saying the sentence *I can do this for you* as they show something they can do.

CUMULATIVE REVIEW

Display the High-Frequency Cards for words previously taught, one card at a time, as children chorally read and spell the word. Mix and repeat. Note words children need to review.

Phonemic Awareness

Objective Identify initial and medial /e/*e*

Materials • **Photo Cards:** *egg, elevator, envelope, jet, net, web* • pocket chart

✔ PHONEME ISOLATION

Tier 2

Model

- Display the **Photo Card** for *egg* in the pocket chart. *Listen for the /e/ sound in* egg, /e/ /g/. Egg *begins with /e/.*

- Display the Photo Card for *net* in a new column in the pocket chart. Explain to children that the /e/ sound can also be heard in the middle of a word. *Listen for the /e/ sound in* net, /n/ /e/ /t/. Net *has the /e/ in the middle.* Repeat with *jet*. Place the picture of the *jet* under the picture of the *net*.

Guided Practice/Practice

- Display the Photo Cards. Children take turns selecting a picture, naming it, telling whether they hear the /e/ sound at the beginning or in the middle and placing the card under the correct picture. *This is a _____. I hear /e/ at the beginning/in the middle of _____.* Guide practice with the first card.

ELL

Extra Practice During the Cumulative Review, pair children at different levels of proficiency and have partners take turns reading and spelling the high-frequency words to each other.

Approaching Level

Phonics

Objective Blend sounds to form words and build fluency
Materials • **Word-Building Cards** • pocket chart

REVIEW

Tier **2**

Model

■ Place **Word-Building Card** *r* in the pocket chart. *The name of this letter is* r. *The letter* r *stands for the /r/ sound. Say /r/. What is the letter? What is the sound?*

■ Repeat with the letters *e* and *d,* forming the word *red. Listen as I blend the three sounds together: /rrreeed/, red. What is the word? Let's say the sounds and blend the word together.*

Guided Practice/Practice

■ Give *r, e,* and *d* cards to three children and ask them to say the sounds for the letters: /r/ /e/ /d/. Then have them blend sounds to say these words: *den, ten, net, Ned,* and *Ed.*

Build Fluency

■ Have children blend *red, den, ten, net, Ned,* and *Ed* as quickly as they can.

Decodable Reader

Objective Reread Decodable Reader *Ed Can, Ted Can*
Materials • **Decodable Reader:** *Ed Can, Ted Can*

REREAD *Ed Can, Ted Can*

■ Have children identify the front cover of the book and read the title. Open to the title page and point out the title. *Let's read the title together.* Have children sound out each word as you run your finger under it. *Look at the picture. What is that a picture of? What do you think this book is going to be about?*

■ Page through the book. Ask children what they see in each picture. Ask them to find and point to the word *do.*

■ Read the book chorally with children. Have them point to each word as they read it. Provide corrective feedback as needed.

■ Ask children to use *do* to talk about the pictures. *What does Ed like to do? He can ride on a sled. What else are children doing in the pictures?*

■ After reading, ask children to recall things they read about.

Corrective Feedback

Blending: Sound Error Model the sound that children missed, then have them repeat the sound. For example, for the word *red,* say: *My turn.* Tap under the letter *e* in the word *red* and say: *Sound? What's the sound?* Then return to the beginning of the word. Say: *Let's start over.* Blend the word with children again.

Decodable Reader

ON YOUR OWN
I Can Do It!

Have children draw a picture of something they like to do, as in the decodable story. Ask them to label the picture with the sentence *I can do it!*

On Level

Decodable Reader

Objective Reread *Ed Can, Ted Can* to develop fluency
Materials • **Decodable Reader:** *Ed Can, Ted Can*

REREAD FOR FLUENCY

- Ask children to look at the illustrations in *Ed Can, Ted Can* and use their own words to retell what the book was about.

- Have children reread a page or two of the story. Model and work with them to read with accuracy and expression. Point out how you used your voice: *When I read, "Ed is set to go. Ed can do it," I said* Ed can do it *with more emphasis. The sentence ended with an exclamation point and I wanted to show that Ed was excited about going down on the sled.*

- Provide time to listen as children read their page(s). Comment on their accuracy and expression, and provide corrective feedback by modeling proper fluency.

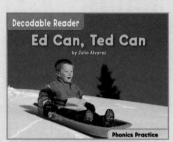

Decodable Reader

Beyond Level

Decodable Reader

Objective Reread *Ed Can, Ted Can* to reinforce fluency and phonics
Materials • **Decodable Reader:** *Ed Can, Ted Can*

REREAD FOR FLUENCY

- Have partners reread *Ed Can, Ted Can*.

- Provide time to listen as children read. Comment on their accuracy and expression, and provide corrective feedback by modeling proper fluency.

INNOVATE

- Have children make a poster to show three things they can do. Ask them to write a title, such as *I Can Do It*. Help them write sentence captions for their drawings.

- For *We Can*, have children add pages to the book by drawing pictures of other things that the people in the book might do. Help them write sentence captions for their drawings. Ask children to read their new pages to partners.

ELL ENGLISH LANGUAGE LEARNERS

Access to Core Content

Content Objective Develop listening comprehension

Language Objective Discuss text using key words and sentence frames

Materials • **ELL Resource Book,** pp. 186–187

PRETEACH BIG BOOK OF EXPLORATIONS

All Language Levels

Use the Interactive Question-Response Guide on **ELL Resource Book** pages 186–187 to preview the **Big Book of Explorations** selections about weather. Preteach the first two selections on Day 3 and the rest on Day 4.

Grammar

Content Objective Identify describing words

Language Objective Speak in complete sentences, using sentence frames

Materials • **Listening Library Audio CD** • **Photo Cards**

DESCRIBING WORDS (ADJECTIVES)

All Language Levels

■ Review describing words (adjectives). Tell children that describing words tell about naming words. Say: *Today is a sunny day. What kind of a day does the sentence tell about?* (sunny) Then ask for other describing words that tell about kinds of days.

> **A Cloud**
> *What brings the rain,*
> *What brings the snow,*
> Open hands, palm up.
> *That showers down on us below?*
> Wiggle fingers, moving downward.
> *When you look up in the high blue sky,*
> Look up.
> *What is the thing you see float by?*
> *A cloud!*

■ Play "A Cloud" from the **Listening Library Audio CD**. Tell children to listen for describing words.

■ Point out the describing words *high* and *blue*. Ask children what these words describe. (sky) Display the **Photo Cards** for *kitten* and *apple*. Point to each and name a word to describe the picture. For example, *fluffy kitten*. Have children repeat the phrase.

PEER DISCUSSION STARTERS

All Language Levels

■ Distribute weather-related Photo Cards such as *cloud* and *sun*.

■ Pair children and have them complete the sentence frame *I see the _____.* Ask them to expand on their sentences by providing as many details as they can. For example: *I see the _____ _____.* Circulate, listen in, and take note of each child's language use and proficiency.

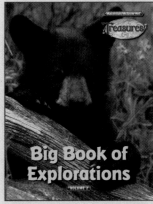

Big Book of Explorations

Puppet

Approaching Level

Phonemic Awareness

Objective Blend sounds to form words

Materials • **Puppet** • **Photo Cards:** *egg, gem, jet, nest, net, shell, vest, web*

PHONEME BLENDING

Tier 2

Model

- Display the **Photo Cards**. *Happy is going to say the sounds in a word: /n/ /e/ /t/. Happy can blend these sounds together: /nnneeet/. Now you blend the sounds to say the word with Happy:* net. Then point to the Photo Card for *net*.

- Repeat with *web*.

Guided Practice/Practice

- Say: *Happy will say some sounds: /e/ /g/. Repeat the sounds Happy said. Now blend the sounds together to make a word: /eeeg/, egg.* Point to the *egg* Photo Card.

- Continue with *jet, nest, vest, gem,* and *shell*.

Phonics

Objective Blend /d/d, /e/e, /f/f, /n/n, /p/p, /r/r, /s/s, /t/t to read words

Materials • **Word-Building Cards**

REVIEW SKILLS: BLEND SOUNDS

Tier 2

Model

- Display **Word-Building Cards** *r, e,* and *d*. Point to the letter *r. What is this letter? What does it stand for?* Have children say /r/: /rrr/. Repeat with the letters *e* and *d*.

- *I put three sounds together to say the word: /rrreeed/, red. We blended /r/ /e/ /d/ together to say the word red.* Children repeat and say the word *red. Now listen again. I'll do another word.* Repeat the blending with the word *fed: /f/ /e/ /d/, /fffeeed/, fed.*

Guided Practice/Practice

- Display Word-Building Cards *s, e, t*. Children walk by the cards and say the sound each letter stands for. Have them repeat, quickly saying the sounds one after the other: /ssseeet/, *set*. Repeat with the following words: *net, pet, pen, den, ten,* and *Ted*.

Approaching Level

Leveled Reader Library

Leveled Reader Lesson 1

Objective Read *Do You Like Rain?* to apply skills and strategies
Materials • **Leveled Reader:** *Do You Like Rain?*

Leveled Reader

BEFORE READING

- **Preview and Predict** Read the title and the name of the author. *Who do you see on the cover? What is happening?* Turn to the title page and point out that it also has the title and the name of the author. *What do you think this book is about?*

- **Model Concepts About Print** *This is the word* rain. *The word is made up of letters. Let's name the letters in* rain *together.*

- **Review High-Frequency Words** Write **this**, **is**, **do**, **you**, **like**, and **the**. Read the words. Guide children to name the letters in each word. Have them find each word in the book and point to it as they read it.

- **Page Through the Book** Name unfamiliar terms and identify rebuses and the pictures.

- **Set a Purpose for Reading** *Let's find out about different kinds of weather.*

Digital Learning

Use the **Leveled Reader Audio CD** for fluency building *after* children read the book with your support during Small Group time.

DURING READING

- Remind children to use the rebuses and illustrations to gain information and to look for the high-frequency words they know. Show children how to self-correct if a word doesn't sound right or doesn't make sense in the sentence. *On page 8, I look at the rebus, and I think, "Do you like the sun?" Then I look at the photograph and see a picture of the sun setting for the night.* Sun *doesn't make sense. The picture doesn't show a sun. I think the word is* sunset. *"Do you like the sunset?" That makes sense.*

- Monitor children's reading and provide help as needed.

ON YOUR OWN
Weather We Like

Have children draw pictures of weather from the book. Then ask them to write the answer to this question: *Do you like this kind of weather?*

I like snow.

AFTER READING

- Ask children to point out words that they had trouble reading and to share strategies they used to help them. Reinforce good behaviors. For example, say: *Colin, I noticed that you looked at the picture after reading the sentence to make sure your sentence made sense.*

- Ask children to retell important facts read in the text and to share information. *Do you like rain? Do you like snow? What is your favorite type of weather? Why?*

Leveled Reader

ELL

Retell Use the Interactive Question-Response Guide Technique to help English Language Learners understand *What Can You Do?* As you read, make meaning clear by pointing to pictures, demonstrating word meaning, paraphrasing text, and asking children questions.

ON YOUR OWN

Draw What You Can Do

Ask children to choose one type of weather from the book. Have them draw and write what they can do in that kind of weather.

On Level

Leveled Reader Lesson 1

Leveled Reader Library

Objective Read *What Can You Do?* to apply skills and strategies

Materials • **Leveled Reader:** *What Can You Do?*

BEFORE READING

- **Preview and Predict** Read the title and the name of the author. *Who is on the cover? What are they doing? What do you think this book is going to be about?* Open and page through the book. Name unfamiliar items and discuss the photographs.

- **Model Concepts About Print** *Listen as I read the title again. The words I say match what is written on the cover of the book. Let's count the words in the title.*

- **Review High-Frequency Words** Write **you**, **do**, and **this** on chart paper. Have children find each word in the book and point to the word as they read it.

- **Set a Purpose for Reading** *Let's find out about different kinds of weather.*

DURING READING

- Have children turn to page 2 and begin by whisper-reading the first two pages.

- Remind them to look for the new high-frequency words and to use the illustrations.

- Monitor children's reading. Stop during the reading and ask open-ended questions to facilitate discussion, such as: *What does the author tell us about weather? What does the author think you should do in different types of weather?* Build on children's responses to develop deeper understanding.

AFTER READING

- Ask children to point out words they had trouble reading and to share strategies they used to figure them out. Reinforce good behaviors.

- **Retell** Have children retell important facts read in the text. Have them share information and help them make a personal connection. *What do you like to do when it rains? What might you like to do in the snow?*

- Have partners take turns asking and answering questions about the text.

Beyond Level

Leveled Reader Lesson 1

Objective Read *Look at the Weather!* to apply skills and strategies

Materials • **Leveled Reader:** *Look at the Weather!*

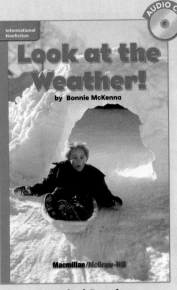

Leveled Reader

BEFORE READING

- **Preview and Predict** Read the title and the name of the author. *What do you see on the cover? What do you think this book is about?* Turn to the title page and point out that it also has the title and the name of the author. Page through the book with children and pause to name unfamiliar items.

- **Introduce Story Words** Point to the word *thermometer* on page 2. Read the sentence. Have children use the picture to explain what a *thermometer* is. Repeat with *icicles* on page 3.

- **Set a Purpose for Reading** Discuss purpose for reading. *Let's find out about things we can do when the temperature changes.*

DURING READING

- Remind children that when they come to an unfamiliar word, they can look for familiar chunks in the word, break the word into syllables and sound out each part. If the word does not sound right or make sense in the sentence, children can self-correct. Have them use picture dictionaries to determine the meanings of unknown words.

- Monitor children's reading and provide help as needed.

AFTER READING

- Ask children to point out words they had trouble reading and to share the strategies they used to figure them out.

- Have children retell important facts read in the text and share information. *When did you use a thermometer? What did it tell you about the weather?*

Guess the Temperature

Have children draw pictures of cold, cool, warm, or hot weather. Children can then trade pictures with partners and figure out the thermometer reading for each type of weather.

- **Synthesize** *Imagine that you are going to take a trip where the weather is different from the way it is where you live. How would you decide what clothes to pack for your trip?*

- Have children work in pairs to study the seven-day forecast for a variety of cities. You may want to print forecasts from an online source ahead of time.

- **Model** Explain to children that they will choose one city as a vacation destination and, based on the weather forecast for that city, write a list of clothing and accessories to pack. For example: *Honolulu, Hawaii: swimsuits, sunscreen, shorts, T-shirts, umbrella.*

Kinds of Weather 1627

Leveled Reader

Vocabulary

Preteach Vocabulary Use the routine in the **Visual Vocabulary Resources**, pages 337–338, to preteach the ELL Vocabulary listed on the inside front cover of the Leveled Reader.

ELL ENGLISH LANGUAGE LEARNERS

Leveled Reader

Content Objective Read to apply skills and strategies
Language Objective Retell information using complete sentences
Materials •**Leveled Reader:** *You Can Do This*

BEFORE READING

All Language Levels

- **Preview** Read the title *You Can Do This*. Ask: *What's the title? Say it again.* Repeat with the author's name. Point to the cover photo and say: *I see three girls.* Point to the girls as you say the word *girl. The girls run.* Now turn to a partner and tell more about what you see in this picture.

- **Page Through the Book** Use simple language to tell about the photo on each page. Immediately follow up with questions, such as: *What is the weather? What can you do?*

- **Review Skills** Use the inside front cover to review the phonics skill and high-frequency words.

- **Set a Purpose** Say: *Let's read to find out about different kinds of weather.*

DURING READING

All Language Levels

- Have children whisper-read each page, or use the differentiated suggestions below. Circulate, listen in, and provide corrective feedback, such as modeling how to identify details.

- **Retell** Stop after every two pages and ask children to state what they have learned so far. Reinforce language by restating children's comments when they have difficulty using story-specific words. Provide differentiated sentence frames to support children's responses and engage children in partner-talk.

Beginning	Intermediate	Advanced
Echo-Read Have children echo-read after you.	**Choral-Read** Have children choral-read with you.	**Choral-Read** Have children choral-read.
Check Comprehension Point to pictures and ask questions such as: *Is it rainy or sunny? Point to the umbrella. Is this a tree?*	**Check Comprehension** Ask questions/prompts such as: *What is the weather? How does it feel when it snows? What can you do when it rains?*	**Check Comprehension** Ask: *Which is your favorite kind of weather in this book? What do you do when it snows? Do you like the rain? Why or why not?*

ELL ENGLISH LANGUAGE LEARNERS

AFTER READING

All Language Levels

Book Talk Children will work with peers of varying language abilities to discuss their books for this week. Display the four **Leveled Readers** read this week: *Look at the Weather!* (Beyond Level), *What Can You Do?* (On Level), *Do You Like Rain?* (Approaching Level), and *You Can Do This* (English Language Learners).

Ask the questions and provide the prompts below. Call on children who read each book to answer the questions or respond to the prompt. If appropriate, ask children to find the pages in the book that illustrate their answers.

- • What kinds of weather did you learn about?
- • What did you lean about rain?
- • What did you learn about snow?
- • What kind of weather do you like? How does it feel?
- • What do you like to do when the sun is out? Tell about it.

Develop Listening and Speaking Skills Tell children to remember the following:

- Share information in cooperative learning interactions. Remind children to work with their partners to retell the story and complete any activities. Ask: *What happened next in the story?*

- Employ self-corrective techniques and monitor their own and other children's language production. Children should ask themselves: *What parts of this passage were confusing to me? Can my classmates help me clarify a word or sentence that I don't understand?*

- Use high-frequency English words to describe people, places, and objects.

- Narrate, describe, and explain with specificity and detail. Ask: *Where did the story take place? Can you describe the setting? What else did you notice?*

- Express opinions, ideas, and feelings on a variety of social and academic topics. Ask: *What do you think about the characters in the story?*

Approaching Level

Phonemic Awareness

Objective Segment words into sounds
Materials
- **Sound Boxes** • markers
- **WorkBoard Sound Boxes; Teacher's Resource Book,** p. 136

 PHONEME SEGMENTATION

Tier 2

Model

- Use the **Sound Boxes**. *Listen for the sounds in the word* men. Men *has three sounds: /m/ /e/ /n/. I will place a marker in each box as I say each sound: /m/ /e/ /n/.*

- *The first sound in* men *is /m/.* Point to the first box and say the sound, /m/. Repeat with the second and third sounds. *Now let's say the word,* men. *Repeat with the word* red.

Guided Practice/Practice

- Distribute a Sound Box and markers to each child. Have children use the Sound Boxes to segment these words: *red, ten, set, Ed, net, pen, den, net, pet, Ted,* and *web.*

ELL

Sound-Letter Relationships Provide additional practice in pronouncing the /e/, /d/, /r/, /f/, /n/ sounds and naming the corresponding letters, as children point to them.

Phonics

Objective Reinforce initial sounds /e/e, /d/d, /r/r, /f/f, /n/n and build fluency
Materials
- **Word-Building Cards**
- **Photo Cards:** *deer, doctor, dog, doll, door, egg, elbow, elevator, exit, fan, farm, feather, feet, fork, nail, net, nose, nurse, nut, rabbit, rake, ring, rock, rope* • pocket chart • **Sound-Spelling WorkBoards**

 BUILD FLUENCY

Tier 2

Model

- Place **Word-Building Cards** *e, d, f, n,* and *r* in the top row of the pocket chart. Have children name the letters and review the sound each letter stands for. Stack the **Photo Cards** facedown.

Guided Practice/Practice

- *Let's do one together.* Draw a card and guide children in naming the picture, identifying the initial sound, and placing the card in the pocket chart under the letter it begins with.

- Children choose a Photo Card, say the picture name, identify the initial sound, and place the card in the pocket chart.

Build Fluency

- Display the Word-Building Cards. Have children say each letter name as quickly as they can. Then ask them to write the letters *e, d, f, n,* and *r* on their **WorkBoards** several times as they say the letters.

Leveled Reader Library

Approaching Level

Leveled Reader Lesson 2

Objective Reread *Do You Like Rain?* to reinforce fluency, phonics, and identifying main idea and details

Materials • **Leveled Reader:** *Do You Like Rain?*

FOCUS ON FLUENCY

■ Tell children that you will read one page of the book and they should read that page right after you. They should follow along in their books and try to read at the same speed and with the same expression that you use.

SKILL IDENTIFY MAIN IDEA AND DETAILS

■ *Look at the pictures in this book. What is this book about? What kinds of weather are shown in the book? Is the weather in this book real or make-believe? How do you know?*

REREAD PREVIOUSLY READ BOOKS

■ Distribute copies of the past six **Leveled Readers**. Discuss the purposes of rereading. Tell children that rereading the books will help them develop their skills and enjoy language.

■ Circulate and listen in as children read. Stop them periodically and ask them how they are figuring out words or checking their understanding. Tell children to read other previously read Leveled Readers during independent reading time.

High-Frequency Words

Objective Review high-frequency words *this, do, you,* and *for*

Materials • **High-Frequency Word Cards:** *this, do, you, for*

BUILD WORD AUTOMATICITY: *this, do, for, you*

■ Distribute copies of the **High-Frequency Word Card** for **do**. Say the word and have children repeat it. Have them name the letters in the word. Repeat with the words **this**, **for**, and **you**.

■ **Build Fluency** Use the High-Frequency Word Cards to review previously taught words. Repeat, guiding children to read more rapidly.

Leveled Reader

Meet Grade-Level Expectations

As an alternative to this day's lesson, guide children through a reading of the On Level Practice Reader. See page 1626. Because both books contain the same vocabulary, phonics, and comprehension skills, the scaffolding you provided will help most children gain access to this more challenging text.

Corrective Feedback

Throughout the lessons, provide feedback based on children's responses. If the answer is correct, ask another question. If the answer is tentative, restate key information to assist the child. If the answer is wrong, provide corrective feedback such as hints or clues, refer to a visual such as a **Sound-Spelling Card** or story illustration, or probe with questions to help the child clarify any misunderstanding.

Leveled Reader

ON YOUR OWN

Make a Prediction

Have children draw and write about what they think the weather will be like tomorrow. Have them display their drawings and tell what they like to do in that kind of weather.

On Level

Leveled Reader Lesson 2

Objective   Reread to apply skills and strategies to retell a story
Materials   • **Leveled Reader:** *What Can You Do?*

BEFORE READING

■ Ask children to look through *What Can You Do?* and recall what the book is about. Reinforce vocabulary by repeating children's sentences using more sophisticated language. For example: *The clouds are white and fluffy. This book shows different types of weather.*

DURING READING

■ Have children join you in a choral-reading of the story. Model reading with expression. *When I read page 3, I emphasized* You can do this *by saying it a little stronger. I used the same strong emphasis on every other page when the sentence* You can do this *was repeated. I wanted to emphasize what the author believes many children can do.* Ask children to use the same kind of expression when they read. Discuss how reading a variety of texts, with expression, can help them enjoy the language.

■ Assign each child a page. Have children practice by whisper-reading. *Follow along as other children read, and be ready to come in when it is your turn. Remember, use lots of expression.*

AFTER READING

■ Have children retell important facts read in the text and share information.

■ *Look at the pictures. What happens on rainy days? What happens on sunny days? What happens on snowy days?* Lead children into discussing what this story is mainly about.

■ Have children make connections to the larger community. *What does weather change in your town? What do people do differently in different weather?*

Leveled Reader Library

Beyond Level

Leveled Reader Lesson 2

Objective   Reread to apply skills and strategies to retell a story

Materials   • **Leveled Reader:** *Look at the Weather!*

BEFORE READING

- Ask children to look back at *Look at the Weather!* and retell important facts from the book. *What was this story mostly about? What were some things the children did when it was cold? What were some things the children did when it was hot?*

DURING READING

- Assign each child a page of the book to read aloud. Have children practice by whisper-reading. *Follow along as each child reads, and be ready to come in when it is your turn. Remember, use lots of expression. Have children ask questions about the text.*

AFTER READING

- Explain that picturing in our mind what a book tells us helps us better understand the ideas. Model the strategy: *When I read about cold weather, I picture icicles on buildings. This helps me understand what cold weather is like. What do you picture in your mind when you read about the hot weather?*

Expand Vocabulary

Objective   Learn and apply the opposite meaning of the words *cold, hot, cool,* and *warm*

Materials   • **Leveled Reader:** *Look at the Weather!*

ENRICH *cold, hot, cool, warm*

Gifted Talented

- Have children reread page 2. Ask them what word describes the temperature outside. *(cold)* Have children give examples of things that are cold. *(snow, ice, water)* Then have children reread page 5. Point out that the word *hot* means the opposite of *cold*. Hot *and* cold *are opposites.* Ask children to name things that are hot.

- Repeat with *cool* (page 6) and *warm* (page 10).

- Use *cold, hot, cool,* and *warm* to begin a chart of opposites. Then have children name opposites for these story words: *like, on, in*. *(hate/dislike, off, out)* Add them to the chart. Have children brainstorm other pairs of opposites. Ask children to use opposites from the chart in sentences: *Ice cream is* cold, *but soup is* hot.

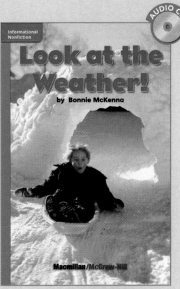

Informational Nonfiction

Look at the Weather!
by Bonnie McKenna

Macmillan/McGraw-Hill

Leveled Reader

ON YOUR OWN

Respond to the Book

Have children draw and write answers to a question from the book, such as *What do you do when it is very cold?* or *What do you do when it is very hot?*

ELL

Partners When children use opposites from the chart in sentences, pair English Language Learners with children who are more proficient.

ELL ENGLISH LANGUAGE LEARNERS

Fluency

Content Objectives Reread the Decodable Reader to develop fluency; develop speaking skills

Language Objective Tell a partner what a selection is about

Materials • **Decodable Reader:** *Ed Can, Ted Can*

REREAD FOR FLUENCY

Beginning

■ Review the high-frequency words **this**, **do**, **are**, **for**, **you**, and **play** using the **Read/Spell/Write** routine.

Intermediate/Advanced

■ Use each word in a sentence that illustrates its use, such as: *You can play with this toy.* Point to a toy. Have children act out playing with it. *This book is for you.* Hand a child a book.

■ Then provide sentence starters for children to complete. Where appropriate, act out children's responses. For example: *This is my hand.*

All Language Levels

■ Guide children through a choral-reading of *Ed Can, Ted Can.* Point to the exclamation mark at the end of the sentence "Ed can do it!" Tell children that when a sentence ends in an exclamation mark, we read it as if we are very excited. Model reading the sentence and have children chorally repeat.

DEVELOP SPEAKING/LISTENING SKILLS

All Language Levels

■ Have children reread *Ed Can, Ted Can* to a partner. Remind them to listen carefully and follow along in their book as their partner is reading. Work with children to read with accuracy and appropriate expression.

■ Ask children to tell their partner about the pictures on each page. Then have the other partner describe the pictures. Circulate, listen in, and provide additional language as needed.

Beginning	Intermediate	Advanced
Confirm Understanding Point to the pictures for partners to identify. Ask: *What do you see?* Restate the correct answer in a complete sentence.	**Express Opinions** Ask partners to tell you which is their favorite picture in the book. Prompt them to explain why it is their favorite picture.	**Compare and Contrast** Have partners compare two different pictures and describe them. Prompt them to explain how they are alike and different.

ELL ENGLISH LANGUAGE LEARNERS

High-Frequency Words

Content Objective Spell high-frequency words correctly

Language Objective Write in complete sentences, using sentence frames

Materials • **Sound-Spelling WorkBoards** • **Sound-Spelling Cards** • **Photo Cards**

Beginning/Intermediate

■ Write the high-frequency words **this** *and* **do** on the board. Have children copy each word on their **WorkBoards**. Then help them say and write sentences for the words. Provide the sentence starters *This is a _____* and *Do you want to _____?*

Advanced

■ Children should first orally state their sentence. Correct as needed. Then they can draw a picture to complete the sentence. For children who are ready, help them spell words using their growing knowledge of English sound-spelling relationships. Model how to segment the word children are trying to spell and attach a spelling to each sound. Use the **Sound-Spelling Cards** to reinforce the spellings for each English sound.

Writing

All Language Levels

■ Dictate the following sound and ask children to write the letter: /e/. Have them write the letter *e* five times as they say /e/. Demonstrate correct letter formation, as needed.

■ Then display a set of **Photo Cards**. Select at least five cards whose picture names begin with /e/ (egg, elbow, elevator, envelope, exit) and three whose picture names begin with /d/ (door, dog, doll).

■ Say the name of each card, stretching the initial sound to emphasize it. You may also need to reinforce the meaning of the word and model correct mouth formation when forming the sound. Use the articulation pictures and prompts on the back of the small Sound-Spelling Cards for support. Tell children that if the picture name begins with /e/, you want them to write the letter *e* on their WorkBoards.

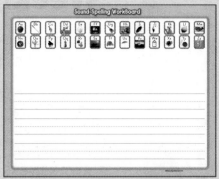

Sound-Spelling WorkBoard

Phonemic Awareness/ Phonics

For English Language Learners who need more practice with this week's phonemic awareness and phonics skills, see the Approaching Level lessons. Focus on minimal contrasts, articulation, and those sounds that do not transfer from the child's first language to English. For a complete listing of transfer sounds, see pages T10–T31.

End-of-Week Assessment

Weekly Assessment

Use your Quick Check observations and the assessment opportunities identified below to evaluate children's progress in key skill areas.

Skills	Quick Check Observations	Pencil and Paper Assessment
PHONEMIC AWARENESS/ PHONICS /e/e 	1569	Activity Book, pp. 4, 9, 12 Practice Book, pp. 141, 145
HIGH-FREQUENCY WORDS *this, do*	1590	Activity Book, pp. 7–8 Practice Book, pp. 143–144
COMPREHENSION Identify Main Idea and Details	1580	Activity Book, pp. 5–6, 11 Practice Book, p. 142

Quick Check Rubric

Skills	1	2	3
PHONEMIC AWARENESS/ PHONICS	Does not connect the /e/ sound with the letter *Ee* and has difficulty blending the CVC words *pen, pet, red, fed, Ted, ten, den, set, met, net, Ned.*	Usually connects the /e/ sound with the letter *Ee* and blends the CVC words *pen, pet, red, fed, Ted, ten, den, set, met, net, Ned* with only occasional support.	Consistently connects the /e/ sound with the letter *Ee* and blends the CVC words *pen, pet, red, fed, Ted, ten, den, set, met, net, Ned.*
HIGH-FREQUENCY WORDS	Does not identify the high-frequency words.	Usually recognizes the high-frequency words with accuracy, but not speed.	Consistently recognizes the high-frequency words with speed and accuracy.
COMPREHENSION	Does not identify the main idea or details using the pictures and text.	Usually identifies the main idea and details using the pictures and text.	Consistently identifies the main idea and details using the pictures and text.

DIBELS LINK	TPRI LINK
PROGRESS MONITORING **Use your DIBELS results to inform instruction.** **IF...** Initial Sound Fluency (**ISF**) 0–34 **THEN...** Evaluate for Intervention	**PROGRESS MONITORING** **Use your TPRI scores to inform instruction.** **IF...** Phonemic Awareness Still Developing Graphophonemic Knowledge Still Developing Listening Comprehension Still Developing **THEN...** Evaluate for Intervention

Diagnose	Prescribe

Review the assessment answers with children. Have them correct their errors. Then provide additional instruction as needed.

PHONEMIC AWARENESS/ PHONICS /e/e	**IF...** **Quick Check Rubric:** Children consistently score 1 or **Pencil and Paper Assessment:** Children get 0–2 items correct	**THEN...** Reteach Phonemic Awareness and Phonics Skills using the **Phonemic Awareness** and **Phonics Intervention Teacher' Editions**. SPIRAL REVIEW Use the Build Fluency lesson in upcoming weeks to provide children practice reading words with /e/e.
HIGH-FREQUENCY WORDS *this, do*	**Quick Check Rubric:** Children consistently score 1 or **Pencil and Paper Assessment:** Children get 0–2 items correct	Reteach High-Frequency Words using the **Phonics Intervention Teacher's Edition**. SPIRAL REVIEW Use the High-Frequency Words lesson in upcoming weeks to provide children practice reading the words *this* and *do*.
COMPREHENSION Skill: Identify Main Idea and Details	**Quick Check Rubric:** Children consistently score 1 or **Pencil and Paper Assessment:** Children get 0–2 items correct	Reteach Comprehension Skill using the **Comprehension Intervention Teacher's Edition**.

Response to Intervention

To place children in Tier 2 or Tier 3 Intervention use the *Diagnostic Assessment.*

- Phonemic Awareness
- Phonics
- Vocabulary
- Comprehension
- Fluency

Week 2 ★ At a Glance

Priority Skills and Concepts

 Comprehension
- **Genre:** Fiction, Folktale, Expository
- **Strategy:** Visualize
- **Skill:** Identify Setting
 - **Skill:** Identify Main Idea and Details

 High-Frequency Words
- *and*, *what*

Oral Vocabulary
- Build Robust Vocabulary: *mild*, *month*, *season*, *shiver*, *warning*

Fluency
- Echo-Read
- Word Automaticity

 Phonemic Awareness
- **Phoneme Isolation**
- **Phoneme Blending**
- **Phoneme Segmentation**

 Phonics
- *Bb, Ll*

Grammar
- Describing Words (Adjectives)

Writing
- Sentences

Key
 Tested in Program   Review Skill

Digital Learning

Digital solutions to help plan and implement instruction

☑ Teacher Resources

LOG ON ▶

ONLINE   www.macmillanmh.com

▶ **Teacher's Edition**
- Lesson Planner and Resources also on CD-ROM

TeacherWorks Plus

▶ **Professional Development**
- Video Library

Professional Development

☑ Student Resources

LOG ON ▶

ONLINE   www.macmillanmh.com

▶ **Leveled Reader Database**

▶ **Activities**
- Oral Language Activities
- Phonics Activities
- Vocabulary/Spelling Activities

AUDIO CD

Listening Library
- Recordings of Literature Big Books, Read-Aloud Trade Books, and Leveled Readers

Weekly Literature

Theme: Seasons

Student Literature

A mix of fiction and nonfiction

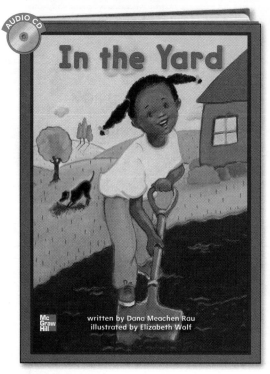

Big Book

Genre Fiction

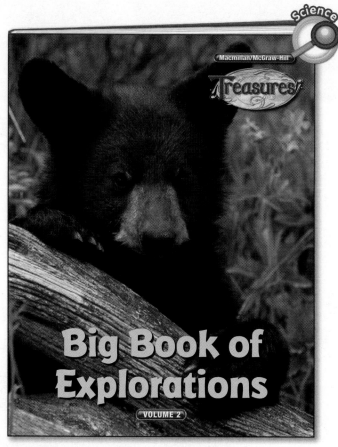

Big Book of Explorations

Genre Expository

Support Literature

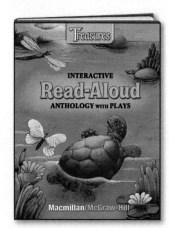

Interactive Read-Aloud Anthology

Genre Folktale

Oral Vocabulary Cards
- Listening Comprehension
- Build Robust Vocabulary

Decodable Reader

Resources for Differentiated Instruction

Leveled Readers

GR Levels A-G

Genre	Fiction

- Same Theme
- Same Vocabulary/Phonics
- Same Comprehension Skills

AUDIO CD

A

Approaching Level

B

On Level

G

Beyond Level

A

ELL

LOG ON ▶ **Leveled Reader Database**
Go to www.macmillanmh.com.

Practice

Activity Book

Practice Book

ELL Practice Book

Response to Intervention

Tier 2

- Phonemic Awareness
- Phonics
- Vocabulary
- Comprehension
- Fluency

Tier 3

Unit Assessment

Assess Unit Skills

- Phonemic Awareness
- Phonics
- High-Frequency Words
- Listening Comprehension

HOME-SCHOOL CONNECTION

- Family letters in English and Spanish
- Take-home stories and activities

Go to **www.macmillanmh.com** for Online Lesson Planner

TeacherWorks *Plus*
All-In-One Planner and Resource Center

Professional Development
Video Library

Big Book

In the Yard

WHOLE GROUP

ORAL LANGUAGE

	DAY 1	DAY 2

• **Oral Vocabulary**

• **Phonemic Awareness**

WORD STUDY

• **Phonics**

• **High-Frequency Words**

READING

• **Listening Comprehension**

• **Apply Phonics and High-Frequency Words**

• **Fluency**

LANGUAGE ARTS

• **Writing**

• **Grammar**

ASSESSMENT

• **Informal/Formal**

DAY 1

❓ Focus Question What are the four seasons?
Build Background, 1650

Oral Vocabulary *mild, month, season, shiver, warning*, 1650

✔ **Phonemic Awareness**
Phoneme Isolation, 1653

✔ **Phonics**
Introduce /b/*b*, 1654
Handwriting: Write *Bb*, 1655
Activity Book, 14
Practice Book, 147

✔ **High-Frequency Words**
and , *what* , 1652

Share the Big Book
In the Yard
Strategy: Visualize, 1651
✔ **Skill:** Identify Setting, 1651

Big Book

Shared Writing
Lists, 1657
Grammar
Describing Words (Adjectives), 1656

Quick Check **Phonemic Awareness**, 1653

DAY 2

❓ Focus Question What do you know about working in a yard in spring, summer, winter, and fall?

Oral Vocabulary *mild, month, season, shiver, warning*, 1658
Words That Compare, 1665

✔ **Phonemic Awareness**
Phoneme Blending, 1666

✔ **Phonics**
Introduce Final /b/*b*, 1666
Blend with /b/*b*, 1677

✔ **Review High-Frequency Words**, 1668

Reread the Big Book
In the Yard
Strategy: Visualize, 1660
✔ **Skill:** Identify Setting, 1660
Retell, 1664
Decodable Reader: *Hot Ben, Hot Lin*, 1668
Activity Book, 15–16
Practice Book, 148
Fluency Echo-Read, 1664

Big Book

Interactive Writing
Sentences, 1669

Quick Check **Comprehension**, 1664

SMALL GROUP Lesson Plan ▶ **Differentiated Instruction 1644–1645**

Priority Skills

Phonemic Awareness/Phonics	High-Frequency Words	Oral Vocabulary	Comprehension
Phonics /b/b, /l/l	*and, what*	Words That Compare	Strategy: Visualize
			Skill: Identify Setting

Half-Day Kindergarten

Teach Core Skills

Focus on tested skill lessons, other lessons, and small group options as your time allows.

DAY 3

? Focus Question What season of the year is it right now?

Oral Vocabulary *mild, month, season, shiver, warning,* 1670

Oral Vocabulary Cards: "Paul Bunyan and the Popcorn Blizzard"

✔ **Phonemic Awareness**
Phoneme Isolation, 1675

✔ **Phonics**
Introduce /l/l, 1676
Handwriting: Write *Ll*, 1677
Activity Book, 19
Practice Book, 151

✔ **High-Frequency Words**
and , what , 1674
Activity Book, 17–18
Practice Book, 149–150
Read for Fluency, 1674

Read the Big Book of Explorations:
"A Year with Bears," 15–20

Text Feature: Photographs, 1672

Big Book of Explorations

Independent Writing
Prewrite and Draft Sentences, 1679

Grammar
Describing Words (Adjectives), 1678

Quick Check **High-Frequency Words,** 1674
Phonemic Awareness, 1675

DAY 4

? Focus Question What is the name of the season of the year that can be cold and snowy?

Oral Vocabulary *mild, month, season, shiver, warning,* 1680

Words That Compare, 1683

✔ **Phonemic Awareness**
Phoneme Blending, 1684

✔ **Phonics**
Picture Sort, 1684
Blend with /l/l, 1685
Activity Book, 20
Practice Book, 152

✔ **Review High-Frequency Words,** 1686

Interactive Read Aloud
Listening Comprehension, 1682

Read Aloud: "How the Turtle Flew South for the Winter"

Decodable Reader: *Hot Ben, Hot Lin,* 1686

Read Aloud

Independent Writing
Revise and Edit Sentences, 1687

Quick Check **Phonics,** 1685

DAY 5
Review and Assess

? Focus Question What time of year or season do you like best and why?

Oral Vocabulary *mild, month, season, shiver, warning,* 1688

Words That Compare, 1690

✔ **Phonemic Awareness**
Phoneme Segmentation, 1691

✔ **Phonics**
Read Words, 1692
Dictation, 1692
Activity Book, 22

✔ **High-Frequency Words**
and , what , this , do , for , you , 1690

Read Across Texts
Strategy: Visualize, 1689
✔ Skill: Identify Setting, 1689
Activity Book, 21

Fluency Word Automaticity, 1690

Independent Writing
Publish and Present Sentences, 1693

✔ **Weekly Assessment,** 1720–1721

Differentiated Instruction

What do I do in small groups?

Teacher-Led Small Groups

Independent Activities

Focus on Skills

IF... children need additional instruction, practice, or extension based on your [Quick Check] observations for the following priority skills

✔ **Phonemic Awareness**
Phoneme Isolation, Blending, Segmentation

✔ **Phonics**
Bb, Ll

✔ **High-Frequency Words**
and , *what*

✔ **Comprehension**
Strategy: Visualize
Skill: Identify Setting

THEN...

Approaching	Preteach and
ELL	Reteach Skills
On Level	Practice
Beyond	Enrich and Accelerate Learning

 Suggested Small Group Lesson Plan

	DAY 1	DAY 2
Approaching Level Tier 2 • **Preteach/Reteach** **Tier 2 Instruction**	• Oral Language, 1694 • High-Frequency Words, 1694 **ELL** High-Frequency Words Review, 1694 • Phonemic Awareness, 1695 • Phonics, 1695 **ELL** Sound-Spellings Review, 1695	• Oral Language, 1700 • High-Frequency Words, 1700 **ELL** • Phonemic Awareness, 1701 • Phonics, 1701
On Level • **Practice**	• High-Frequency Words, 1696 • Phonemic Awareness/Phonics, 1696 **ELL**	• Phonics, 1702
Beyond Level • **Extend/Accelerate** **Gifted and Talented**	• High-Frequency Words/Vocabulary, 1697 **ELL** Expand Oral Vocabulary, 1697 • Phonics, 1697	• Phonics, 1702
ELL • **Build English Language Proficiency** • See **ELL** in other levels.	• Oral Language Warm-Up, 1698 • Academic Language, 1698 • Vocabulary, 1699	• Access to Core Content, 1703

1644 Unit 7 Week 2

Small Group

Focus on Leveled Readers

Levels A–G

Approaching

On Level

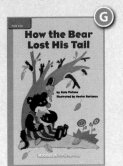
Beyond

ELL

Additional Leveled Readers

Leveled Reader Database
www.macmillanmh.com

Search by
- Comprehension Skill
- Content Area
- Genre
- Text Feature
- Guided Reading Level
- Reading Recovery Level
- Lexile Score
- Benchmark Level

Subscription also available

Manipulatives

Sound-Spelling WorkBoards

Sound-Spelling Cards

Photo Cards

High-Frequency Word Cards

Visual Vocabulary Resources

DAY 3

- High-Frequency Words, 1704 **ELL**
- Phonemic Awareness, 1704
- Phonics, 1705
- Decodable Reader, 1705

- Decodable Reader, 1706 **ELL**

- Decodable Reader, 1706

- Access to Core Content, 1707
- Grammar, 1707

DAY 4

- Phonemic Awareness, 1708
- Phonics, 1708 **ELL**
- Leveled Reader Lesson 1, 1709

- Leveled Reader Lesson 1, 1710 **ELL**

- Leveled Reader Lesson 1, 1711
- Evaluate, 1711

- Leveled Reader, 1712–1713

DAY 5

- Phonemic Awareness, 1714
- Phonics, 1714 **ELL**
- Leveled Reader Lesson 2, 1715
- High-Frequency Words, 1715

- Leveled Reader Lesson 2, 1716

- Leveled Reader Lesson 2, 1717 **ELL**
- Expand Vocabulary, 1717

- Fluency, 1718
- High-Frequency Words, 1719
- Writing, 1719

Managing the Class

What do I do with the rest of my class?

Teacher-Led Small Groups

Independent Activities

- Activity Book
- Practice Book
- ELL Practice Book
- Leveled Reader Activities
- Literacy Workstations
- Online Activities
- Buggles and Beezy

Classroom Management Tools

Weekly Contract

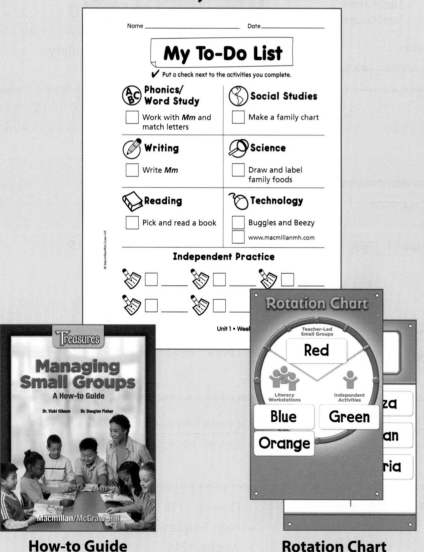

Name _____ Date _____

My To-Do List

✔ Put a check next to the activities you complete.

Phonics/Word Study
☐ Work with *Mm* and match letters

Social Studies
☐ Make a family chart

Writing
☐ Write *Mm*

Science
☐ Draw and label family foods

Reading
☐ Pick and read a book

Technology
☐ Buggles and Beezy
☐ www.macmillanmh.com

Independent Practice

Unit 1 • Week

How-to Guide

Treasures
Managing Small Groups
A How-to Guide
Dr. Vicki Gibson Dr. Douglas Fisher
Macmillan/McGraw-Hill

Rotation Chart

Rotation Chart
Teacher-Led Small Groups
Red
Literacy Workstations Independent Activities
Blue **Green**
Orange

Digital Learning

Phonics Activities

- Match Letters
- Match Letters to Sounds
- Blend Words

Meet the Author/Illustrator

Karma Wilson

- Karma grew up an only child in Idaho.
- Reading was Karma's first love. By the age of 11, she read about one novel a day.
- Karma's books have been translated into dozens of languages.

Other books by Karma Wilson
- Wilson, Karma, and Jane Chapman. *Bear Snores On*. New York: Margaret K. McElderry, 2002.
- Wilson, Karma, and Douglas Cushman. *Never Ever Shout in a Zoo*. New York: Little, Brown Young Readers, 2004.

- Read Other Books by the Author or Illustrator

Practice

Activity Book

Practice Book

ELL Practice Book

Independent Activities

ONLINE INSTRUCTION www.macmillanmh.com

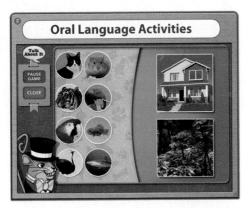

Oral Language Activities

- Focus on Vocabulary and Concepts
- English Language Learner Support

Vocabulary/Spelling Activities

- Differentiated Lists and Activities

Leveled Reader Database

- Leveled Reader Database
- Search titles by level, skill, content area, and more

Available on CD

LISTENING LIBRARY
Recordings of selections
- Literature Big Books
- Read-Aloud Trade Books
- Leveled Readers
- ELL Readers

NEW ADVENTURES WITH BUGGLES AND BEEZY
Phonemic awareness and phonics activities

Leveled Reader Activities

Approaching

On Level

Beyond

ELL

See inside cover of all Leveled Readers.

Literacy Workstations

Reading — Phonics/Word Study — Writing — Science/Social Studies

See lessons on pages 1648–1649

Managing the Class

What do I do with the rest of my class?

Reading

Objectives
- Read and discuss a book with a group
- Read a nonfiction book aloud

Phonics/Word Study

Objectives
- Make posters for the letters *b*, *e*, and *l*, using words and pictures
- Sort words by sounds and identify rhymes

Reading — **Book Club** — 20 Minutes

Read and talk about a book as a group.

❶ Sit in a circle.　❷ Read the book together.　❸ Talk about it.

Do More
- Talk about the setting.
- Read the book as you listen to the CD.

For more book titles, go to the Meet the Author/ Illustrator page on www.macmillanmh.com

39

© Macmillan/McGraw-Hill

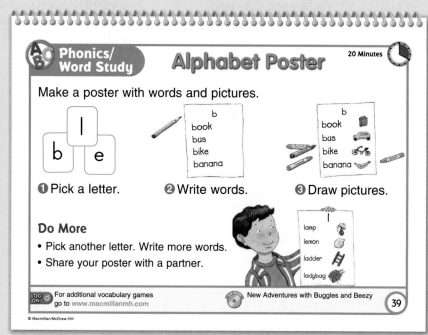

Phonics/Word Study — **Alphabet Poster** — 20 Minutes

Make a poster with words and pictures.

❶ Pick a letter.　❷ Write words.　❸ Draw pictures.

Do More
- Pick another letter. Write more words.
- Share your poster with a partner.

For additional vocabulary games go to www.macmillanmh.com

New Adventures with Buggles and Beezy

39

© Macmillan/McGraw-Hill

Reading — **Book Buddies** — 20 Minutes

Read a fiction book aloud to a buddy.

❶ Make a buddy.　❷ Read to your buddy.

Do More
- Talk with a partner about where the stories you read take place.

For more book titles, go to the Meet the Author/ Illustrator page on www.macmillanmh.com

40

© Macmillan/McGraw-Hill

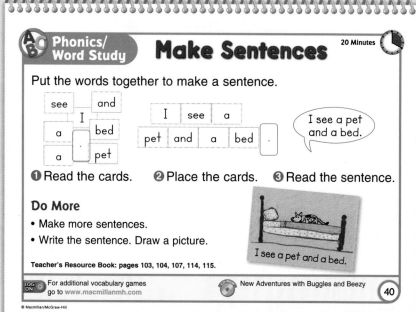

Phonics/Word Study — **Make Sentences** — 20 Minutes

Put the words together to make a sentence.

I see a pet and a bed.

❶ Read the cards.　❷ Place the cards.　❸ Read the sentence.

Do More
- Make more sentences.
- Write the sentence. Draw a picture.

I see a pet and a bed.

Teacher's Resource Book: pages 103, 104, 107, 114, 115.

For additional vocabulary games go to www.macmillanmh.com

New Adventures with Buggles and Beezy

40

© Macmillan/McGraw-Hill

Literacy Workstations

Reading

Phonics/ Word Study

Writing

Science/ Social Studies

Literacy Workstation Flip Charts

 Writing

Objectives

- Find words that begin with *Bb* and *Ll*
- Write a riddle

Content Literacy

Objectives

- Match fabrics with the seasons in which they are worn
- Make a chart that shows the different jobs that are done in each season

Writing — Find Bb and Ll — 20 Minutes

Find words that begin with Bb or Ll.

My Bb and Ll Words

❶ Write a title. ❷ Cut out Bb and Ll words. ❸ Glue Bb and Ll words.

Do More
- Add more Bb or Ll words.
- Write a sentence using Bb and Ll words.

I love blue.

39

© Macmillan/McGraw-Hill

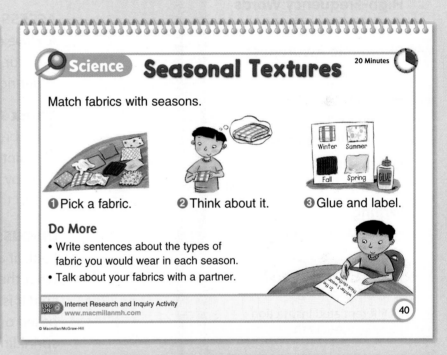

Science — Seasonal Textures — 20 Minutes

Match fabrics with seasons.

❶ Pick a fabric. ❷ Think about it. ❸ Glue and label.

Do More
- Write sentences about the types of fabric you would wear in each season.
- Talk about your fabrics with a partner.

LOG ON ▶ Internet Research and Inquiry Activity
www.macmillanmh.com

40

© Macmillan/McGraw-Hill

Writing — Write Riddles — 20 Minutes

Write a riddle.

I like a nap and sound like hat.

I am a cat.

❶ Draw a picture. ❷ Write a riddle. ❸ Write an answer.

Do More
- Try to solve your partner's riddles.
- Create new riddles for everyone to solve.

40

© Macmillan/McGraw-Hill

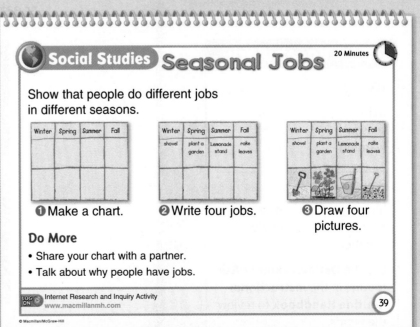

Social Studies — Seasonal Jobs — 20 Minutes

Show that people do different jobs in different seasons.

Winter	Spring	Summer	Fall

Winter	Spring	Summer	Fall
shovel	plant a garden	Lemonade stand	rake leaves

Winter	Spring	Summer	Fall
shovel	plant a garden	Lemonade stand	rake leaves

❶ Make a chart. ❷ Write four jobs. ❸ Draw four pictures.

Do More
- Share your chart with a partner.
- Talk about why people have jobs.

LOG ON ▶ Internet Research and Inquiry Activity
www.macmillanmh.com

39

© Macmillan/McGraw-Hill

Oral Language
• Build Background

✔ **Comprehension**
• Read *In the Yard*
• Strategy: Visualize
• Skill: Identify Setting

✔ **High-Frequency Words**
• Introduce *and*, *what*

✔ **Phonemic Awareness**
• Phoneme Isolation

✔ **Phonics**
• Introduce /b/*b*
• Handwriting: Write *Bb*

Grammar
• Describing Words (Adjectives)

Writing
• Shared Writing: Lists

SMALL GROUP

• Differentiated Instruction, pages 1694–1719

Oral Vocabulary

Week 2

mild	month
season	shiver
warning	

Review

blustery	chilly
cloud	drizzle
weather	

Use the **Define/Example/Ask** routine in the **Instructional Routine Handbook** to review the words.

Oral Language

Talk About It

Build Background: *Seasons*

ACCESS PRIOR KNOWLEDGE

Tell children that this week they will be talking and reading about the **seasons**. Explain that a season is a time of year. *There are four seasons in a year, each with a different kind of weather.*

Write the following question on the board: *What are the names of the four seasons?* Track the print as you read aloud the question. Remind children that we read from left to right and top to bottom. Then prompt children to answer the question.

ACCESS PRIOR KNOWLEDGE

■ Have children discuss the seasons and the **months** in which they occur. Ask: *What is your favorite season? What do you like to do during those months?*

Think Aloud Let's look at this picture. It is a girl holding an umbrella. It is raining, and she has her hand out in the rain. (Point to the girl, the umbrella, and her hand.) It looks like she enjoys being in the rain because she is smiling. Which season do you think it is? How can you tell?

DISCUSS THE PHOTOGRAPH

Look at and discuss the photograph with children. Have them notice what the girl is wearing. What can they tell about how warm or cold it is by her clothes? How can you figure out what season it is based on what she is wearing? Ask children to tell you if it is lightly sprinkling or if it is raining hard. How do they know? Have children speak audibly and clearly.

Teaching Chart 46

Share the Big Book

Listening Comprehension

Big Book

PREVIEW AND PREDICT Display the cover. *I see a girl shoveling dirt. Behind her, there is a dog digging a hole.* Point to the girl, shovel, and dog as you talk. *What do you think this story will be about based on the title and illustrations?*

Read the title and the names of the author and the illustrator as you track the print. *Where do you think the girl is?*

GENRE: LITERARY TEXT: FICTION *This story is* **fiction**, *which means the story did not really happen, but it could. What is the purpose for listening to fiction stories?*

 STRATEGY Monitor Comprehension: Visualize

EXPLAIN/MODEL Tell children that picturing in our minds where and when a story takes place helps us monitor our understanding of what is happening in the story.

Think Aloud I see a girl digging in the dirt. I see part of a house. I can picture the rest of the house and the yard in my mind.

 SKILL Identify Setting

EXPLAIN/MODEL Remind children that the setting is where and when a story takes place. *What is the purpose for knowing the setting?*

Think Aloud I can see dirt and trees and grass. There is a house behind the girl. All of this tells me that the setting is in a yard in the spring or summer.

Read the Big Book

SET PURPOSE Tell children to think about how the setting will change during each season. Use the **Define/Example/Ask** routine to teach the story words on the inside back cover.

Respond to Literature

MAKE CONNECTIONS Have children name their favorite part. *How did the yard change? How do you know? Point to evidence in the book that shows this.* Have children draw a picture of the girl in the yard.

Objectives

- Discuss the theme
- Use oral vocabulary words *season* and *month*
- Discuss a photograph
- Listen and respond to a story
- Visualize/identify setting

Materials

- Teaching Chart 46
- Big Book: *In the Yard*

ELL

Use the **Interactive Question-Response Guide** for *In the Yard*, **ELL Resource Book** pages 188–193, to guide children through a reading of the book. As you read *In the Yard*, make meaning clear by pointing to the pictures, demonstrating word meanings, paraphrasing text, and asking children questions.

Digital Learning

Story on **Listening Library Audio CD**

Objectives

- Read the high-frequency words *and, what*
- Identify the words *and* and *what* in speech and text
- Review high-frequency words *for, you, this, do*

Materials

- High-Frequency Word Cards: *and, what, for, you, this, do*
- Teaching Chart 47

High-Frequency Words

 and, what

INTRODUCE Display the **High-Frequency Word Cards** for **and** and **what**. Use the **Read/Spell/Write** routine to teach the words.

- **Read** Point to and say the word *and. My favorite sports are soccer and baseball.*

- **Spell** *The word* and *is spelled* a-n-d. *What's the first sound in* and? *That's right. The first sound in* and *is /a/. That's why the first letter is* a. *After the* a, *I see* n *and* d. *Let's read and spell* and *together.*

- **Write** *Now let's write the word* and *on our papers. Let's spell aloud the word as we write it:* and, a-n-d.

- Repeat the routine with *what.*

SPIRAL REVIEW **REVIEW** *for, you, this, do* Display each card and have children read the words one at a time.

READ THE RHYME AND CHIME
Have children point to *and, what, do,* and *you.* Repeat the rhyme together for fluency. Then add *and* and *what* to the class Word Wall.

Look, Bear, Look!

Look, Bear, look!
And what do you see?
A ladybug on a leaf
and a bird in a tree.
Listen, Bear, listen!
What do you hear?
Lambs saying, "Baaa!"
and bees buzzing in my ear.

Teaching Chart 47

For Tier 2 instruction, see page 1694.

TIME TO MOVE!

Have children follow simple nonstop instructions using the word *and. Jump and clap and touch your toes and raise your hands.*

Phonemic Awareness

Phoneme Isolation

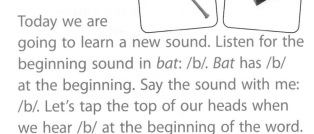

Model

Display the **Photo Card** for *bat*.

Today we are going to learn a new sound. Listen for the beginning sound in *bat*: /b/. *Bat* has /b/ at the beginning. Say the sound with me: /b/. Let's tap the top of our heads when we hear /b/ at the beginning of the word.

Repeat with the Photo Card for *box*.

Say the "Look, Bear, Look!" Rhyme and Chime again. Have children tap every time they hear /b/.

Look, Bear, look!
And what do you see?
A ladybug on a leaf
and a bird in a tree.
Listen, Bear, listen!
What do you hear?
Lambs saying, "Baaa!"
and bees buzzing in my ear.

Review /e/, /r/

Display the Photo Card for *egg*.

Repeat for *rock*.

This is an *egg*. The beginning sound in *egg* is /e/. Listen: /eeeg/. (Stretch the beginning sound.) What is the sound?

Guided Practice/Practice

Display and name the Photo Cards one at a time. Children identify the initial sound. Guide practice with the first card using the same routine. Continue orally with *end, red, big, run*.

Say each picture name with me. Tell me the sound at the beginning of the word.

Quick Check

Can children identify the initial sound /b/?

During **Small Group Instruction**

If No → **Approaching Level**   Provide additional practice, page 1695.

If Yes → **On Level**   Children blend words with /b/, page 1696.

Beyond Level   Children blend words with /b/, page 1697.

Objectives

- Identify initial /b/
- Review initial /e/ and /r/

Materials

- Photo Cards: *balloon, bat, bike, book, box, bus, envelope, exit, egg, elevator, rock, rabbit, ring, rope*

ELL

Pronunciation Display and have children name **Photo Cards** from this and prior lessons to reinforce phonemic awareness and word meanings. Point to a card and ask: *What do you see?* (a bat) *What is the sound at the beginning of the word bat?* (/b/). Repeat using Photo Cards with words that begin with the sounds /e/ and /r/.

Objectives

- Match the letter *b* to the sound /b/
- Handwriting: write *B* and *b*

Materials

- Sound-Spelling Card: *Bat*
- Teaching Chart 47
- Word-Building Cards
- Handwriting
- Handwriting Teacher's Edition
- Activity Book, p. 14
- Practice Book, p. 147

ELL

Variations in Language
Speakers of Hmong, Cantonese, and Korean may have difficulty perceiving and pronouncing /b/. Use the Approaching Level Phonics lessons for additional pronunciation and decoding practice.

Sound Pronunciation

See **Sound Pronunciation CD** for a model of the /b/ sound. Play this for children needing additional models.

Phonics

✓ Introduce /b/b

Model

Display the *Bat* **Sound-Spelling Card**.

This is the *Bat* card. The beginning sound is /b/. The /b/ sound is spelled with the letter *b*. Say it with me: /b/. This is the sound you hear at the beginning of the word *bat*. Listen: /b/ /b/ /b/...*bat*.

What is the name of this letter? What sound does it stand for?

Read the "Look, Bear, Look!" Rhyme and Chime. Reread the title. Point out that the word *Bear* begins with the letter *B*. Model placing a self-stick note below the *B* in *Bear*.

Look, Bear, Look!

Look, Bear, look!
And what do you see?
A ladybug on a leaf
and a bird in a tree.
Listen, Bear, listen!
What do you hear?
Lambs saying, "Baaa!"
and bees buzzing in my ear.

Unit 7
Rhyme and Chime

High-Frequency Words: and, what
Phonics: /b/b, /l/l

Weather Week 2 47

Teaching Chart 47

Guided Practice/Practice

Read the rhyme. Stop after each line. Children place self-stick notes below words that begin with the letter *b*. Guide practice with *Bear* in line 1.

Let's put a sticky note below the word in the line that begins with /b/. The word *bear* begins with the letter *b*.

Corrective Feedback

If children have difficulty with /b/b, review the word *bees* together. *This is the /b/ sound in the beginning of* bees: /b/ /ē/ /z/, bees. *Let's say* bees *together:* /b/, bees.

Build Fluency: Sound-Spellings

 Display the following **Word-Building Cards**: *a, b, c, d, e, f, h, i, m, n, o, p, r, s, t*. Have children chorally say each sound. Repeat and vary the pace.

Handwriting: Write *Bb*

MODEL Model holding up your writing hand. Say the handwriting cues as you write the capital and lowercase forms of *Bb* on the board. Then trace the letters on the board and in the air.

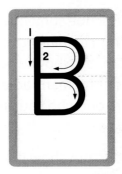 *Straight down. Go back to the top. Around and in, around and in.*

 *Straight down. Go to the dotted line. Around all the way.*

PRACTICE Ask children to hold up their writing hand.

- Say the cues together as children trace with their index finger the letters you wrote on the board.

- Have children write *B* and *b* in the air as they say /b/ multiple times.

- Distribute handwriting practice pages. Observe children's pencil grip and paper position, and correct as necessary. Have children say /b/ every time they write the letter *b*.

For Tier 2 instruction, see page 1695.

For Tier 2 instruction, see page 1695.

> ### Daily Handwriting
> Check that children form letters starting at the top and moving to the bottom. See **Handwriting Teacher's Edition** for ball-and-stick and slant models.

Activity Book, page 14
Practice Book, page 147

Objective

- Recognize describing words (adjectives)

Materials

- Big Book: *In the Yard*
- Photo Cards: *bird, book, crown, farm, feather, fire, mop, mouse, ostrich, sun, volcano, watermelon, wheel*

Corrective Feedback

Linguistic Differences In the first-person present tense, many speakers of African American Vernacular English will properly use *I am* or *I'm,* but say it more like "uhm." Focus on pronunciation.

ELL

Basic and Academic Vocabulary Display the **Photo Cards** from this lesson and pair English Language Learners with fluent speakers. Explain to partners that they have to talk as if they were the objects or animals pictured on the cards. Prompt partners to elaborate on their descriptions.

Grammar

Describing Words (Adjectives)

MODEL Use the **Big Book** *In the Yard* to discuss describing words. Point to the illustrations on pages 4–5 as you say: *Mom and daughter plant small red flowers.* Ask: *What kind of flowers?* Explain that the words *small* and *red are* describing words. Say the sentence without the describing words: *Mom and daughter plant flowers.* Explain that by using describing words, we get more information and are better able to picture the story in our minds.

- Tell children that you are going to describe someone. The class will figure out who you are describing. *I'm thinking of someone, and he's a boy.* Ask children if they can tell who the person is by the description. Then give a description using many adjectives of a boy in the class. Have the class figure out who you are describing.

PRACTICE

Hold the watermelon **Photo Card** but do not show it to the class. Describe the picture in the first person. *I am a type of fruit. I am red on the inside and green outside. I am heavy. I am big. I taste sweet. What am I?* Have children figure out what it is and then have them identify the describing words that were used. (*big, heavy, red, green, sweet*)

- Have children choose a Photo Card and describe the object in the first person using as many describing words as possible. Guide children if they need help.

> *I am a tall bird, with long legs.*
>
> *I am a very small furry animal with a long tail.*

- Have the class identify what is on the Photo Card and tell describing words that were used.

Writing

Shared Writing: Lists

BRAINSTORM

Remind children that in the story *In the Yard,* they read about a family who spent time in their yard during all four **seasons**. Plan a draft of the sentences children will write later in the week. *What are some of the different things the family did in their yard?*

WRITE

■ Create four lists as shown below. Read each heading together as you track the print.

■ Tell children they will write about what the family did in each season. Model by reading pages 2–5 of the **Big Book** and say: *It is spring. The child and her mom dig holes and plant flowers, so I will write* dig *and* plant *under the heading* Spring is a time to.

■ Continue by reading pages 10–11, 12–15, and 18–20. After you read each group of pages, have children tell you what to write. Read the completed lists together as you track the print.

■ Save the lists to refer to in other writing activities this week.

Spring is a time to	Summer is a time to
dig	grow
plant	weed
water	mow
dance	

Fall is a time to	Winter is a time to
rake	shovel
pick	play
bake	rest

Write About It

Ask children to draw and label a picture. Suggest that they draw a picture of a flower. Help them to write a caption using a descriptive word.

Objective

• Write lists

Materials

• Big Book: *In the Yard*

5-Day Writing

Sentences	
DAY 1	Shared: Lists
DAY 2	Interactive: Sentences
DAY 3	Independent: Prewrite and Draft Sentences
DAY 4	Independent: Revise and Edit Sentences
DAY 5	Independent: Publish and Present

ELL

Use New Language Read the lists chorally and have children act out the actions as they read. Then say: *Tell me something you do in a yard in the spring.* Repeat with the other seasons.

Transitions That Teach

While children are packing up, ask them to talk about the **seasons**. Ask: *Which season is good for flying kites? Why?*

WHOLE GROUP

Oral Language
- Build Robust Vocabulary

✓ **Comprehension**
- Reread *In the Yard*
- Strategy: Visualize
- Skill: Identify Setting
- Fluency: Echo-Read

Vocabulary
- Words That Compare
- Story Words: *dance, sway*

✓ **Phonemic Awareness**
- Phoneme Blending

✓ **Phonics**
- Introduce Final /b/*b*
- Blend with /b/*b*
- Decodable Reader:
  Hot Ben, Hot Lin

Writing
- Interactive Writing: Sentences

SMALL GROUP

- Differentiated Instruction,
  pages 1694–1719

Oral Vocabulary

Week 2

mild	month	season
shiver	warning	

Review

blustery	chilly	cloud
drizzle	weather	

Use the **Define/Example/Ask** routine in the **Instructional Routine Handbook** to review the words.

Oral Language

 Talk About It

Build Robust Vocabulary

INTRODUCE WORDS

Tell children that today they will be talking about the different months and seasons of the year.

Vocabulary Routine

Use the routine below to discuss the meaning of each word.

Define: There are twelve **months** in one year. January is the first month of the year. December is the last month. Say the word with me.
Example: September is the first month of fall.
Ask: In what month were you born?

Define: A **season** is a time of year. Winter, spring, summer, and fall are the four seasons. Say the word with me.
Example: My favorite season is summer because I like the warm weather.
Ask: Which season has your favorite kind of weather?

CREATE A CHART

Create a three-column chart, or use **Teaching Chart G4**. Read the title and headings as you track the print. *The Big Book* In the Yard *shows the family in spring first, so I will write* spring *under* Season. *Spring starts in the month of March. I will write* March *under* Months. *What are the next two months in spring? What is the weather like in spring?* Have children share information and ideas by speaking audibly and clearly.

Help children name the months for each season and discuss what the weather is like in each season where you live. Record children's responses. Read the completed chart with children as you track the print. Point out that you wrote commas to separate the names of the months. Read the chart together as you track the print.

Season	Months	Weather
spring	March, April, May	
summer	June, July, August	
fall	September, October, November	
winter	December, January, February	

Listen for Alliteration

IDENTIFY ALLITERATION
Remind children that alliteration is when the same sounds are repeated as in the rhyme Wee Willie Winkie. Tell children that this rhyme also uses alliteration. Have them listen for words beginning with the same sound.

RHYME ABOUT WEATHER
Let's say a rhyme about a type of weather. Play the rhyme "One Misty, Moisty Morning," using the **Listening Library Audio CD**. Then teach children the words and recite the rhyme together.

Ask: *Which words begin with the same sounds?* (misty, moisty, morning) *What type of weather is it?* Explain to children that when the weather is misty, there is a very light rain.

One Misty, Moisty Morning

One misty, moisty morning
When cloudy was the weather,
I met a little old man
Who had clothes of leather.

He began to compliment,
And I began to grin,
How do you do, and how do you do,
And how do you do again?

 ELL ENGLISH LANGUAGE LEARNERS

Beginning

Confirm Understanding Review oral vocabulary using the **Big Book** *In the Yard*. Show pages that clearly illustrate the seasons, such as pages 8–9. Say: *The sun shines in the summer. When does the sun shine?* (in the summer) Continue with other seasons.

Intermediate

Enhance Understanding Ask children to describe what the characters do during each season. For example: *Who mows the grass?* (Dad mows the grass.) *When does Dad mow the grass?* (Dad mows the grass in the summer.)

Advanced

Describe Details Ask children to explain how they can tell what season is shown in each picture. Prompt children to elaborate by asking them to describe specific picture details.

Objectives
- Discuss the theme
- Complete a chart
- Use oral vocabulary words *season* and *month*
- Recognize alliteration

Materials
- **Big Book:** *In the Yard*
- **Graphic Organizer; Teaching Chart G4**
- **Listening Library Audio CD**

Rhyme on Listening Library Audio CD

Objectives

- Visualize
- Identify setting
- Develop fluency

Materials

- Big Book: *In the Yard*
- Retelling Cards
- Activity Book, pp. 15–16
- Practice Book, p. 148

Big Book

Digital Learning

Story on **Listening Library Audio CD**

ELL

Gesture and Talk Use gesturing and talking to help make the text comprehensible.

p. 3

dig: Point to the illustration of the girl and the shovel. Gesture digging with an imaginary shovel. Say: *I dig.* Have children repeat.

pp. 4–5

plants: Gesture planting in the ground. Point to the book and say: *Mom plants.* Ask children to gesture while saying: *We plant.*

Reread the Big Book
Listening Comprehension

CONCEPTS ABOUT PRINT Display the cover and read the title as you track the print. Ask children to tell what they remember.

 STRATEGY Monitor Comprehension: Visualize

Ask children to think about and visualize the sensory details. Sensory details use the senses to help us become more involved in the story's events. Some examples are how the dirt feels when planting, how the leaves crunch when raking, or how good the apples taste.

 SKILL Identify Setting

Remind children that where a story takes place is called the setting. Paying attention to the setting helps to understand the story better.

Think Aloud The story's setting is in the family's yard. As I read, I'll pay attention to how the setting changes.

Read the **Big Book** and use the prompts on the inside covers.

page 3

SETTING

- *Where does this story take place?* (It takes place in the girl's yard.)

CONCEPTS ABOUT PRINT

- *How many words are in this sentence?* (2)

pages 4–5

VISUALIZE

Think Aloud The words are *Mom plants.* I see the mother holding a flower with dirt around the roots. I can picture her putting the roots in a hole in the dirt and then patting the dirt down.

Develop Comprehension

pages 6–7

 SETTING

- *What do you see in the yard?* (Possible answer: trees, flowers, grass, people, a dog) *Why is the father watering the flowers?* (to help them grow)

pages 8–9

SETTING

- *What **season** do you think is pictured? What **month** might it be? How can you tell?* (It is summer. It might be June. The grass is green. The sun is shining, and it looks warm.)

pages 10–11

SETTING

- *I see the mother is carrying a tray with drinks on it. Where do you think she was?* (in the kitchen in the house) *Do you have any questions about the setting or where this is taking place?*

pages 12–13

VISUALIZE

- *What season is it now? Can you picture, in your minds, what the trees looked like before the leaves fell?*

Comprehension

Visualize
- (pages 4–5) I can picture the mother putting the root ball in a hole in the dirt and then patting the dirt down around it. Then it will look like the other flowers, which have already been planted.

Setting
- (page 3) Where does this story take place?
- (pages 8–9) I can tell that it is summer in the yard. The grass is green and growing. The sun is shining and it looks warm.

Story Words
(page 7) dance   (page 17) sway

About the Illustrator: Elizabeth Wolf
Elizabeth Wolf lives in Idaho, which gets lots of snow in the winter. In the spring and summer, her yard is mostly covered with sagebrush.

**Big Book
Inside Back Cover**

ELL

pp. 6–7
dance: Point to the illustration of the girl and her mother dancing. Ask children to dance as they say: *We dance.*

pp. 8–9
shines: Point to the sun and run your fingers out from the center, like sun rays. Have children repeat the sentence: *Sun shines.*

pp. 10–11
mows: Point to Dad mowing the lawn and to the part of the illustration that shows that the grass is shorter. Gesture pushing a lawn mower. Have children gesture and say: *We mow.*

pp. 12–13
leaves: Point to the leaves. Ask children to count the leaves falling in the air with you.

Identify Setting

Explain Remind children that when they answer a question, they must support their answer with text evidence.

Discuss Have children look at and listen to pages 6–7 and 16–17. Ask: *How are the settings different?* Have children point to the place in the book where they found their answer.

ELL

pp. 14–15
pick: Point to the girl reaching for an apple. Demonstrate picking with your hand. Tell children to repeat the action and story sentence with you.

pp. 16–17
blow, sway: Point to the trees bending in the wind and make a wind-blowing noise. Say *blow.* Have children blow like the wind, too. Then sway back and forth like the trees. Say *sway.* Repeat the story sentences with children.

pp. 18–19
shovel: Point to the shovel. Dramatize digging snow. Tell children to shovel, too. Then have children point to and name the shovel.

Develop Comprehension

pages 14–15

MAKE INFERENCES

■ *What kind of pies do you think the father is making?* (apple pies) *Where do you think he got the apples?* (The girl and her mother picked them from the tree in the yard.)

pages 16–17

 VISUALIZE

Think Aloud I can picture the wind blowing and the trees swaying.

 SETTING

■ *Now what season is it? How can you tell?* (It is winter. There is lots of snow.)

pages 18–19

 MAIN IDEA AND DETAILS

Think Aloud The family is in the yard again. I think the main idea is about all the things you can do in a yard throughout the year. We've seen pictures of the yard in spring, summer, fall, and winter.

pages 20–21

HIGH-FREQUENCY WORDS

■ *Can you find the word* and?

pages 22–23

SETTING

■ *Where is the family now?*
(Now they are in
the house.)

VISUALIZE

■ *What do you think the yard
looks like?*

Respond to Literature

TALK ABOUT IT Have children talk about the words and illustrations
they liked and refer to the book as they answer these questions.

■ *Where does the story take place?* LOCATE (in the yard and in the house)

■ *What did the family do in the yard in each* **season**? COMBINE (dig, plant,
and weed in the spring and summer; rake leaves in the fall; shovel
and build snowmen in the winter)

■ *How does the setting in each picture help you understand which
season it is?* CONNECT (I find clues in the pictures about the weather
which helps me figure out the season.)

■ *What do you think will happen next?*

■ *How do you think the author feels about all the different seasons?*

Activity Book, pages 15–16
Practice Book, page 148

Retelling Rubric

(4) Excellent

Retells the selection without prompting, in sequence, and using supporting details. Clearly describes the setting, main characters, and complete plot.

(3) Good

Retells the selection with little guidance, in sequence, and using some details. Generally describes the setting, main characters, and plot.

(2) Fair

Retells the selection with some guidance, mostly in sequence, and using limited details. Partially describes the setting, main characters, and plot.

(1) Unsatisfactory

Retells the selection only when prompted, out of sequence, and using limited details. Does not describe the main characters or plot.

Retell

Retelling Cards

GUIDED RETELLING

Remind children that as they listened to *In the Yard,* they used the words and illustrations to understand the book. Now they will use the pictures on these cards to retell the story.

- Display **Retelling Card 1**. Based on children's needs, use either the Guided, Modeled, or ELL prompts. The ELL prompts contain support for English Language Learners based on levels of language acquisition.

- Repeat the procedure with the rest of the Retelling Cards, using the prompts to guide children's retelling.

- Discuss the book. *Do you think the family has fun in the yard throughout all the **months** of the year? Why or why not?*

- Have children act out their favorite parts of the book.

Fluency: Echo-Read

MODEL Reread pages 6–7, using an excited tone of voice for the exclamatory sentence on page 7. Guide children in recognizing that your intonation and volume help to express the girl's excitement. Then reread pages 16–17 and have children echo-read as you track the print.

Quick Check

Can children identify setting to understand a story?
Can children retell a story?

Vocabulary

Words That Compare

Chant the following jingle:

I see three kids;	*I see three pencils;*
One is tall,	*One is* long,
One is taller,	*One is* longer,
One is the tallest*!*	*One is the* longest*!*

- Repeat the first four lines and name the words that compare size. Repeat with the other lines.

- Display the pocket chart with three paper rectangles or pictures of objects of different lengths. Place rectangles in size order. As you point to each rectangle, ask children to tell which is long, longer, or longest.

NAME WORDS THAT COMPARE Have children arrange classroom objects in size order. Then have them describe the objects by pointing and saying *tall, taller, tallest* or *long, longer, longest*.

Story Words: *dance, sway*

Display page 7 of *In the Yard* and point out the word *dance* and the picture of the mom and girl. Ask: *Do you like to dance?* Ask children if they know any dances.

Display page 17 and point out the word *sway* and the picture of trees moving in the wind. Explain that *sway* means "swinging back and forth from side to side." *Can you* sway? *When do you* sway?

Ask children to dance like a tree in a storm. Say: *Sway to the left and sway to the right. Wave your branches [arms] high and low. Bend to the front and bend to the back.*

Objectives

- **Use words that compare**
- **Learn the story words** *dance* **and** *sway*
- **Sort rectangles or pictures of objects into size order**

Materials

- **Big Book:** *In the Yard*
- **3 paper rectangles or pictures of objects of different sizes**

Digital Learning

LOG ON ▶ For children who need additional language support and oral vocabulary development, use the activities found at **www.macmillanmh.com.**

ELL

Reinforce Meaning
Demonstrate and emphasize words that compare. For example, have three children stand in size order. Hold your hand above their heads as you say, *tall, taller, tallest.* Then ask the rest of the children to point to the *tall, taller,* and *tallest* child. Repeat displaying three paper strips, each a different length. Describe them as *long, longer, longest.*

Objectives

- Orally blend sounds to form words with /b/*b*
- Review initial /b/*b*
- Introduce final /b/*b*
- Match letters *b, n, d,* to final sounds /b/, /n/, /d/
- Blend sounds in words with /b/*b*

Materials

- Puppet
- Photo Cards: *web, fan, bird*
- Sound Box
- WorkBoard Sound Boxes; Teacher's Resource Book, p. 136
- Word-Building Cards; Teacher's Resource Book, pp. 95–102
- pocket chart

Phonemic Awareness

Phoneme Blending

Model

Use the **Puppet** to model how to blend sounds in the word *bed*.

Repeat with *bin*.

Happy is going to say the sounds in a word. Listen to Happy as he says each sound: /b/ /e/ /d/. Happy can blend these sounds to say a word: *bed*. Now you can say the sounds with Happy: /b/ /e/ /d/, /beeed/. Now say the word with Happy: *bed*.

Guided Practice/Practice

Use the Puppet to say the sounds. Children blend the sounds to form words.

Guide practice with the first word.

Happy is going to say the sounds in a word. Listen to Happy as he says each sound. Blend the sounds to say the word.

/b/ /e/ /t/   /b/ /o/ /b/   /b/ /ī/ /t/

/t/ /a/ /b/   /b/ /e/ /n/   /b/ /i/ /b/

Phonics

Introduce Final /b/*b*

b n d

Model

Display **Word-Building Card** *b* in the pocket chart. Show the **Photo Card** for *web*.

Repeat the routine for final /n/ and /d/. Use the Photo Cards for *fan* and *bird*.

This is a picture of a *web*. The word *web* has the /b/ sound at the end.

I know that the letter *b* stands for the /b/ sound. I will place the card for *b* in the last box of the Sound Box because I hear the /b/ sound at the end of the word *web*.

Guided Practice/Practice

Distribute **Word-Building Cards** *b, d,* and *n* and the **Sound Boxes**. Say each word. Children place the Word-Building Card for the final sound in the Sound Boxes. Guide practice with first word.

Listen to the sound at the end of each word. Place the Word-Building Card in the last box that stands for the sound you hear.

bib	lid	tin	rib	red	club
den	Bob	sad	cob	can	job

Build Fluency: Sound-Spellings

Display Word-Building Cards *a, b, c, d, e, f, h, i, m, n, o, p, r, s, t*. Have children chorally say each sound. Repeat and vary the pace.

Blend with /b/*b*

Model

Place Word-Building Card *b* in the pocket chart.

This letter is *b*. The letter *b* stands for the /b/ sound. Say /b/.

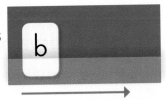

Place Word-Building Card *e* next to *b*. Move your hand from left to right.

This is the letter *e*. The letter *e* stands for the /e/ sound. Listen as I blend the two sounds together: /beee/. Now you say it. (/beee/)

Place Word-Building Card *d* next to *be*. Move your hand from left to right.

Repeat the routine with the word *bat*.

This is the letter *d*. The letter *d* stands for the /d/ sound. Listen as I blend the three sounds together: /beeed/, *bed*. Now you say it. (/beeed/, *bed*)

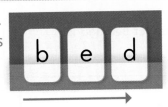

Guided Practice/Practice

Children blend sounds to form words. Guide practice with first word.

bin	bit	Bob	bat
bet	bib	Ben	ban

Objectives

- Read decodable words with /b/b, /l/l
- Read the words *and, what*
- Reread for fluency

Materials

- Decodable Reader: *Hot Ben, Hot Lin*
- High-Frequency Word Cards: *a, and, are, do, is, what*
- pocket chart

Decodable Text

For additional decodable passages, see pages 29–30 of the **Teacher's Resource Book**.

Decodable Reader

Read *Hot Ben, Hot Lin*

Decodable Reader

Hot Ben, Hot Lin
by Liz Ray

Phonics Practice

Hot Ben, Hot Lin

 REVIEW HIGH-FREQUENCY WORDS Display the **High-Frequency Word Cards** for **a**, **is**, **and**, **are**, **what**, and **do** in the pocket chart. Review words using the **Read/Spell/Write** routine.

MODEL CONCEPTS ABOUT PRINT
I hold the book so that it is not upside down. I open the book by turning the cover. Then I turn each page as I read it.

PREDICT Ask children to describe the cover. *What season is it? How do you know? What do you think this book is about?*

FIRST READ Have children point to each word, sounding out the decodable words and saying the sight words quickly. Children should chorally read the story the first time through.

DEVELOP COMPREHENSION Ask the following:

- *Where are the children?* (baseball field, pool, puddle, skating rink)

- *What* **season** *is it when the children are ice skating?* (winter)

 SECOND READ Have partners reread the book together. Circulate, listen in, and provide corrective feedback.

PARTNERS

It is hot, hot, hot.
Lin and Ben are hot.

2

Dad let Ben hop in.

3

It is hot, hot, hot.

4

Bob had a red cap on.
Bob ran, ran, ran.

5

It is not hot.
What can fit on Deb?

6

They can fit on Deb.

7

It is not hot.
Mom let Tim hop in!

8

Decodable Reader

Writing

Interactive Writing: Sentences

REVIEW
Display and read aloud the lists that children created for the Shared Writing activity.

WRITE

■ *Today we are going to write two sentences about a **season** that we like. The first sentence will be a question. The next sentence will be the answer to the question.*

■ Collaborate with children to write the following sentence frames. Read the sentences and point out the question mark and period.

> What is _____?
> _____ is a time to
> _____ and _____.

■ Say: *My favorite season is summer.* Write *summer* in the question, having children help by writing any letters they know.

■ Explain that the first word of the second sentence frame will answer the question, so the first word will be *Summer*. Write *Summer*, pointing out that a sentence begins with a capital letter.

■ Have children suggest words for the second sentence from the Day 1 list. Write the words to complete the sentence. Read the completed sentences aloud as you track the print.

■ Save the sentences to use in other Writing activities this week.

■ To extend the lesson, work with children to write sentences about one of the things on the list that they like to do.

Write About It
Have children draw a picture of what they like to do in their favorite season and write the caption: *I do this in _____.*

Objectives

• Write sentences
• Use letter knowledge to write letters in a word

Materials

• Shared Writing lists from Day 1

5-Day Writing

Sentences	
DAY 1	Shared: Lists
DAY 2	Interactive: Sentences
DAY 3	Independent: Prewrite and Draft Sentences
DAY 4	Independent: Revise and Edit Sentences
DAY 5	Independent: Publish and Present

ELL

Prewriting Planning Ask children what their favorite season is and what they like to do during that season. List their responses as ideas for what they can draw. Then help children complete their captions.

Transitions That Teach

While children are lining up, have them talk about the **months** of the year. Name each and have them describe it.

Oral Language
- Build Robust Vocabulary
- Oral Vocabulary Cards: "Paul Bunyan and the Popcorn Blizzard"

✔ **Comprehension**
- Read "A Year with Bears"
- Text Feature: Photographs

✔ **High-Frequency Words**
- Review *and*, *what*

✔ **Phonemic Awareness**
- Phoneme Isolation

✔ **Phonics**
- Introduce /l/
- Handwriting: Write *Ll*

Grammar
- Describing Words (Adjectives)

Writing
- Independent Writing: Sentences

SMALL GROUP

- Differentiated Instruction, pages 1694–1719

Additional Vocabulary

To provide 15–20 minutes of additional vocabulary instruction, see Oral Vocabulary Cards 5-Day Plan. The pre- and posttests can be found in the **Teacher's Resource Book**, pages 226–227.

Oral Language

 Talk About It

Build Robust Vocabulary

BUILD BACKGROUND

Introduce the story "Paul Bunyan and the Popcorn Blizzard" using **Oral Vocabulary Card 1** and read the title aloud. Explain that a *blizzard* is a very windy snowstorm. *In what season or month would you expect to see a snowstorm?* Ask children to tell what they think will happen in the story.

■ Read the story on the back of the cards. Pause at each oral vocabulary word and read the definition. Check children's understanding using the Compare and Contrast, Sequence of Events, and Words with Multiple Meanings prompts.

Oral Vocabulary Cards

Vocabulary Routine

Use the routine below to discuss the meaning of each word.

Define: When you **shiver**, your whole body shakes or trembles. Say the word with me.
Example: The children were shivering when they came out of the cold lake.
Ask: What does shivering look like? What makes you shiver?

Define: When the weather is **mild**, it is not too hot and not too cold. Say the word with me.
Example: A bright sun and mild temperatures are perfect for playing outside.
Ask: If you are outside and sweating, is the weather mild or not mild? How do you know?

Define: A **warning** is a way of telling that something bad is going to happen. Say the word with me.
Example: The yellow sign was a warning that the floor was slippery.
Ask: What are some examples of warning signs that help us stay safe?

 SPIRAL REVIEW

■ Use the routine on Cards 1 and 2 to review the words **month** and **season**.

■ Review last week's words: *blustery, chilly, cloud, drizzle,* and *weather.*

Listen for Alliteration

IDENTIFY ALLITERATION

Remind children that alliteration is when two or more words have the same beginning sound.

Tell children they will recite a rhyme about rain and the sound it sometimes makes. Play the rhyme "Pitter, Patter" and have children recite the rhyme and tap with their fingers. Ask children which words begin with the same sound. (*pitter, patter*)

Generate alliteration by modeling how to change the beginning /p/ sound to /b/ to say "Bitter, Batter." Guide children to repeat with /l/ and /d/.

Pitter, Patter

Oh, where do you come from,

You little drops of rain.

Pitter, patter, pitter, patter

Tap fingers on table or floor.

Down the windowpane.

Tell me, little raindrops,

Is that the way you play?

Pitter, patter, pitter, patter

Tap fingers on table or floor.

All the rainy day.

Objectives

- Listen and respond to a tall tale
- Use oral vocabulary words *mild, month, season, shiver,* and *warning*
- Recognize and generate alliteration

Materials

- Oral Vocabulary Cards: "Paul Bunyan and the Popcorn Blizzard"

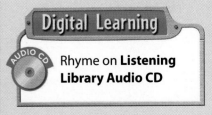

Digital Learning

Rhyme on **Listening Library Audio CD**

Objectives

- Retell and respond to expository text
- Analyze text features
- Understand time sequence in an expository selection about bears
- Relate particular months to seasons of the year

Material

- Big Book of Explorations, Vol. 2: "A Year with Bears"
- classroom calendar
- copy of calendar for the current year

Content Vocabulary

den a place where wild animals sleep

cub a very young bear

bedding usually sheets and blankets but in this text, it is leaves

Informational Text

Genre

Big Book of Explorations

INFORMATIONAL TEXT: EXPOSITORY
Tell children that this nonfiction selection is **expository** text. Access children's prior knowledge about months. Ask children if they know the month and date of their birth. Record these by month order, listing each child's name and birth date under the appropriate month. Say that they will read how two cubs grow through one year.

READ "A YEAR WITH BEARS"

- **Preview and Predict** Display the first page and read the title as you track the print. Point to the bear on page 15. *What animal is this?* Turn the pages and point out each page has different months of the year. *What do you think this selection will be about? What animal will we learn about?*

- **Content Vocabulary** Introduce and discuss the vocabulary words.

- **Text Feature: Photographs** Explain that this nonfiction selection uses photographs to give information about how real black bear cubs in the wild grow and change. Have children compare growth changes of the cub pictured on page 16 with the one pictured on page 19.

CONTENT FOCUS

- Read page 15 aloud. Have children describe the mother bear. Then point to the boldfaced word for *January.* Show January on a calendar and say that January is a month of the winter season.

- Read pages 16 and 17 to children. Have children describe the cub. Then show these months on the calendar. Tell children that February and most of March are part of the winter season. Explain that the season of spring begins on March 21. Show and say this date on the calendar. Ask children what season the months April and May are part of. (spring)

- As you read pages 18 and 19, show these months on the calendar. Point to and say the date that summer begins.

- Read page 20 to children. Point to *September, October, November* and *December* on the calendar. Say the dates that the seasons fall and winter begin. Define *den* and point it out in the photograph.

page 15

pages 16–17

pages 18–19

page 20

Retell and Respond

- *In which month were the cubs born?* (January)

- *In which months do the bears begin their long nap?* (November and December)

Connect to Content

Science: A Year in Your Life

- Each group will need a sheet of poster board. Assign a season to each of four groups.

- Review the life cycle of the bear as shown in "A Year With Bears." Review the names of the months in each season.

- Have one group member write the name of the group's season on the poster. Then have children draw activities that bears and people do at that time of year. Help them write labels.

- Display the posters, and have groups present them to the class in this order: winter, spring, summer, fall.

ELL

Beginning

Gesture and Talk For page 16, ask children to help you gesture being asleep and cuddling with your cubs.

Intermediate

Ask Questions After reading each page, ask questions to support vocabulary and key concepts. page 15: *Where does the mother bear stay in January?* page 17: *In which months do the plants start to grow?* page 19: *What kind of food do bears eat?*

Advanced

Develop Concepts Ask children more in-depth questions about key concepts. page 20: *How do the cubs help prepare for the winter?*

Objective

- Read the high-frequency words *and, what*

Materials

- High-Frequency Word Cards: *What, do, and, see, you, I, a*
- pocket chart
- Photo Cards: *ball, balloon, goat, gorilla, ladybug, leaf*
- 2 index cards with: period mark, question mark
- Activity Book, pp. 17–18
- Practice Book, pp. 149–150

Activity Book, pages 17–18
Practice Book, pages 149–150

High-Frequency Words

 and, what

SPIRAL REVIEW **REVIEW** Display the **High-Frequency Word Card** for **and**. Review the word using the **Read/Spell/Write** routine.

Repeat the routine for the word **what**.

APPLY Build sentences in the pocket chart using High-Frequency Word Cards and **Photo Cards**. Read each sentence aloud, then have children chorally read it as you track the print with your finger. Use the question and answer below and the following: *I see a ladybug and a leaf. I see a goat and a gorilla.*

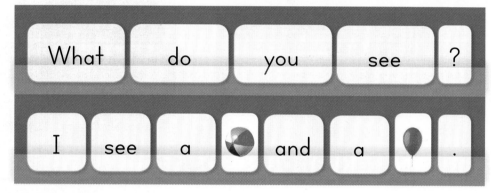

READ FOR FLUENCY Chorally read the Take-Home Book with children. Then have them reread the book to review high-frequency words and build fluency.

Quick Check

Can children read the words *and* and *what*?

During **Small Group Instruction**

If No → **Approaching Level** Provide additional practice with high-frequency words, page 1704.

If Yes → **On Level** Children are ready to read the Take-Home Book.

Beyond Level Children are ready to read the Take-Home Book.

TIME TO MOVE!

Have children form a circle for a Cat and Mouse game. Ask one child to walk around the outside tapping several children. The child says: *I tap Billy and Natalie and Annie and . . . you are it!* The last child chases the tapper around the circle and then tries to make it back to his or her seat.

Phonemic Awareness

Phoneme Isolation

Model

Display the **Photo Card** for *leaf*.

Today we are going to learn a new sound. Listen for the beginning sound in *leaf*: /l/. *Leaf* has /l/ at the beginning. Say the sound with me: /l/. What is the sound?

Repeat with the Photo Card for *ladybug*.

We'll make a loop with our fingers when we hear a word that begins with /l/.

Say the "Look, Bear, Look!" Rhyme and Chime again.

Look, Bear, look!
And what do you see?
A ladybug on a leaf
and a bird in a tree.
Listen, Bear, listen!
What do you hear?
Lambs saying, "Baaa!"
and bees buzzing in my ear.

Model making a loop with your fingers after you say "Look."

Review /b/, /r/, /e/
Display the Photo Card for *bus*.

This is a bus. The sound at the beginning of *bus* is /b/. What is the sound?

Repeat for *ring* and *egg*.

Guided Practice/Practice

Display and name each Photo Card.

Say each picture name with me. Tell me the sound at the beginning of the word.

Children identify the initial sound. Guide practice with the first card.

Quick Check

Can children identify the initial sound /l/?

During **Small Group Instruction**

If No → | Approaching Level | Provide additional practice, page 1704.

If Yes → | On Level | Children blend words with /l/, page 1696.

| Beyond Level | Children blend words with /l/, page 1697.

Objectives

- Identify initial sound /l/
- Review initial sounds /r/, /b/, and /e/

Materials

- Photo Cards: *leaf, lemon, ladder, lock, ladybug, lamp, egg, elbow, exit, balloon, box, bus, ring, rock, rose*

ELL

Pronunciation Display and have children name **Photo Cards** from this and prior lessons to reinforce phonemic awareness and word meanings. Point to a card and ask: *What do you see?* (a leaf) *What is the sound at the beginning of the word* leaf? (/l/). Repeat using Photo Cards with words that begin with the sounds /r/, /b/, and /e/.

Objectives

- Match the letter *l* to the sound /l/
- Handwriting: write *Ll*

Materials

- Sound-Spelling Card: *Lemon*
- Teaching Chart 47
- Handwriting
- Handwriting Teacher's Edition, pp. 62–64
- Activity Book, p. 19
- Practice Book, p. 151

ELL

Variations in Languages

Speakers of Korean may have difficulty perceiving and pronouncing /l/. Use the Approaching Level Phonics lessons for additional pronunciation and decoding practice.

Corrective Feedback

Linguistic Differences

Many speakers of African American Vernacular English drop the /l/ sound in words, particularly in words with *-ool* and *-oal* spelling patterns, such as *cool* and *coal*, and when the letter *l* precedes the consonant *p, t,* or *k* as in *help, belt,* and *milk*. These children will drop the *l* when spelling these words, as well. Provide additional articulation support prior to reading and spelling these words.

Phonics

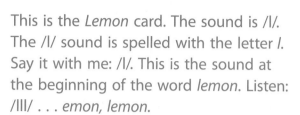

 ## Introduce /l/l

Model

Display the *Lemon* **Sound-Spelling Card**.

This is the *Lemon* card. The sound is /l/. The /l/ sound is spelled with the letter *l*. Say it with me: /l/. This is the sound at the beginning of the word *lemon*. Listen: /lll/ . . . *emon, lemon.*

What is the name of this letter? What sound does this letter stand for?

Read the "Look, Bear, Look!" Rhyme and Chime. Point out that *Look* begins with the letter *L*. Reread the title. Model placing a self-stick note below the *L* in *Look*.

Teaching Chart 47

Guided Practice/Practice

Read the rest of the rhyme. Stop after each line.

Children place self-stick notes below words that begin with *l*. Guide with *Look* in line 1.

Let's put a sticky note below the word in the line that begins with /l/. The word *Look* begins with the capital letter *L*.

Build Fluency: Sound-Spellings

 SPIRAL REVIEW Display the following **Word-Building Cards**: *a, b, c, d, e, f, h, i, l, m, n, o, p, r, s, t.* Have children chorally say each sound. Repeat and vary the pace.

Handwriting: Write *Ll*

MODEL Model holding up your writing hand. Say the handwriting cues as you write the capital and lowercase forms of *Ll* on the board. Then trace the letters on the board and in the air as you say /l/.

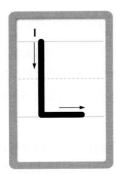

Straight down. Straight across the bottom line.

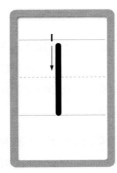

Straight down.

PRACTICE Ask children to hold up their writing hand.

■ Say the cues together as children trace with their index finger the letters you wrote on the board.

■ Have children write *L* and *l* in the air as they say the /l/ multiple times.

■ Distribute handwriting practice pages. Observe children's pencil grip and paper position, and correct as necessary. Have children say /l/ every time they write the letter *l*.

For Tier 2 instruction, see page 1705.

Daily Handwriting

Check that children form letters starting at the top and moving to the bottom. See **Handwriting Teacher's Edition** for ball-and-stick and slant models.

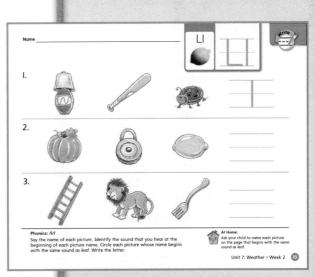

Activity Book, page 19
Practice Book, page 151

Objective

- Recognize describing words (adjectives)

Materials

- Big Book of Explorations, Vol. 2: "A Year with Bears"
- Photo Cards: *berries, ball, box, carrots, envelope, fish, globe, key, lamp, nail*

Grammar

Describing Words (Adjectives)

MODEL Use the **Big Book of Explorations** selection "A Year with Bears" to discuss describing words. Remind children that describing words tell more about something. Turn to page 15 and read the sentence. *There is little food in the woods.* Ask: *Which word describes how much food is in the woods?* (little) *Yes,* little *is the describing word in this sentence.*

- *How would you describe the bear in this picture?* (big, black, furry)

- Turn to page 17. Ask: *How would you describe this setting?* (green, grassy, hilly) Tell children that describing words help the reader to visualize, or get pictures in the mind, about what is happening in a book.

PRACTICE Play a game with children. Say: *I'm thinking of something in this classroom that is brown. It is made of smooth wood. We have many of them in the classroom. You sit on the flat part of it. What is it?* (chair) *What are the describing words?* (brown, smooth, many, flat)

- Have children take turns describing objects in the classroom. Tell them to use as many describing words as possible. Prompt them by asking if the object is smooth, rough, or shiny. Ask what color the object is. Tell children not to look at the object that they are describing so they don't give it away.

- When the class figures out the object, have children tell the describing words that were used. Ask the class which word helped them figure out what was being described.

- If children cannot find something in the class to describe, give them the following **Photo Cards**: *berries, ball, box, carrots, envelope, fish, globe, lamp, key,* and *nail.*

Writing

Independent Writing: Sentences

Display the lists of activities from the Shared Writing activity.

BRAINSTORM

WRITING TRAIT: WORD CHOICE Explain that children will write sentences about what they like to do in their favorite **season** or **month**. First they need to choose the words they want to use.

Think Aloud Good writers make sure to use the best word. I want to write about summer. I like to play in the water, but what I really like to do is swim and dive. So I'll use the words *swim* and *dive*.

Ask children to think of their favorite season and what they like to do then. List children's ideas for them to use as a reference.

PREWRITE

Write the following sentence frame on the board and read it aloud:

> _____ is a time to _____ and _____.

Complete the sentence by writing the words *Summer*, *swim*, and *dive* in the frames. Read the sentence aloud as you track the print.

- Have children choose a season and what they like to do in that season. Guide them to use the class Word Wall to select words to use in their writing.

DRAFT

- Have children write the sentence frame and then complete it by writing the name of a season and two activities. Have children add a drawing to illustrate their sentence.

- Collect and save children's work to use tomorrow.

Write About It

Ask children to draw a picture of their home or neighborhood during the fall or winter and write a sentence.

Objectives

- Write a sentence
- Begin to use writing trait: word choice
- Use letter knowledge to write letters in a word

Materials

- children's writing from Day 2

5-Day Writing

	Sentences
DAY 1	Shared: Lists
DAY 2	Interactive: Sentences
DAY 3	Independent: Prewrite and Draft Sentences
DAY 4	Independent: Revise and Edit Sentences
DAY 5	Independent: Publish and Present

ELL

Use New Language Ask children: *What season are we in? What things do you like to do during this season?* List children's answers and ask them to make a drawing of themselves doing one of the seasonal activities on the list.

Transitions That Teach

While lining up, have children describe **mild** weather and what they like to do on mild weather days.

DAY 4
At a Glance

WHOLE GROUP

Oral Language
- Build Robust Vocabulary

✓ Comprehension
- Read Aloud: "How the Turtle Flew South for the Winter"

Vocabulary
- Words That Compare
- Story Words: *dance, sway*

✓ Phonemic Awareness
- Phoneme Blending

✓ Phonics
- Picture Sort
- Blend with /l/
- Decodable Reader: *Hot Ben, Hot Lin*

Writing
- Independent Writing: Revise and Edit Sentences

SMALL GROUP
- Differentiated Instruction, pages 1694–1719

Oral Language

 Talk About It

Build Robust Vocabulary

ANIMALS AND SEASONS

Name the **seasons** of the year with children. Then discuss what animals do in each season. Remind children to speak clearly.

- *Which animals do you see in the spring, summer, fall, and winter months? What do the animals do in each season?*

CREATE A WORD WEB

Draw a word web and label as shown below, or use **Teaching Chart G1**. Read aloud the words as you track the print.

Think Aloud In the spring I often see birds building nests, so I will write *birds building nests* on our web under *Spring*. In the summer I see turtles swimming in ponds, so I'll write *turtles swimming in ponds* under *Summer*. What other animals can we add to our web for each of the four seasons?

As children discuss the animals they see in each season and what those animals do, add their ideas to the web. Then read all the words on the web with children as you track the print.

Winter
birds looking for berries
bears hibernate

Spring
birds building nests
ants building anthills

Animals in the Seasons

Fall
geese flying south
squirrels gathering nuts

Summer
turtles swimming in ponds
bees buzzing around flowers

ELL   ENGLISH LANGUAGE LEARNERS

Beginning	Intermediate	Advanced
Confirm Understanding Show children pictures of familiar baby animals and ask children in what season of the year they think each of the baby animals is born.	**Enhance Understanding** Show children pictures of animals commonly found in parks. Ask children to talk about how they think these animals find food in summer and in winter.	**Share Information** Ask children to share what they know about what some animals do in each season of the year. Elaborate on what children say.

Listen for Alliteration

IDENTIFY ALLITERATION

Remind children that alliteration is when the beginning sound in a group of words is repeated.

Theme: *Seasons*

RHYME ABOUT THE WEATHER

Tell children that they will recite the rhyme "One Misty, Moisty Morning" that they learned earlier in the week. Play the rhyme and have children join in. Have children identify the alliterative words.

Point out that the words *misty, moisty,* and *morning* all begin with the same sound. Have children generate other alliterative words, such as: *One **mild** Monday morning when wonderful was the weather.*

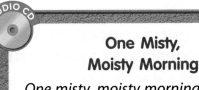

One Misty, Moisty Morning

One misty, moisty morning

When cloudy was the weather,

I met a little old man

Who had clothes of leather.

He began to compliment,

And I began to grin,

How do you do, and how do you do,

And how do you do again?

Objective

- Listen and respond to a folktale

Materials

- Read-Aloud Anthology: "How the Turtle Flew South for the Winter," pp. 101–104

ELL

Background Knowledge
Remind children of how the four seasons were illustrated in the **Big Book** *In the Yard*. Browse through the book to review the features of each season.

Readers Theater

BUILDING LISTENING AND SPEAKING SKILLS
Distribute copies of "So Long as There's Weather," Read-Aloud Anthology pages 185–186. Have children practice performing the play throughout the unit. Assign parts and have children present the play or perform it as a dramatic reading at the end of the unit.

Interactive
Read Aloud

Listening Comprehension

GENRE: LITERARY TEXT/FOLKTALE

Tell children that "A Year with Bears" was about how bears live throughout the **months** of the year. Explain that the purpose of today's folktale was to teach children how birds and turtles respond to the changing **seasons**. Compare the settings in this folktale with the story *In the Yard*.

Read Aloud

CULTURAL PERSPECTIVES

This tale is a Sioux Native American tale. Today the Sioux are one of the largest groups of Native Americans. They live mostly in North and South Dakota, Minnesota, Nebraska, and Montana.

READ "HOW THE TURTLE FLEW SOUTH FOR THE WINTER"

- **MODEL ASKING QUESTIONS ABOUT VISUALIZING** Use the Think Alouds provided at point of use for the strategy.

- **MODEL FLUENT READING** Read aloud the folktale with fluent expression. Stop occasionally so that children can predict what will happen next.

- **EXPAND VOCABULARY** See page 101 of the **Read-Aloud Anthology** to teach new words using the **Define/Example/Ask** routine.

Respond to Literature

TALK ABOUT IT Children retell important events from the folktale.

- *What season is it at the beginning of the story?* (fall) *Why are the birds in the story flying south?*

- *What happened to the turtle when he opened his mouth?*

- *Which events can really happen and which ones are imagined?*
  (Possible answers: seasons really change, animals cannot talk)

Write About It
Ask children to draw their favorite part of the folktale and have them write a label or sentence about their drawing.

Vocabulary

Words That Compare

REVIEW WORDS THAT COMPARE
I am going to read a story that uses words that compare. When you hear a word that compares two or more things, hold up your hand.

Read the following story:

> *Tanya went to the zoo with her mom to see the animals. They looked at the giraffes. "Which one do you like?" asked her mom. Tanya said, "I like the* tall *one." "I like the* taller *mother giraffe," said her mom. The* tallest *giraffe stood still, so they took its picture. Then they looked at the snakes. "Which one do you like?" asked her mom. Tanya said, "I like the* long *one." "I think the* longer *one is the best," said her mom. The* longest *snake slithered and stuck out its tongue. So they took its picture!*

Display pictures of the same item in different sizes. Have children sort the pictured items into categories of "big, bigger, biggest" or "small, smaller, smallest".

Story Words: *dance, sway*

Display page 7 of *In the Yard.* Ask children how they like to dance. *Do you like to dance fast or slow? With music or without?* Display pages 14–15. Ask children to name other things that *sway* in the wind. (flowers, grasses, bushes)

TIME TO MOVE!

Have children dance to fast music, moving around and picking up their feet. Then have them pretend to be swaying trees. Have them sway to slow music, with both feet on the floor and arms at sides.

Objectives

- **Use words that compare**
- **Review story words** *dance, sway*

Materials

- **pictures of the same item in different sizes**
- **Big Book:** *In the Yard*

ELL

Reinforce Meaning Have children pick crayons in three different sizes and sort them as *long, longer,* and *longest.*

Objectives

- Orally blend sounds to form words with /l/
- Sort picture names with initial *l, b, e*
- Review sound-spellings for /b/b, /e/e, /l/l
- Blend with *l*
- Read simple one-syllable words

Materials

- Puppet
- Photo Cards: *bicycle, book, bowl, bus, envelope, egg, exit, ladybug, lamp, lock*
- Word-Building Cards
- pocket chart
- Activity Book, p. 20
- Practice Book, p. 152

ELL

Pronunciation Display and have children name **Photo Cards** from this and prior lessons to reinforce sound-letter relationships and word meanings. Point to a card and ask: *What do you see?* (a bicycle) *What is the sound at the beginning of the word* bicycle? (/b/) *What is the letter at the beginning of the word* bicycle? (b)

Phonemic Awareness

Phoneme Blending

Model

Use the **Puppet** to model how to blend sounds in the word *lap*.

Repeat the routine with *lip*.

Happy is going to say the sounds in a word. Listen to Happy as he says each sound: /l/ /a/ /p/. Happy can blend these sounds to say the word: /lllaaap/, *lap*. Say the sounds with Happy: /l/ /a/ /p/, /lllaaap/. Now say the word with Happy. (*lap*)

Guided Practice/Practice

Say the sounds.

Children blend the sounds to form words. Guide practice with the first word.

Happy is going to say the sounds in a word. Listen as he says each sound. Blend the sounds to say the word.

/l/ /e/ /t/   /s/ /e/ /l/   /l/ /o/ /t/   /l/ /i/ /t/

/l/ /i/ /d/   /f/ /i/ /l /   /l/ /e/ /d/   /b/ /e/ /l/

Phonics

Picture Sort

b l e

Model

Place **Word-Building Card** *b* in the pocket chart.

This is the letter *b*. The letter *b* stands for the sound /b/. Say /b/.

Repeat for *l* and *e*.

The letter *l* stands for the /l/ sound. Say /l/.

Hold up the **Photo Card** for *bus*.

Repeat with *lock* and *egg*.

Here is a picture of a *bus*. *Bus* begins with /b/. The letter *b* stands for the /b/ sound. I will place the *bus* under *b*.

Guided Practice/Practice

Children sort the Photo Cards. Guide practice with the first card.

Build Fluency: Sound-Spellings

 Display the following **Word-Building Cards**: *a, b, c, d, e, f, h, i, l, m, n, o, p, r, s, t*. Have children chorally say each sound. Repeat and vary the pace.

 ## Blend with /l//

Model

Place Word-Building Card *l* in the pocket chart.

This letter is *l*. The letter *l* stands for the /l/ sound. Say /l/.

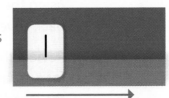

Place Word-Building Card *e* next to *l*. Move your hand from left to right.

This is the letter *e*. The letter *e* stands for the /e/ sound. Listen as I blend the two sounds together: /llleee/. Now you say it. (/llleee/)

Place Word-Building Card *t* next to *le*. Move your hand from left to right.

This is the letter *t*. The letter *t* stands for the /t/ sound. Listen as I blend the three sounds together: /llleeet/, *let*. Now you say it. (/llleeet/, *let*)

Repeat with *led*.

Guided Practice/Practice

Children blend sounds to form words. Guide practice with the first word.

lid	lad	lab	lap	lip
lit	lid	led	let	lot

Corrective Feedback

Blending: Sound Error Model the sound that children missed, then have them repeat the sound. For example, for the word *let*, say: *My turn.* Tap under the letter *t* in the word *let* and say: *Sound? What's the sound?* Then return to the beginning of the word. Say: *Let's start over.* Blend the word with children again.

CCVC: Initial Blends

Explain Display Word-Building Cards *f, l*. F *and* l *together stand for the sounds* /fl/ *as in* flip. *What sounds do the letters* fl *stand for together?* Hold up the Word-Building Cards *s, l*. S *and* l *together stand for the sounds* /sl/ *as in* sled. Repeat with *cl* and the word *clam*.

Model Place Word-Building Cards *f, l* in the pocket chart. *The letters* f *and* l *stand for* /fl/. *Place the* i *to the right of* fl. *This is the letter* i. *It stands for* /i/. *Let's blend* fl *and* i: /fliii/. *This is the letter* p. *It stands for* /p/. *Listen as I blend all four sounds:* /fliiip/, flip. *Say it with me.* Have children repeat. Continue by modeling the words *flat, slot, clip, sled, slip, clap.*

Guided Practice/Practice Using Word-Building Cards, assist children in blending the word *slab*. Continue with *flab, flat, slip, clip, clam, slam, slap.*

Activity Book, page 20
Practice Book, page 152

Objectives

- Read decodable words with /b/b, /l/l
- Read the words *and, what*
- Reread for fluency

Materials

- Decodable Reader: *Hot Ben, Hot Lin*
- High-Frequency Word Cards: *a, is, and, are, what, do*
- Sound-Spelling Cards: *Bat, Lemon*

Decodable Text

For additional decodable passages, see pages 29–30 of the **Teacher's Resource Book**.

Decodable Reader

Read *Hot Ben, Hot Lin*

REVIEW Review this week's high-frequency words and phonics skills using the word lists on the inside back cover of *Hot Ben, Hot Lin*.

Decodable Reader

Hot Ben, Hot Lin
by Liz Ray

Phonics Practice

Hot Ben, Hot Lin

Review the high-frequency words for **a**, **is**, **and**, **are**, **what**, and **do** using the **Read/Spell/Write** routine. Then have children chorally read the high-frequency word list.

Review phonics skills /b/b and /l/l using the *Bat* and *Lemon* **Sound-Spelling Cards**. Have children chorally read the decodable word list. Model blending and take note of children who struggle reading these words. Provide additional practice during Small Group time.

MODEL CONCEPTS ABOUT PRINT

Guide children to follow along. *I open the book by turning the cover. Then I turn each page as I read it, starting with the first page and ending with the last page. Now I want you to read the book.*

PARTNERS

REREAD FOR FLUENCY Have children reread the book with a partner. Have partners take turns asking and answering questions from each other. Circulate and listen in, providing corrective feedback. Then have children reread the book independently.

It is hot, hot, hot.
Lin and Ben are hot.

2

Dad let Ben hop in.

3

4

It is hot, hot, hot.

Bob had a red cap on.
Bob ran, ran, ran.

5

It is not hot.
What can fit on Deb?

6

They can fit on Deb.

7

8

It is not hot.
Mom let Tim hop in!

Decodable Reader

Writing

Independent Writing: Sentences

REVISE AND EDIT

Distribute children's sentences from Day 3. Have children reread them and check for the following:

- Did I write my name?

- Did I write the name of a **season** or **month** in my sentence?

- Did I use the best words to say what I mean?

- Did I begin my sentence with a capital letter?

- Did I end my sentence with a period?

Have children use their phonetic knowledge and understanding of spelling conventions to self-correct any errors in their work. Circulate and help children as they review and revise their sentences. Have children share their sentences with a partner.

Keisha

Fall is a time to pick and eat.

Write About It

Have children draw a picture of a holiday during one of the four seasons. Have them write a sentence or label their drawings with the season or the month. Encourage them to use describing words in their sentence or label.

Objectives

- Revise and edit sentences
- Use letter knowledge to write letters in a word

Materials

- children's sentences from Day 3
- Writer's Checklist; Teacher's Resource Book, p. 205

5-Day Writing

Sentences	
DAY 1	Shared: Lists
DAY 2	Interactive: Sentences
DAY 3	Independent: Prewrite and Draft Sentences
DAY 4	Independent: Revise and Edit Sentences
DAY 5	Independent: Publish and Present

ELL

Prewriting Planning Ask children to help you list holidays and sort them according to the season in which they take place. Then tell children to make a drawing of their favorite holiday and write the season in which it takes place.

Transitions That Teach

While children pack up, have them talk about what happens when they get a **shiver** from feeling cold.

Oral Language
- Build Robust Vocabulary

Comprehension
- Strategy: Visualize
- Skill: Identify Setting
- Read Across Texts

Vocabulary
- Review High-Frequency Words
- Review Words That Compare

Phonemic Awareness
- Phoneme Segmentation

Phonics
- Read Words
- Dictation

Writing
- Independent Writing: Publish and Present

- Differentiated Instruction, pages 1694–1719

Review and Assess
Oral Language
Build Robust Vocabulary

REVIEW WORDS
Review this week's oral vocabulary words with children. Explain that all of the words will be used to discuss the weather. Talk about how the weather changes from season to season where you live. Remind children that a season is a time of year.

Use the following questions to check children's understanding:

- Why might you **shiver** if you go outside without a jacket when it is cold?

- Which **season** is the hottest?

- Name a **month** when the weather might be cold.

- Why is it a good idea to listen to a **warning** about a heavy rainstorm that is coming?

- What is an activity you like to do in **mild** weather?

REVIEW RHYMES ABOUT WEATHER
Say the rhyme "One Misty, Moisty Morning" and ask children to join in and recite the rhyme with you. Have children name the words that rhyme. (*weather, leather*)

Recite "Pitter, Patter" with children. Have children name the rhyming words. (*rain, windowpane; play, day*) Have children identify the alliterative words for each rhyme. (misty, moisty, morning, pitter, patter)

Review and Assess
Comprehension

STRATEGY Monitor Comprehension: Visualize

REFLECT ON THE STRATEGY Tell children that visualizing helps to understand the setting that is not shown in the illustrations or photographs in a book.

Think Aloud I will create pictures in my mind to help me understand the setting. Creating pictures in my mind also helps me to monitor and adjust my understanding of the text.

SKILL Identify Setting

Review *In the Yard* and "How the Turtle Flew South for the Winter." Then use the following questions to review the setting in each story.

- *In which two places does* In the Yard *take place? Where does "How the Turtle Flew South for the Winter" take place?*

- *What happened in each* **season** *in* In the Yard? *What happened in each season in "How the Turtle Flew South for the Winter"?*

Reading Across Texts

Guide children connect ideas across texts. Then create a chart to compare the fiction story *In the Yard* and the expository selection "A Year with Bears." You may also wish to add a third column for the folktale "How the Turtle Flew South for the Winter." Have children draw or write about the settings and characters in the selections. Guide them to express their opinions.

In the Yard	A Year with Bears
fiction	expository
illustrations	photographs
lines that rhyme	does not rhyme
setting is in the family's yard in different seasons	setting is outside where bears live in different seasons
about things that people could really do	about real animals and what they do
about how people live as the seasons change	about how bears live as the **months** and seasons change

Objectives
- Recognize alliteration
- Review the strategy and skill
- Discuss purposes for listening to various texts
- Compare and contrast genres, stories, and characters
- Listen to and share information

Materials
- Big Book: *In the Yard*
- Big Book of Explorations, Vol. 2: "A Year with Bears"
- Read-Aloud Anthology: "How the Turtle Flew South for the Winter"
- Activity Book, p. 21

Activity Book, page 21

Objectives

- Review the high-frequency words *and, what, this, do, for, you*
- Review words that compare

Materials

- High-Frequency Word Cards: *this, do, and, what, for, you*
- words that compare on index cards: *tall, taller, tallest; long, longer, longest*
- 3 paper rectangles or pictures of the same object in different sizes
- pocket chart

Fluency

Connected Text Have children reread this week's **Decodable Reader** with a partner. Circulate, listen in, and note those children who need additional instruction and practice reading this week's decodable and sight words.

Review and Assess
Vocabulary

 ## ✓ High-Frequency Words

Distribute one of the following **High-Frequency Word Cards** to each child: **and**, **what**, **this**, **do**, **for**, and **you**. *When you hear the word that is on your card, stand and hold up your Word Card.*

- *I know how to read* this *word!*
- Do *you like to sing songs?*
- *My mother* and *father are here at school.*
- What *color is* this *jacket?*
- *If* you *sing, I will play the piano* for you.

Build Fluency: Word Automaticity

Display the High-Frequency Word Cards *and, what, this, do, for,* and *you*. Point quickly to each card, at random, and have children read the word as quickly as they can.

and	what	this	do

Words That Compare

Have children say the words as quickly as they can as you display index cards. Display the pocket chart with paper rectangles of three sizes set vertically and say words that compare with children: *tall, taller, tallest.* Then turn the rectangles horizontally and have children say words that compare: *long, longer, longest.* You may also use pictures of the same object in three different sizes.

TIME TO MOVE!

Play "Simon Says" with words that compare. For example: *Simon says, stand up tall. Simon says, stand up taller. Stand up the tallest!* Repeat with crouch down *low, lower, lowest.*

Review and Assess
Phonemic Awareness

Phoneme Segmentation

Objective
• Segment words into sounds

Materials
• Photo Cards: *lock, bus*
• Sound Box
• WorkBoard Sound Boxes; Teacher's Resource Book, p. 136
• markers

Guided Practice

Display the **Photo Cards** for *lock* and *bus*.

Repeat with *bus*.

Let's say the sounds in the word *lock* together: /l/ /o/ /k/. For each sound, let's put a marker in a box: /l/ /o/ /k/. We'll count the sounds as we say them: /l/ /o/ /k/. There are three sounds. Say the sounds in *lock*: /l/ /o/ /k/. Now say the word: *lock*.

Practice

Distribute Sound Boxes. Children put a marker in a box for each sound and then say the word. Guide practice with the first word.

I will say a word. Say the sounds in the word. Place a marker in the Sound Box for each sound you hear.

let, /l/ /e/ /t/   *bell*, /b/ /e/ /l/

bed, /b/ /e/ /d/   *tab*, /t/ /a/ /b/

bit, /b/ /i/ /t/   *lap*, /l/ /a/ /p/

lot, /l/ /o/ /t/   *led*, /l/ /e/ /d/

Objectives

- Read decodable words
- Read simple one-syllable words
- Write simple one-syllable words

Materials

- index cards (blank)
- 7 index cards with: *This, trip, is, a, lot, of, fun,* exclamation mark
- 5 index cards with: *What, is, a, bib,* question mark
- WorkBoard Sound Boxes; Teacher's Resource Book, p. 136
- Activity Book, p. 22

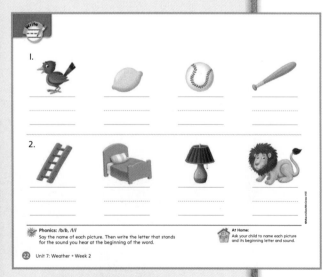

Activity Book, page 22

Review and Assess
Phonics

Build Fluency: Sound-Spellings

Rapid Naming Display the following **Word-Building Cards**: *a, b, c, d, e, f, h, i, l, m, n, o, p, r, s, t.* Have children chorally say each sound as quickly as they can.

 ## Read Words

Apply

Distribute the first set of cards. Have children stand in sequence.	Let's read the sentence together. *This trip is a lot of fun!*
Repeat using the other set of cards.	*What is a bib?*
Write the following sentences on the board.	Let's read the sentence together. *The frog can hop.* *I can go on the sled.*

 ## Dictation

Apply

Dictate sounds for children to spell.

Have children write the letters.

Listen as I say a sound. Repeat the sound, then write the letter that stands for the sound.

/e/	/l/	/d/	/r/	/o/	/f/
/b/	/h/	/k/	/i/	/t/	/a/

Then dictate words for children to spell. Model for children how to use the Sound Boxes to segment the word. Have them repeat.

Write the letters and words on the board for children to self-correct.

Now let's write some words. I will say a word. I want you to repeat the word, then think about how many sounds are in the word. Use your Sound Boxes to count the sounds. Then write one letter for each sound you hear.

bat	bet	let	lot	hot	hat
had	bad	bed	red	fed	led
lad	lap	lit	it	bit	sit

Review and Assess
Writing

Independent Writing: Sentences

PUBLISH
Explain to children that you will gather their sentences to make a class book about the seasons.

- Have children brainstorm a title, such as "All Year Long."

- Have a few children work on the cover. Write the title.

- Make holes along the edges of the cover and each page.

- Bind the pages together with yarn.

PRESENT
Have children take turns reading their sentences to the class and telling what the pictures show.

LISTENING, SPEAKING, AND VIEWING

- Remind children to speak clearly and to be good listeners when a classmate is speaking.

- Praise children for their hard work and display the finished book for everyone to enjoy. Children may wish to add a copy of their work to their Writing Portfolios.

Nathan

Spring is a time to plant and water.

Write About It
In their Writer's Notebooks, have children draw and label a picture of their favorite **month** at school.

Objective
- Publish and present sentences on the seasons

Materials
- children's writing from Day 4

5-Day Writing

	Sentences
DAY 1	Shared: Lists
DAY 2	Interactive: Sentences
DAY 3	Independent: Prewrite and Draft Sentences
DAY 4	Independent: Revise and Edit Sentences
DAY 5	Independent: Publish and Present

Transitions That Teach

While children are waiting in line, have them tell about a time they heard a **warning** about the weather.

Write About the Season

Have children draw pictures showing what they like to do in the current season of the year. Help them write sentences telling what they like to do.

I like to fly a kite.

ELL

Partners When pairing children to make up sentences, pair English Language Learners with children who are more proficient. Write their sentences, read them together, and point out the high-frequency words.

Approaching Level

Oral Language

Objective	Preteach oral vocabulary
Materials	• none

THEME WORDS: *season, month*

- Tell children that a **season** is a time of the year. *There are four seasons in a year. Each season has different weather. What are the names of the seasons? What is your favorite season? What do you like to do during those* **months***?*

- Discuss the words with children. Ask: *What season is it now? What month is it now? Describe some of the things that you see that help you know the season.*

- Have children use the following sentence frames to generate complete oral sentences using the words: *My favorite season is _____. I know it will be that season in the month of _____.*

High-Frequency Words

Objective	Preteach high-frequency words *and, what*
Materials	• **High-Frequency Word Cards:** *and, what*

PRETEACH WORD: *and, what*

- Display the **High-Frequency Word Card** for **and**.

- **Read** Point to and say the word *and. This is the word* and. *It is a word we use when we talk about more than one. I like spaghetti and meatballs.*

- **Spell** *The word* and *is spelled* a-n-d. Have children read and spell *and*.

- **Write** Finally, have children write the word *and*. Repeat the routine using the word **what**.

- Have children work with a partner to make up sentences using the words *and* and *what*. Ask them to talk about what they like to do during the summer season.

HIGH-FREQUENCY WORDS REVIEW

Display the High-Frequency Word Cards for words previously taught, one card at a time, as children chorally read and spell the word. Mix and repeat. Note words children need to review.

Tier 2

Approaching Level

Phonemic Awareness

Objective Identify initial sound /b/
Materials • **Photo Cards:** bike, book, bus, banana, balloon

✔ PHONEME ISOLATION

Model

- Display the **Photo Card** for bike. *This is a bike. Listen for the beginning sound in* bike: bike, /b/. *Bike begins with* /b/. Repeat for bus.

Guided Practice/Practice

- Display the Photo Cards. Have children take turns selecting a picture, naming it, and saying the initial sound: *This is a _____. _____ begins with* /b/. Guide practice with the first card.

Phonics

Objective Recognize words with initial /b/b
Materials • **Sound-Spelling Card:** Bat • **Word-Building Cards**
• **Photo Cards:** bat, balloon, banana, bike, book, bus

✔ PRETEACH: RECOGNIZE /b/b

Model

- Display the Photo Cards for bat and banana and the Bat **Sound-Spelling Card**. Say: *The name of this letter is* b. B *stands for the /b/ sound that you hear at the beginning of* bat. *I will place a* b *on the bat because* bat *begins with* /b/. Repeat with banana.

- Say /b/ and trace the b on your **Word-Building Card**.

Guided Practice/Practice

- Display the Photo Cards. Say: *This is the picture of a bike. What sound do you hear at the beginning of* bike? *What letter stands for /b/? Let's place a* b *on the bike because* bike *begins with* /b/. Repeat with remaining Photo Cards for /b/b.

- Guide children to trace the letter b on their Word-Building Cards.

- For additional practice, point out children and objects in the classroom with names that begin with initial /b/.

SOUND-SPELLINGS REVIEW

Tier 2

Display Word-Building Cards *m, a, s, p, t, i, n, c, o, f, h, d, r, e,* and *b,* one at a time. Have children chorally say the sound. Repeat and vary the pace.

On Level

High-Frequency Words

Objective Review high-frequency words *and, what, do, this, are, play*

Materials • **High-Frequency Word Cards:** *and, what, this, do, are, play*

REVIEW

- Display the **High-Frequency Word Card** for **and**.

- **Read** Point to and say the word *and. This is the word* and. *It is a word we use when we talk about more than one person, place, or thing. Meg and Paul came to the party.*

- **Spell** *The word* and *is spelled* a-n-d. Have children read and spell *and*.

- **Write** Finally, have children write the word *and*.

- Repeat with **what**, **this**, **do**, **are**, and **play**. Then have partners make up sentences using the words.

Phonemic Awareness/Phonics

Objective Review recognizing and blending initial /b/*b*, /e/*e*, /l/*l*

Materials • **Word-Building Cards** • pocket chart • **Puppet**

PHONEME BLENDING

Model

- *Listen as Happy says the sounds for* bet. *Say* /b/ /e/ /t/. *Now Happy will blend the sounds:* /beeet/, bet. *Happy blended* /b/ /e/ /t/ *together to say the word* bet.

Practice

- Have **Puppet** say /b/ /e/ /l/. Have children repeat. *Now blend the sounds and say the word:* /b/ /e/ /l/, bell. Repeat with:

/k/ /a/ /b/   /b/ /a/ /t/   /b/ /i/ /n/   /b/ /i/ /t/   /t/ /a/ /b/

/l/ /e/ /d/   /l/ /a/ /b/   /l/ /e/ /t/   /l/ /o/ /t/   /b/ /a/ /n/

REVIEW /b/*b*, /e/*e*, and /l/*l*

- Display **Word-Building Card** *b. The name of this letter is* b. B *stands for the* /b/ *sound at the beginning of* bib. *I'll hold up the* b *because* bib *begins with* /b/. *Repeat with* e *and* end. *Use the routine with* l *and* let *on Day 3 when the letter* l *is introduced.*

- Say: *bib, bed, edge, bet, bit, echo, egg, enter.* Children hold up the corresponding small Word-Building Cards and say the first sound of each word. Guide Practice with the first two words.

- For practice on Day 3 with /l/*l*, use *lit, lab, big, egg, late, bat,* and *lap* for children to identify /l/*l*, /b/*b*, /e/*e*.

Puppet

Partners When pairing children to make up sentences, pair English Language Learners with children who are more proficient. Write their sentences, read them together, and point to the high-frequency words.

Beyond Level

High-Frequency Words/Vocabulary

Objective   Review high-frequency words

Materials   • none

✔ ACCELERATE

- Write *eat* and *there* on the board.

- **Read** Point to and say the word *eat. This is the word* eat. *It means "to put into the mouth, chew, and swallow." I like to eat fruit.*

- **Spell** *The word* eat *is spelled* e-a-t. Have children read and spell *eat.*

- **Write** Have children write the word *eat.* Repeat with *there.*

- Have children work with a partner to make up oral sentences using the words *eat* and *there.*

EXPAND ORAL VOCABULARY

- **Synonyms** Review the meaning of the oral vocabulary word *warning* with children. Then explain that a *synonym* is a word that means the same thing as another word.

- Say: *A synonym for the word* warning *is* caution. *The word* caution *on a sign tells people they should be careful. The sign* Caution— Road Work Ahead *means drivers should slow down and drive carefully because there are workers in the road.*

- Have children take turns using the new word *caution* in a sentence. Then tell children that they will work with a partner to discuss times when they should be careful, or use *caution.*

Phonics

Objective   Read words with initial and final /b/*b* and /l/*l*

Materials   • **Sound-Spelling Cards:** *Bat, Lemon*   • **Word-Building Cards**
            • pocket chart

✔ ENRICH

- Display the *Bat* **Sound-Spelling Card**. Remind children that *Bb* stands for the /b/ sound. Bat *begins with the /b/ sound.* Cob *has /b/ at the end.* Repeat the routine for *l* with the words *lit* and *tall.*

- Write these words on the board: *ball, mall, small, bell, tell, back, black, lend, blend, last, blast, rib, crib, grab, club.* Model blending.

- Display **Word-Building Cards** *a, b, c, d, e, f, i, j, k, l, n, o, s, t, u, w,* and *x.* Have partners make as many words as they can. Provide time for children to share their lists.

ELL

Partners When pairing children to make up sentences, pair English Language Learners with children who are more proficient. Write their sentences, read them together, and point to the high-frequency words.

Corrective Feedback

If needed, review the letter-sound relationship for initial /b/*b*. Say: *The /b/ sound is at the beginning of* bat: */b/ /a/ /t/.* Ask children to echo the sound after you: */baaat/.* Repeat with *bell, bid, ban.*

ELL ENGLISH LANGUAGE LEARNERS

Oral Language Warm-Up

Content Objective Learn theme vocabulary

Language Objective Repeat and act out a fingerplay to demonstrate understanding

Materials • **Listening Library Audio CD** • **Visual Vocabulary Resources** • **Teaching Chart 46**

BUILD BACKGROUND KNOWLEDGE

All Language Levels

- Continue developing vocabulary around the unit theme "Weather" using the fingerplay "Pitter, Patter." Display a picture of rain or a rainy day, such as one of the **Visual Vocabulary Resources** or **Teaching Chart 46**. Teach the word *raindrops* as you point to the picture. Have children repeat the word three times.

- Play "Pitter, Patter" on the **Listening Library Audio CD**. Act out the lines as you chant the fingerplay.

- Then teach children the fingerplay hand motions. Emphasize the key words that connect to motions and where the rain falls: *pitter patter; Down the window pane.*

- Play the fingerplay several times until children correctly repeat it.

- Ask children to tell what rainy days are like. Build on their responses to model speaking in complete sentences.

Academic Language

Language Objective Use academic language in classroom conversations

All Language Levels

- This week's academic words are **boldfaced** throughout the lesson. Define the word in context and provide a clear example from the selection. Then ask children to generate an example or a word with a similar meaning.

Academic Language Used in Whole Group Instruction

Oral Vocabulary Words	Vocabulary and Grammar Concepts	Strategy and Skill Words
mild month season shiver warning	words that compare describing words	visualize setting describing words question

Cognates

Help children identify similarities and differences in pronunciation and spelling between English words and Spanish cognates:

Cognates

visualize	*visualizar*

ELL ENGLISH LANGUAGE LEARNERS

Vocabulary

Language Objective Demonstrate understanding and use of key words by describing seasons

Materials • **Visual Vocabulary Resources**

PRETEACH KEY VOCABULARY

All Language Levels

Use the **Visual Vocabulary Resources** to preteach the weekly oral vocabulary words *mild, month, season, shiver,* and *warning*. Focus on one or two words per day. Use the following routine that appears in detail on the cards.

- Define the word in English and provide the example given.
- Define the word in Spanish, if appropriate, and indicate if the word is a cognate.
- Display the picture and explain how it illustrates or demonstrates the word.
- Then engage children in structured partner-talk about the image, using the key word.
- Ask children to chorally say the word three times.
- Point out any known sound-spellings or focus on a key aspect of phonemic awareness related to the word.

PRETEACH FUNCTION WORDS AND PHRASES

All Language Levels

Use the Visual Vocabulary Resources to preteach the function words and phrases *work hard* and *in the yard*. Focus on one word per day. Use the detailed routine on the cards.

- Define the word in English and, if appropriate, in Spanish. Point out if the word is a cognate.
- Refer to the picture and engage children in talk about the word. For example, children will partner-talk using sentence frames, or they will listen to sentences and replace a word or phrase with the new function word.
- Ask children to chorally repeat the word three times.

TEACH BASIC WORDS

Beginning/Intermediate

Use the Visual Vocabulary Resources to teach the basic words *shovel, mow, rake, dig, pick,* and *weed*. Teach these "things we do in the yard" words using the routine provided on the card.

Visual Vocabulary Resources

Approaching Level

Oral Language

Objectives Reinforce oral vocabulary; speak in complete sentences
Materials • none

THEME WORDS: *season, month*

- Say: *We have talked about how there are four* **seasons** *in a year: fall, winter, spring, and summer. Each season takes place during certain* **months** *of the year.*

- *Would it be summer if it were snowing? Why or why not? Does fall occur in October or July? How do you know?* Have children answer in complete sentences.

- *What is the current season? How do you know?*

- *In which month(s) would you expect to see flowers blooming? In which month(s) do the leaves fall from the trees?*

High-Frequency Words

Objective Reteach high-frequency words
Materials • **High-Frequency Word Cards:** *and, what*
• **Sound-Spelling WorkBoards**

RETEACH WORDS: *and, what*

Tier 2

- Distribute a **WorkBoard** to each child. Then display the **High-Frequency Word Card** for **and**.

- Use the **Read/Spell/Write** routine to reteach the word. Point to and say the word. *This is the word* and. *It is a word we use when we talk about more than one person, place, or thing: Teri and Matt are leaving.* And *is spelled* a-n-d.

- Have children read and spell *and*. Then have them write the word on their WorkBoards. Repeat the routine with the word **what**.

- Have children work with a partner to make up sentences using the words *and* and *what*. Have them ask each other what their favorite months are.

CUMULATIVE REVIEW

Display the High-Frequency Word Cards for words previously taught, one card at a time, as children chorally read and spell the word. Mix and repeat. Note words children need to review.

ELL

Partners When pairing children to make up sentences, pair English Language Learners with children who are more proficient. Write their sentences, read them together, and point out the high-frequency words.

Approaching Level

Phonemic Awareness

Objective Identify and blend with /b/
Materials • **Puppet**

Puppet

PHONEME ISOLATION

Tier 2

Model

- *Listen as Happy says the sounds for* bet. *Say* /b/ /e/ /t/. *Now Happy will blend the sounds:* /beeet/, bet. *Happy blended* /b/ /e/ /t/ *together to say the word* bet. *Now listen again. I'll do another word.* Repeat the blending with the word *bed:* /b/ /e/ /d/, /beeed/, *bed.*

Practice

- Have the **Puppet** say /b/ /e/ /l/. Say: *Now you blend the sounds and say the word with Happy:* /b/ /e/ /l/, bell. *Repeat:*

/k/ /a/ /b/	/b/ /a/ /t/	/b/ /a/ /n/
/b/ /i/ /n/	/b/ /i/ /t/	/t/ /a/ /b/
/k/ /o/ /b/	/b/ /e/ /t/	/n/ /a/ /b/

Phonics

Objective Reinforce letter-sound correspondence for /b/*b*
Materials • **Sound-Spelling Card:** *Bat* • **Sound-Spelling WorkBoards**
           • **Word-Building Card** • **Decodable Reader** *Hot Ben, Hot Lin*

RECOGNIZE /b/*b*

Model

- Display the *Bat* **Sound-Spelling Card.** *The letter* b *stands for the* /b/ *sound as in* bat. *What is this letter? What sound does it stand for?* Repeat with *bike.*

- Trace *b* on a small **Word-Building Card.** *I will say a sentence. We'll* trace *b* when we hear /b/. Say: *Bob bought bread and butter.*

Guided Practice/Practice

- Distribute a **WorkBoard** to each child. Say: *bike, bug, cut, bacon, boat, basket, desk, big.* Children write *b* on their WorkBoard when they hear a word with /b/. Guide them with the first two words.

- **Read the Decodable Reader** Read *Hot Ben, Hot Lin* with children. Have them echo-read each page. Chorally reread the story.

CUMULATIVE REVIEW

Display Word-Building Cards *m, a, s, p, t, i, n, c, o, f, h, d, r, e,* and *b,* one at a time. Point to the letters in a random order. Have children chorally say the sound. Repeat and vary the pace.

Decodable Reader

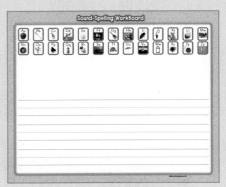

Sound-Spelling WorkBoard

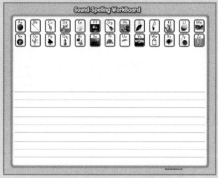

Sound-Spelling WorkBoard

On Level

Phonics

Objectives Review recognizing and blending initial /b/b, /l/l, /t/t, and /n/n; preteach /e/e

Materials • **Word-Building Cards** • pocket chart
• **Sound-Spelling WorkBoards**

✓ REVIEW /b/b, /e/e, /l/l, /t/t, and /n/n

- Display **Word-Building Card** b. *The name of this letter is* b. *B stands for the /b/ sound at the beginning of* bat. *I'll hold up the* b *because* bat *begins with /b/.* Repeat with l and *lemon,* t and *turtle,* n and *nut.* Preteach /e/e with *egg* which is introduce on Day 3.

- **Blend Words** Place Word-Building Cards b, a, t, in the pocket chart. Point to each letter for children to identify. Move your hand from left to right below the letters as you blend the word: /baaat/. *What is the word?* Continue blending with: *bit, lit, lot, not, hot, hat,* and *bat.* Blend e words with *Ben, bet, let, Len, ten,* and *net.*

- Have children write b, e, l, l on their **WorkBoards** and say /b/, /e/, and /l/. Repeat with b, e, n; b, e, t; l, e, t; l, e, n; t, e, n; and n, e, t.

- **Read the Decodable Reader** Read *Hot Ben, Hot Lin.* Have children reread each page. Then chorally reread the story.

Beyond Level

Phonics

Objective Read words with /a/a and /ā/a_e

Materials • **Sound-Spelling Cards:** *Bat, Lemon*
• **Word-Building Cards** • pocket chart

✓ ACCELERATE

- Display Word-Building Cards m, a, d. Read the word. Add e. *When I add the* e, *the* e *is silent, but the vowel sound changes to say its name.* Say *mad* and *made* to compare the vowel sounds.

- Write these word pairs for children to blend.

mad	made	rat	rate	mat	mate
fad	fade	fat	fate	tap	tape
Sam	same	stag	stage	plan	plane

ELL ENGLISH LANGUAGE LEARNERS

Access to Core Content

Content Objective Develop listening comprehension
Language Objective Discuss text using key words and sentence frames
Materials • **ELL Resource Book**, pp. 188–193

PRETEACH BIG BOOK

All Language Levels

Use the Interactive Question-Response Guide on **ELL Resource Book** pages 188–193 to introduce children to *In the Yard*. Preteach half of the selection on Day 1 and half on Day 2.

■ Use the prompts provided in the guide to develop meaning and vocabulary. Use the partner-talk and whole-class responses to engage children and increase student talk.

■ When completed, revisit the selection and prompt children to talk about the illustrations. Provide sentence starters as needed and build on children's responses to develop language.

ELL Resource Book

Big Book

Beginning	Intermediate	Advanced
Use Visuals During the Interactive Reading, select several pictures. Describe them and have children summarize what you said.	**Summarize** During the Interactive Reading, select a few lines of text. After you read them and explain them, have children summarize the text.	**Expand** During the Interactive Reading, select a larger portion of text. After you read it and explain it, have children summarize the text.

Approaching Level

High-Frequency Words

Objective Recognize high-frequency words *and, what, this, do*
Materials
- **High-Frequency Word Cards:** *and, what, this, do*
- **Word-Building Cards**

REVIEW WORDS: *and, what, this, do*

- Display the **High-Frequency Word Card** for **what**. Say the word and have children repeat it. Point to each letter and have children name it.

- Distribute **Word-Building Cards** *w, h, a, t*. Model putting the letters together to form *what*. Then have children form *what*.

- Repeat the above routines with the words **and**, **this**, and **do**.

- Have children use the words in questions, such as: *What is this? What can you do?* Answers should include the words, if possible.

CUMULATIVE REVIEW

Display the High-Frequency Cards for words previously taught, one card at a time, as children chorally read and spell the word. Mix and repeat. Note words children need to review.

Phonemic Awareness

Objective Identify initial and final sound /l/
Materials
- **Photo Cards:** *lamp, ladder, ladybug, lemon, lock, nail, pencil, seal, doll, quail, shell, bowl* • markers
- **WorkBoard Sound Boxes; Teacher's Resource Book**, p. 136

PHONEME ISOLATION

Model

- Display the **Photo Card** for *lamp. This is a lamp. Listen for the /l/ sound at the beginning of* lamp: /lllaaammmp/, *lamp. Lamp begins with /l/. I'll put a marker in the first box of the Sound Box to show that I hear /l/ at the beginning of* lamp. Repeat for *ladder*.

- Display the Photo Card for *nail. The /l/ sound can also be heard at the end of a word: /nālll/.* Nail *has /l/ at the end. I'll put a marker in the last box to show I hear /l/ at the end of* nail.

Guided Practice/Practice

- Distribute **Sound Boxes** and markers. Display the Photo Cards. Children take turns selecting a picture and naming it. Have children listen for /l/ and place the marker in the first or last box as they say: *This is a(n) _____. I hear /l/ at the beginning/end of _____.* Guide practice with the first card.

ELL

Extra Practice During the Cumulative Review, pair children at different levels of proficiency and have partners take turns reading and spelling the high-frequency words to each other.

Corrective Feedback

Lingusitic Differences Many speakers of African American Vernacular English drop the /l/ sound in words, particularly in words with *-ool* and *-oal* spelling patterns, such as *cool* and *coal*, and when the letter *l* precedes the consonants *p, t,* or *k* as in *help, belt,* and *milk*. These children will drop the *l* when spelling these words, as well. Provide additional articulation support prior to reading and spelling these words.

Approaching Level

Phonics

Objective Recognize words that begin with /l/l

Materials • **Sound-Spelling Card:** *Lemon* • **Word-Building Cards**
• **Photo Cards:** *lamp, ladder, ladybug, lemon, lock*

RECOGNIZE /l/l

Tier 2

Model

- Display the **Photo Card** for *lamp* and the *Lemon* **Sound-Spelling Card**. *This is the letter* l. *L stands for /l/ you hear at the beginning of* lamp. *I'll place an* l *on the lamp because* lamp *begins with /l/. Repeat with* ladder.

- Say /l/ and trace the *l* on your **Word-Building Card**.

Guided Practice/Practice

- Display the Photo Cards. *This is a lemon. What sound do you hear at the beginning of* lemon? *What letter stands for /l/? Let's place an* l *on the lemon because* lemon *begins with /l/. Repeat with remaining Photo Cards for /l/l.*

- Guide children to trace the letter *l* on their Word-Building Cards.

- For additional practice, point out children and objects in the classroom with names that begin with initial /l/. Hold the *l* card next to each while children say the name chorally.

Decodable Reader

Objective Reread Decodable Reader *Hot Ben, Hot Lin*

Materials • **Decodable Reader:** *Hot Ben, Hot Lin*

REREAD *Hot Ben, Hot Lin*

- Have children identify the front cover of the book and read the title. Open to the title page. Have children sound out each word of the title as you run your finger under it. *Look at the picture. What is this book about?*

- Page through the book. Ask children what they see in each picture. Have them find and point to the words *and* and *what*.

- Read the book chorally. Have children point to each word as they read it. Provide corrective feedback as needed.

- Ask children to use *and* to discuss the pictures. *What are Ben and Lin doing? What else do you see children doing?*

- After reading, ask children to recall things they read about.

Corrective Feedback

Association Error If children have difficulty identifying initial and final /l/, say: *My turn: /beeelll/,* bell. *I hear the /l/ sound at the end of* bell: */beeelll/. What is the sound? What is the letter? Let's start over.* Repeat with the word *lap* for children to identify the position of /l/.

Decodable Reader

ON YOUR OWN

Generate Alliteration

Ask children to make alliterative sentences using /b/ or /l/, such as: *Lin and Lou like lemonade.* Then have them write and illustrate their sentences.

Ben and Bob bat the ball.

Write Words for a Character

Children draw scenes from *Hot Ben, Hot Lin* and write what the characters might say.

We hop in. We swim!

Decodable Reader

On Level

Decodable Reader

Objective   Reread *Hot Ben, Hot Lin* to develop fluency
Materials   • **Decodable Reader:** *Hot Ben, Hot Lin*

REREAD FOR FLUENCY

- Ask children to look back at the pictures in *Hot Ben, Hot Lin* and use their own words to tell what the book was about.

- Have children read a page or two of the story. Model and work with them to read with accuracy and expression.

- Point out how you used your voice to say the words: *When I read, "It is hot, hot, hot," I said* hot *with more emphasis. I wanted to emphasize how hot Lin and Ben were.*

- Provide time to listen as children read. Comment on their accuracy and expression and provide corrective feedback.

Beyond Level

Decodable Reader

Objective   Reread *Hot Ben, Hot Lin* to reinforce fluency and phonics
Materials   • **Decodable Reader:** *Hot Ben, Hot Lin*

REREAD FOR FLUENCY

- Have partners reread *Hot Ben, Hot Lin*.

- Provide time to listen as children read. Comment on their accuracy and expression and provide corrective feedback.

INNOVATE

- Point out that the story has pictures of what children do in the summer, winter, and spring. Have children add pages to the book by drawing pictures of an activity that can be done in the fall. Help them write a sentence caption for their drawings.

ELL ENGLISH LANGUAGE LEARNERS

Access to Core Content

Content Objective Develop listening comprehension
Language Objective Discuss text using key words and sentence frames
Materials • **ELL Resource Book**, pp. 194–195

PRETEACH BIG BOOK OF EXPLORATIONS

All Language Levels

Use the Interactive Question-Response Guide on **ELL Resource Book** pages 194–195 to preview the **Big Book of Explorations** selection "A Year with Bears." Preteach half of the selection on Day 3 and half on Day 4.

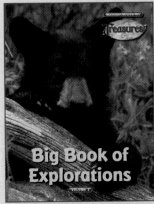

Big Book of Explorations

Grammar

Content Objective Identify describing words
Language Objective Speak in complete sentences, using sentence frames
Materials • **Listening Library Audio CD** • **Photo Cards**

DESCRIBING WORDS (ADJECTIVES)

All Language Levels

■ Review describing words (adjectives). Tell children that describing words tell about naming words. Say: *White snow falls from the sky. What kind of snow does the sentence tells about?* (white) Then ask for other describing words about snow.

One Misty, Moisty Morning

One misty, moisty morning,
When cloudy was the weather,
I met a little old man,
Who had clothes of leather.

He began to compliment,
And I began to grin,
How do you do, and how do you do,
And how do you do again?

■ Play the first stanza of "One Misty, Moisty Morning" from the **Audio CD**. Tell children to listen for describing words.

■ Point out the describing words *misty* and *moisty*. Explain that *misty* and *moisty* are other ways to describe something wet. Ask children what these words describe. (morning) Display the **Photo Cards** for *ant, fire,* and *wheel*. Point to each and name a word to describe the picture, for example: *tiny ant*. Have children repeat the phrase.

PEER DISCUSSION STARTERS

All Language Levels

■ Distribute yard-related Photo Cards such as *leaf* and *rake*.

■ Pair children and have them complete the sentence frame *I see the _____.* Ask them to expand on their sentences by providing as many details as they can. For example: *I see the _____ _____.* Circulate, listen in, and provide feedback.

Puppet

Approaching Level

Phonemic Awareness

Objective	Blend sounds to form words
Materials	• **Puppet** • **Photo Cards:** *bat, lamp, doll, lock, nail, ladder, lemon, girl, circle, shell, wheel, whale* • pocket chart

 PHONEME BLENDING

Tier 2

Model

■ Display the **Photo Cards** in the pocket chart and hold up the **Puppet**. *Happy is going to say the sounds in a word: /l/ /a/ /m/ /p/. Happy can blend these sounds together: /lllaaammmp/, lamp.* Say *lamp* as you point to the *lamp* Photo Card. *Now listen again, I'll do another word.* Repeat the blending with the word *bat*: */b/ /a/ /t/, /baaat/, bat.* Say *bat* as you point to the *bat* Photo Card.

Guided Practice/Practice

■ Say: *Happy will say some sounds: /l/ /o/ /k/.* Ask children to repeat. *Now you blend the sounds and say the word with Happy: /llloook/,* lock. Guide children to blend the sounds together to make *lock* and then point to the correct picture. Follow the same procedure for *nail, ladder, lemon, girl, doll, circle, shell, wheel,* and *whale*.

Phonics

Objective	Blend with /b/b, /d/d, /e/e, /l/l, /t/t
Materials	• **Word-Building Cards** • pocket chart

 REVIEW SKILLS

Tier 2

Model

■ Display **Word-Building Cards** *l, e,* and *t* in the pocket chart. Point to the letter *l. The name of this letter is* l. *The letter* l *stands for the /l/ sound.* Repeat with the letters *e* and *t*.

■ Walk by the word and say the sound each letter stands for: */l/ /e/ /t/. Now I blend the three sounds together: /llleeet/,* let.

Guided Practice/Practice

■ Keep the Word-Building Cards in the pocket chart. Have children take turns walking by the cards, saying the letter sounds, and blending the word: */l/ /e/ /t/, /llleeet/, let.* Repeat with *bat, bet, bed, led, lid, did, rid, rip, lip,* and *lap*.

Corrective Feedback

Mnemonic Display the *Lemon* **Sound-Spelling Card**. Say: *This is the* Lemon *Sound-Spelling Card. The sound is /l/. The /l/ sound is spelled with the letter* l. *Say /l/ with me: /lll/. This is the sound at the beginning of* lemon. *What is the letter? What is the sound? What word begins with /l/?* Lemon *is the word we can use to remember the sound for* l, */l/.*

ELL

Extra Practice Provide additional practice in recognizing and naming letters for children whose native languages do not use the symbols of the Latin alphabet.

Approaching Level

Leveled Reader Lesson 1

Objective   Read *What Can Len Do?* to apply skills and strategies
Materials   • **Leveled Reader:** *What Can Len Do?*

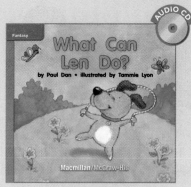

Leveled Reader

BEFORE READING

- **Preview and Predict** Read the title and the name of the author. Turn to the title page and again point out the title and author's name. *What do you think will happen in this story?*

- **Model Concepts About Print** Display pages 2–3. *This is the top of the page. I start reading at the top and read from left to right.* Guide children to follow in their books.

- **Review High-Frequency Words** Write and read the words **I**, **like**, **to**, **and**, **what**, **do**, **you**. Guide children to name the letters in each word and then find the words in the book. Have children point out the difference between a letter and a word.

- **Page Through the Book** Name unfamiliar terms and identify rebuses and the pictures.

- **Set a Purpose for Reading** *Let's find out what Len can do in each season of the year.*

DURING READING

- Remind children to use the rebuses and illustrations to gain information and to look for the high-frequency words they know.

- Show children how to monitor comprehension and self-correct if a word doesn't sound right or doesn't make sense. *On page 2, I look at the rebus and think, "Ben can float and play." Then I see that the word starts with an* s. Float *doesn't start with an* s, *but* swim *does. I think the word is* swim. *"Ben can swim and play." That makes sense.*

- Monitor children's reading and provide help as needed.

AFTER READING

- Ask children to point out words that they had trouble reading and share strategies they used. Reinforce good behaviors: *Jack, I noticed that you tracked the words with your finger as you read each sentence.*

- Ask children to retell the story and share personal responses. *What does Len do? Does Len do things you like to do? What does Ben do? What else do you like to do?*

Digital Learning

Use the **Leveled Reader Audio CD** for fluency building *after* children read the book with your support during Small Group time.

ON YOUR OWN

You and Len

Have children draw a picture showing their favorite part of the story. Ask them to include themselves and Len in the picture. Have children write a sentence telling about their favorite part.

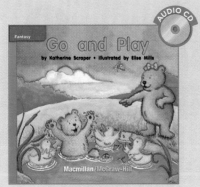

Leveled Reader

ELL

Retell Use the Interactive Question-Response Guide Technique to help English Language Learners understand *Go and Play*. As you read, make meaning clear by pointing to pictures, demonstrating word meaning, paraphrasing text, and asking children questions.

ON YOUR OWN

Predict What Cub Will Do

Have children write and illustrate what they think Cub will do when he wakes up after his winter sleep.

Cub plays.

On Level

Leveled Reader Lesson 1

Leveled Reader Library

Objective Read *Go and Play* to apply skills and strategies
Materials • **Leveled Reader:** *Go and Play*

BEFORE READING

- **Preview and Predict** Read the title and the name of the author. *Who is on the cover? What are they doing? What do you think this book might be about?* Open and page through the book. Read *Cub* and point to him. Ask: *What is a* cub?

- **Model Concepts About Print** *Words can be spoken, and they can be written down. Listen as I read the title again. The words I say match what is written on the cover of the book. The first word I said was* Go. *Point to the word* Go *in the title.*

- **Review High-Frequency Words** Write **see**, **what**, **and**, **do**, **go**, **to**, **play**. Have children find each word in the book and point to the word as they read it.

- **Set a Purpose for Reading** *Let's find out what animals do in each season.*

DURING READING

- Have children turn to page 2 and begin by whisper-reading the first two pages.

- Remind children to look for the new high-frequency words and to use the illustrations.

- Monitor children's reading. Stop during the reading and ask open-ended questions to facilitate discussion, such as: *What is the author telling us about the seasons? What does the author tell us about how different animals act in each season?* Build on children's responses to develop deeper understanding of the text.

AFTER READING

- Ask children to point out words they had trouble reading and to share strategies they used. Reinforce good behaviors: *Jesse, I noticed you looked at the picture after you read the sentence.*

- **Retell** Have children retell the story. Help them make a personal connection. *What season do you think Cub likes most? Why? What is your favorite season? Why?*

- Have partners take turns asking and answering questions about the text.

Beyond Level

Leveled Reader Lesson 1

Objective Read *How the Bear Lost His Tail* to apply skills and strategies
Materials • **Leveled Reader:** *How the Bear Lost His Tail*

BEFORE READING

- **Preview and Predict** Read the title and the name of the author. *Who do you see on the cover? What is he doing? What do you think is going to happen in this story?* Turn to the title page and point out that it also has the title and the name of the author. Page through the book with children and pause to name unfamiliar items.

- **Introduce Story Words** Point to the word *stuck* on page 12. Read the sentence and ask children to explain what *stuck* means.

- **Set a Purpose for Reading** Discuss the purpose for reading different kinds of text. *Let's find out how a bear loses his tail.*

DURING READING

- Ask children to use self-monitoring comprehension strategies to understand text read orally: assess and revise predictions, use picture clues, self-question, and clarify meaning or self-correct meaning. Have them use picture dictionaries to determine the meanings of unknown words.

- Monitor children's reading and provide help as needed.

AFTER READING

- Ask children to point out words they had trouble reading and to share the strategies they used.

- Have children retell the story and share personal responses. *What other stories about bears have you read or heard?*

- Have partners take turns asking and answering questions about the text.

- **Evaluate** *How would you feel if someone tricked you when you asked for help? How might Fox have helped bear?*

- Provide another version of this folktale, and have partners read it aloud together. Then have them compare and contrast the two versions, filling in a preprinted Venn diagram.

- **Model** Explain to children that they will use their completed Venn diagrams to write a review. They will compare and contrast the two versions of the folktale. Reviews should answer these questions: *Which version do you prefer? Why?*

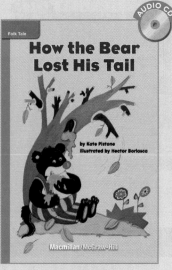

Leveled Reader

Predict What Bear Will Do

Have children look at the last page in the book. Tell them to write and illustrate what they think Bear might say or do when he sees Fox again.

Leveled Reader

Vocabulary

Preteach Vocabulary Use the routine in the **Visual Vocabulary Resources**, pages 339–340, to preteach the ELL Vocabulary listed on the inside front cover of the Leveled Reader.

ELL ENGLISH LANGUAGE LEARNERS

Leveled Reader

Content Objective Read to apply skills and strategies
Language Objective Retell information using complete sentences
Materials • **Leveled Reader:** *You Can Play*

BEFORE READING

All Language Levels

- **Preview** Read the title *You Can Play*. Ask: *What's the title? Say it again.* Repeat with the author's name. Point to the cover illustration and say: *I see a cub.* Point to the cub. *The cub is a baby bear. This cub is in the water. Now turn to a partner and tell more about what you see in this picture.*

- **Page Through the Book** Use simple language to tell about the illustration on each page. Immediately follow up with questions, such as: *What will the cub do? Can you do it, too?*

- **Review Skills** Use the inside front cover to review the phonics skill and high-frequency words.

- **Set a Purpose** Say: *Let's read to find out about what the cub will play.*

DURING READING

All Language Levels

- Have children whisper-read each page, or use the differentiated suggestions below. Circulate, listen in, and provide corrective feedback, such as modeling how to describe the setting.

- **Retell** Stop after every two pages and ask children to state what they have learned so far. Reinforce language by restating children's comments when they have difficulty using story-specific words. Provide differentiated sentence frames to support children's responses and engage children in partner-talk.

Beginning	Intermediate	Advanced
Echo-Read Have children echo-read after you.	**Choral-Read** Have children choral-read with you.	**Choral-Read** Have children choral-read.
Check Comprehension Point to pictures and ask questions such as: *Does the cub play with ducks? Is this a duck or a rabbit?*	**Check Comprehension** Ask questions/prompts such as: *What is the cub doing? Who is he playing with? What do bears do?*	**Check Comprehension** Ask: *Which is your favorite thing to do in this book? What do you like to play?*

ELL ENGLISH LANGUAGE LEARNERS

AFTER READING

All Language Levels

Book Talk Children will work with peers of varying language abilities to discuss their books for this week. Display the four **Leveled Readers** read this week: *How the Bear Lost His Tail* (Beyond Level), *Go and Play* (On Level), *What Can Len Do?* (Approaching Level), and *You Can Play* (English Language Learners).

Ask the questions and provide the prompts below. Call on children who read each book to answer the questions or respond to the prompt. If appropriate, ask children to find the pages in the book that illustrate their answers.

- **How did the animals in your story have fun?**
- **Can you do the things the animals can do?**
- **Tell about the weather in your book.**
- **What new things did you read about?**
- **What is your favorite picture in the book? Tell about it.**

Develop Listening and Speaking Skills Tell children to remember the following:

- Share information in cooperative learning interactions. Remind children to work with their partners to retell the story and complete any activities. Ask: *What happened next in the story?*

- Employ self-corrective techniques and monitor their own and other children's language production. Children should ask themselves: *What parts of this passage were confusing to me? Can my classmates help me clarify a word or sentence that I don't understand?*

- Use high-frequency English words to describe people, places, and objects.

- Narrate, describe, and explain with specificity and detail. Ask: *Where did the story take place? Can you describe the setting? What else did you notice?*

- Express opinions, ideas, and feelings on a variety of social and academic topics. Ask: *What do you think about the characters in the story?*

Approaching Level

Phonemic Awareness

Objective Segment words into sounds
Materials • **WorkBoard Sound Boxes; Teacher's Resource Book**, p. 136
• markers • **Sound Box**

PHONEME SEGMENTATION

Tier 2

Model
- Use the **Sound Box**. Say: *Listen for the sounds in the word* lock. Lock *has three sounds: /l/ /o/ /k/*. Name each sound as you place a marker in a box. Repeat with *let*.

Guided Practice/Practice
- Distribute Sound Boxes and markers. *I will say a word. Say each sound in the word as you place a marker in a box. Then tell me the sounds.* Say these words and have children say each sound as they place a marker in a box.

bed, /b/ /e/ /d/	bit, /b/ /i/ /t/	lot, /l/ /o/ /t/
bell, /b/ /e/ /l/	tab, /t/ /a/ /b/	lap, /l/ /a/ /p/
led, /l/ /e/ /d/	lip, /l/ /i/ /p/	bat, /b/ /a/ /t/

Phonics

bjective Reinforce initial sounds /b/b, /e/e, /l/l and build fluency
Materials • **Photo Cards:** *bat, balloon, banana, bike, book, bus, egg, elbow, elevator, envelope, exit, ladder, ladybug, lamp, lemon, lock* • pocket chart
• **Word-Building Cards** • **Sound-Spelling WorkBoards**

BUILD FLUENCY: LETTER-SOUND CORRESPONDENCE

Tier 2

Model
- Place **Word-Building Cards** *b, e,* and *l* in the top row of the pocket chart. Then stack the **Photo Cards** facedown. Choose a card. Say the name of the picture, identify the initial sound, and place the card in the pocket chart under the letter that stands for the sound.

Guided Practice/Practice
- Have each child choose a Photo Card, say the name of the picture, identify its initial sound, and place the card under the letter that stands for the sound. Guide practice as needed.

Build Fluency
- Display Word-Building Cards *b, e, l*. Have children say each letter name as quickly as they can. Ask them to write the letters on their **WorkBoards** several times as they say the sounds.

ELL

Sound-Letter Relationships Provide additional practice in pronouncing the /b/, /e/, /l/ sounds and naming the corresponding letters as children point to them.

Approaching Level

Leveled Reader Library

Leveled Reader Lesson 2

Objective Reread *What Can Len Do?* to reinforce fluency, identify setting

Materials • **Leveled Reader:** *What Can Len Do?*

FOCUS ON FLUENCY

- Tell children that you will read one page of the book and they should read that page right after you. They should follow along in their books and try to read at the same speed and with the same expression that you use.

SKILL IDENTIFY SETTING

- *Look at pictures in this book. In which season do Ben and Len sled and skate? In which do they rake? When do they swim? Where do they swim?*

REREAD PREVIOUSLY READ BOOKS

- Distribute copies of the past six **Leveled Readers**. Tell children that rereading the different books will help them develop their skills and enjoy language. Ask children to think about how the settings are different in the various texts.

- Circulate and listen in as children read. Stop them periodically and ask them how they are figuring out words or checking their understanding. Tell children to read other previously read Leveled Readers during independent reading time.

High-Frequency Words

Objective Review high-frequency words *what, do, and, this, are, play* and build fluency

Materials • **High-Frequency Word Cards:** *what, do, and, this, are, play*

BUILD WORD AUTOMATICITY: *what, do, and, this, are, play*

- Distribute copies of the **High-Frequency Word Card** for **what**. Say the word and have children repeat it. Have children name the letters in the word. Repeat with the words **do**, **and**, **this**, **are**, and **play**.

- **Build Fluency** Use the High-Frequency Word Cards to review previously taught words. Repeat, guiding children to read more rapidly.

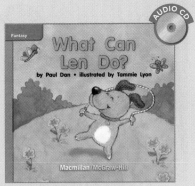

Leveled Reader

Meet Grade-Level Expectations

As an alternative to this day's lesson, guide children through a reading of the On Level Leveled Reader. See page 1710. Since both books contain the same vocabulary, phonics, and comprehension skills, the scaffolding you provided will help most children gain access to this more challenging text.

ON YOUR OWN

Draw Illustrations

Have children draw pictures that show children doing things in the winter, spring, summer, or fall. Children display their pictures, and others figure out the season.

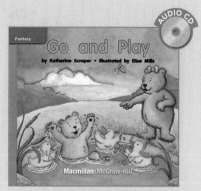

Leveled Reader

Write Captions

Have children draw pictures to show what one animal does in one of the seasons. Help children write captions for their pictures.

On Level

Leveled Reader Lesson 2

Objective   Reread to apply skills and strategies to retell a story
Materials   • **Leveled Reader:** *Go and Play*

BEFORE READING

■ Ask children to look through *Go and Play* and recall what the book is about. Reinforce vocabulary by repeating children's sentences using more sophisticated language. For example: *I wonder in which month the bears go to sleep. This book shows all four seasons.*

■ Discuss the purposes for reading various texts. Have children compare the seasonal settings in this book with the settings in *In the Yard*.

DURING READING

■ Have children join you in a choral reading of the story. Model reading with expression. *When I read page 2, I emphasized* You can too! *by saying it a little stronger. I used the same strong emphasis on every other page when it repeated the sentence* You can too! *I wanted to emphasize what the character thinks Cub can do.* Ask children to use the same kind of expression when they read.

■ Assign each child a page. Have children practice by whisper-reading. *Follow along as other children read, and be ready to come in when it is your turn. Remember, use lots of expression.*

AFTER READING

■ Have children retell the selection in their own words.

■ *Look at the pictures. Where does Cub see birds? What season of the year is it?* Lead children into discussing the setting of the book.

■ Have children make connections to their own experiences. *What are some things that you do only in winter?* Repeat with spring, summer, and fall.

Beyond Level

Leveled Reader Lesson 2

Objective   Reread to apply skills and strategies to retell a story
Materials   • **Leveled Reader:** *How the Bear Lost His Tail*

BEFORE READING

- Ask children to look back at *How the Bear Lost His Tail* and recall what the book is about. *Where does the story take place? What season did this story take place in? How do you know?*

- Discuss the purposes for reading various texts.

DURING READING

- Assign each child a page of the book to read aloud. Have children practice by whisper-reading. *Follow along as each child reads, and be ready to come in when it is your turn.*

AFTER READING

- Explain that if we picture in our minds what happens in a story, it helps us understand the story characters. Model the strategy: *When I read about Bear's tail stuck in the ice, I picture Bear trying to stand up and tugging on his tail.* Have children tell how they visualize Bear as they read. If they have difficulty, suggest they look at the pictures, reread, and/or ask for help.

Expand Vocabulary

Objective   Learn and apply the multiple meanings of the words *spring* and *fall*
Materials   • **Leveled Reader:** *How the Bear Lost His Tail*

ENRICH: *spring, fall*

Gifted Talented

- Have children reread page 2. Ask them to point to *spring* and tell what it means in the sentence. Have children use *spring* in sentences to describe springtime.

- Then explain that *spring* has other meanings, too. Say: *My cat can* spring *up onto the bed.* Ask what *spring* means in that sentence. (jump) Have children demonstrate the meaning. Ask what other meanings for *spring* children know. (a stream, a curly device that goes up and down)

- Repeat with *fall* (page 4).

- Use *spring* and *fall* to begin a chart of multiple-meaning words. Have children find other words in the book that have more than one meaning to add to the chart and use in sentences. (*bear, honey, den, hard, stand*)

Leveled Reader

ON YOUR OWN

Write a Play

Ask partners what Bear and Fox might say to each other after Fox tricks Bear. Have one child in each pair write what Bear might say and the other write what Fox might say. Have partners act out their plays.

ELL

Partners When children write about another animal living in the park, pair English Language Learners with children who are more proficient.

ELL ENGLISH LANGUAGE LEARNERS

Fluency

Content Objectives Reread the Decodable Reader to develop fluency; develop speaking skills

Language Objective Tell a partner what a selection is about

Materials • **Decodable Reader:** *Hot Ben, Hot Lin*

REREAD FOR FLUENCY

Beginning

■ Review the high-frequency words **and**, **what**, **for**, **you**, **this**, and **do** using the **Read/Spell/Write** routine.

Intermediate/Advanced

■ Use each word in a sentence that illustrates its use, such as: *This book is for you and me.* Act out sharing a book with a child. *What is your name?* Have a child tell his or her name.

■ Then provide sentence starters for children to complete. Where appropriate, act out children's responses, for example: *This pen is for writing.*

All Language Levels

■ Guide children through a choral reading of *Hot Ben, Hot Lin*. Model reading sentences with words you want to emphasize with expression, such as reading the repeated words *hot, ran,* and *hop* stronger. Model reading several sentences using appropriate expression and have children chorally repeat.

DEVELOP SPEAKING/LISTENING SKILLS

All Language Levels

■ Have children reread *Hot Ben, Hot Lin* to a partner. Remind them to listen carefully and follow along in their book as their partner is reading. Work with children to read with accuracy and appropriate expression.

■ Ask children to tell their partner about the pictures on each page. Then have the other partner describe the pictures. Circulate, listen in, and provide additional language as needed.

Beginning	Intermediate	Advanced
Confirm Understanding Point to the pictures for partners to identify. Ask: What do you see? Restate the correct answer in a complete sentence.	**Express Opinions** Ask partners to tell you which is their favorite picture in the book. Prompt them to explain why it is their favorite picture.	**Compare and Contrast** Have partners compare two different pictures and describe them. Prompt them to explain how they are alike and different.

ELL ENGLISH LANGUAGE LEARNERS

High-Frequency Words

Content Objective Spell high-frequency words correctly
Language Objective Write in complete sentences, using sentence frames
Materials • Sound-Spelling WorkBoards • Sound-Spelling Cards • Photo Cards

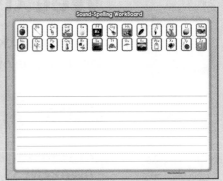

Sound-Spelling WorkBoard

Beginning/Intermediate

- Write the high-frequency words **and** and **what** on the board. Have children copy the words on their **WorkBoards**. Then help them say each word and write a sentence for it. Provide the sentence starters *I can run and _____. What do you _____?*

Advanced

- Children should first orally state each sentence. Correct as needed. Then they can draw a picture to complete the sentence. For children who are ready, help them spell words using their growing knowledge of English sound-spelling relationships. Model how to segment the word children are trying to spell and attach a spelling to each sound. Use the **Sound-Spelling Cards** to reinforce the spellings for each English sound.

Writing

All Language Levels

- Tell children that at night they sleep in a bed. Dictate the word *bed* and ask children to write it. Have them write the word five times as they say *bed*. Demonstrate correct letter formation, as needed. Repeat with the word *let*. Use the word in a sentence and explain the meaning as needed.

- Then display a set of **Photo Cards**. Select at least five cards whose picture names begin with /b/ (*bed, balloon, banana, bike, book*) and five whose picture names begin with /l/ (*lamp, ladder, lock, leaf, light*).

- Say the name of each card, stretching or reiterating the initial sound to emphasize it. You may also need to reinforce the meaning of the word and model correct mouth formation when forming the sound. Use the articulation pictures and prompts on the back of the small Sound-Spelling Cards for support. Tell children to write the first letter of each picture name on their WorkBoards.

Phonemic Awareness/ Phonics

For English Language Learners who need more practice with this week's phonemic awareness and phonics skills, see the Approaching Level lessons. Focus on minimal contrasts, articulation, and those sounds that do not transfer from the child's first language to English. For a complete listing of transfer sounds, see pages T10–T31.

Weekly Assessment

Use your Quick Check observations and the assessment opportunities identified below to evaluate children's progress in key skill areas.

Skills	Quick Check Observations	Pencil and Paper Assessment
✔ **PHONEMIC AWARENESS/ PHONICS** /b/b, /l/l **b l**	1653, 1675	Activity Book, pp. 14, 19–20, 22 Practice Book, pp. 147, 151–152
✔ **HIGH-FREQUENCY WORDS** *and, what* **and**	1674	Activity Book, pp. 17–18 Practice Book, pp. 149–150
✔ **COMPREHENSION** Identify Setting	1664	Activity Book, pp. 15–16, 21 Practice Book, p. 148

Quick Check Rubric

Skills	1	2	3
✔ **PHONEMIC AWARENESS/ PHONICS**	Does not connect the sounds /b/, /l/ with the letters *Bb, Ll* and has difficulty blending the CVC words *Bob, bib, tab, bed, Ben, bit, bet, lap, let, lit, lot, lip, led, lid.*	Usually connects the sounds /b/, /l/ with the letters *Bb, Ll* and blends the CVC words *Bob, bib, tab, bed, Ben, bit, bet, lap, let, lit, lot, lip, led, lid* with only occasional support.	Consistently connects the sounds /b/, /l/ with the letters *Bb, Ll* and blends the CVC words *Bob, bib, tab, bed, Ben, bit, bet, lap, let, lit, lot, lip, led, lid.*
✔ **HIGH-FREQUENCY WORDS**	Does not identify the high-frequency words.	Usually recognizes the high-frequency words with accuracy, but not speed.	Consistently recognizes the high-frequency words with speed and accuracy.
✔ **COMPREHENSION**	Does not identify the setting using the pictures and text.	Usually identifies the setting using the pictures and text.	Consistently identifies the setting using the pictures and text.

DIBELS LINK

PROGRESS MONITORING

Use your DIBELS results to inform instruction.

IF...
Initial Sound Fluency (**ISF**)   0–34

THEN...
Evaluate for Intervention

TPRI LINK

PROGRESS MONITORING

Use your TPRI scores to inform instruction.

IF...
Phonemic Awareness   Still Developing
Graphophonemic Knowledge   Still Developing
Listening Comprehension   Still Developing

THEN...
Evaluate for Intervention

Diagnose		Prescribe
Review the assessment answers with children. Have them correct their errors. Then provide additional instruction as needed.		
PHONEMIC AWARENESS/ PHONICS /b/b, /l/l	**IF...** **Quick Check Rubric:** Children consistently score 1 or **Pencil and Paper Assessment:** Children get 0–2 items correct	**THEN...** Reteach Phonemic Awareness and Phonics Skills using the **Phonemic Awareness** and **Phonics Intervention Teacher' Editions.** SPIRAL REVIEW Use the Build Fluency lesson in upcoming weeks to provide children practice reading words with /b/b and /l/l.
HIGH-FREQUENCY WORDS *and, what*	**Quick Check Rubric:** Children consistently score 1 or **Pencil and Paper Assessment:** Children get 0–2 items correct	Reteach High-Frequency Words using the **Phonics Intervention Teacher's Edition.** SPIRAL REVIEW Use the High-Frequency Words lesson in upcoming weeks to provide children practice reading the word *and* and *what*.
COMPREHENSION Skill: Identify Setting	**Quick Check Rubric:** Children consistently score 1 or **Pencil and Paper Assessment:** Children get 0–2 items correct	Reteach Comprehension Skill using the **Comprehension Intervention Teacher's Edition.**

Response to Intervention

To place children in **Tier 2** or **Tier 3** Intervention use the *Diagnostic Assessment.*

- Phonemic Awareness
- Phonics
- Vocabulary
- Comprehension
- Fluency

Week 3 ★ At a Glance

Priority Skills and Concepts

 Comprehension
- **Genre:** Fantasy, Folktale, Expository
- **Strategy:** Visualize
- **Skill:** Distinguish Between Fantasy and Reality

 Skill: Identify Setting

 High-Frequency Words
- *this*, *do*, *and*, *what*

Oral Vocabulary
- Build Robust Vocabulary: *clear*, *cozy*, *experience*, *hibernate*, *retreat*

Fluency
- Echo-Read
- Word Automaticity

 Phonemic Awareness
- **Phoneme Isolation**
- **Phoneme Blending**
- **Phoneme Segmentation**

 Phonics
- *Bb, Ee, Ll*

Grammar
- Describing Words (Adjectives)

Writing
- Sentences

Key  Tested in Program  Review Skill

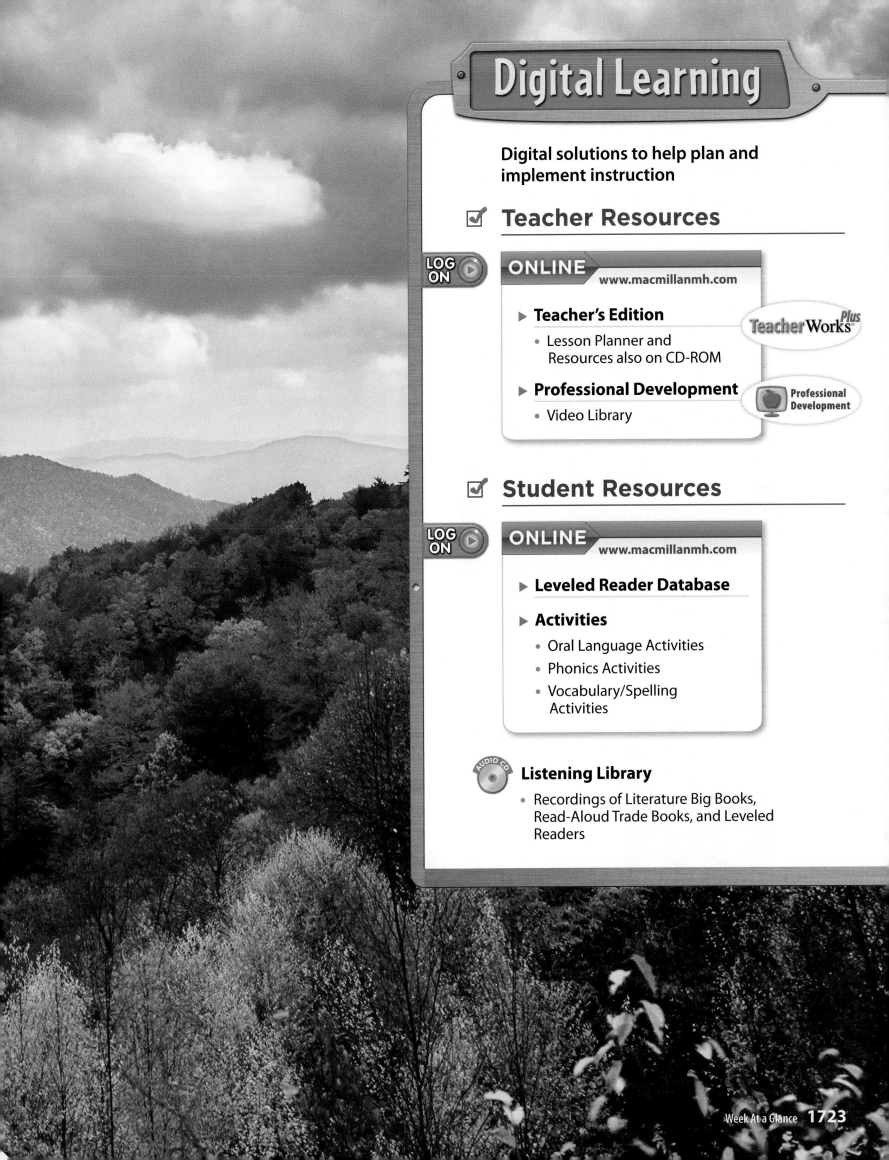

Digital Learning

Digital solutions to help plan and implement instruction

☑ Teacher Resources

LOG ON ▶

ONLINE www.macmillanmh.com

▶ **Teacher's Edition**
- Lesson Planner and Resources also on CD-ROM

TeacherWorks Plus

▶ **Professional Development**
- Video Library

Professional Development

☑ Student Resources

LOG ON ▶

ONLINE www.macmillanmh.com

▶ **Leveled Reader Database**

▶ **Activities**
- Oral Language Activities
- Phonics Activities
- Vocabulary/Spelling Activities

AUDIO CD **Listening Library**
- Recordings of Literature Big Books, Read-Aloud Trade Books, and Leveled Readers

Theme: How Weather Affects Us

Student Literature

A mix of fiction and nonfiction

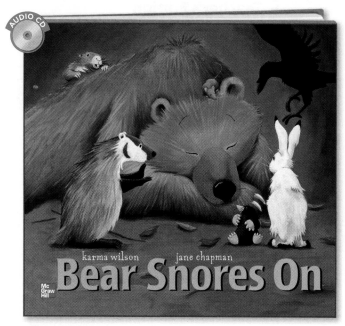

Trade Book

Genre	Fantasy

Big Book of Explorations

Genre	Expository

Support Literature

Interactive Read-Aloud Anthology

Genre	Folktale

Oral Vocabulary Cards

- Listening Comprehension
- Build Robust Vocabulary

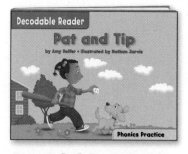

Decodable Reader

Resources for Differentiated Instruction

Leveled Readers

GR Levels A–G

Genre	Fiction

- Same Theme
- Same Vocabulary/Phonics
- Same Comprehension Skills

A

What Can We Do?

Approaching Level

C

In the Snow
by Michael Price • Illustrated by Steve Haskamp

On Level

G

The Woodpecker
by Pam Frame
Illustrated by Jared Lee

Beyond Level

B

Snow
by Michael Price • Illustrated by Steve Haskamp

ELL

LOG ON ▶ **Leveled Reader Database**
Go to www.macmillanmh.com.

Practice

Unit 7 · WEATHER

Treasures

KINDERGARTEN · ACTIVITY BOOK

Activity Book

Treasures

Practice Book
- Phonemic Awareness
- Phonics
- High-Frequency Words
- Comprehension

Macmillan/McGraw-Hill

Practice Book

Treasures

English
Language
Learner
Practice Book

Macmillan/McGraw-Hill

ELL Practice Book

Response to Intervention

Tier 2

- Phonemic Awareness
- Phonics
- Vocabulary
- Comprehension
- Fluency

Tier 3

Unit Assessment

Treasures

Unit and Benchmark Assessment

Macmillan/McGraw-Hill

Assess Unit Skills
- Phonemic Awareness
- Phonics
- High-Frequency Words
- Listening Comprehension

HOME-SCHOOL CONNECTION

Treasures

Home-School Connection
- Parent Letters in 6 languages
- Homework Activities
- Take-Home Stories

Macmillan/McGraw-Hill

- Family letters in English and Spanish
- Take-home stories and activities

Suggested Lesson Plan

Go to **www.macmillanmh.com** for Online Lesson Planner

 **TeacherWorks** *Plus*
All-In-One Planner and Resource Center

🍎 **Professional Development**
Video Library

Trade Book

Bear Snores On

WHOLE GROUP

⏱ ORAL LANGUAGE

- Oral Vocabulary

- Phonemic Awareness

⏱ WORD STUDY

- Phonics

- High-Frequency Words

⏱ READING

- Listening Comprehension

- Apply Phonics and High-Frequency Words

- Fluency

⏱ LANGUAGE ARTS

- Writing

- Grammar

ASSESSMENT

- Informal/Formal

DAY 1

❓ Focus Question What do you like to do at this time of the year?
Build Background, 1734
Oral Vocabulary *clear, cozy, experience, hibernate, retreat*, 1734

✔ **Phonemic Awareness**
Phoneme Isolation, 1737

✔ **Phonics**
Review /l/l, /b/b, /e/e, 1738
Handwriting: Review *Ll, Bb,* and *Ee*, 1739
Activity Book, 24
Practice Book, 153
✔ **High-Frequency Words**
this , do , and , what , 1736

Share the Trade Book
Bear Snores On
Strategy: Visualize, 1735
✔ **Skill:** Distinguish Between Fantasy and Reality, 1735

Trade Book

Shared Writing
A Chart, 1741
Grammar
Describing Words (Adjectives), 1740

Quick Check Phonemic Awareness, 1737

DAY 2

❓ Focus Question What do bears and some other animals do when it is cold?

Oral Vocabulary *clear, cozy, experience, hibernate, retreat*, 1742

Review Sound Words, 1749
✔ **Phonemic Awareness**
Phoneme Blending, 1750

✔ **Phonics**
Review /b/b, /l/l, /e/e, /d/d, 1750
Blend with *-in*, 1751

✔ **Review High-Frequency Words**, 1752

Reread the Trade Book
Bear Snores On
Strategy: Visualize, 1744
✔ **Skill:** Distinguish Between Fantasy and Reality, 1744
Retell, 1748
Decodable Reader:
Pat and Tip, 1752
Activity Book, 25; Practice Book, 154
Fluency Echo-Read, 1748

Trade Book

Interactive Writing
Sentences, 1753

Quick Check Comprehension, 1748

⏱ **SMALL GROUP Lesson Plan** ▷ **Differentiated Instruction 1728–1729**

Priority Skills

Phonemic Awareness/Phonics	High-Frequency Words	Oral Vocabulary	Comprehension
Review /b/b, /l/l, /e/e; -it, -ip, -id	*this, do, and, what*	Words That Compare	Strategy: Visualize Skill: Distinguish Between Fantasy and Reality

Half-Day Kindergarten

Teach Core Skills
Focus on tested skill lessons, other lessons, and small group options as your time allows.

DAY 3

❓ Focus Question What do you like best about cold weather?

Oral Vocabulary *clear, cozy, experience, hibernate, retreat,* 1754

Oral Vocabulary Cards: "Animals in Winter"

✔ **Phonemic Awareness**
Phoneme Segmentation, 1759

✔ **Phonics**
Review /b/b, /l/l, /e/e, 1760

Blend with -ip, 1761

✔ **High-Frequency Words**
this, do, and, what, 1758

Activity Book: "This Is What I Can Do!" 27–28

Practice Book, 155–156

Read for Fluency, 1758

Read the Big Book of Explorations:
"Let It Snow," 21–24

Text Feature: Photographs, 1756

Big Book of Explorations

Independent Writing
Prewrite and Draft Sentences, 1763

Grammar
Describing Words (Adjectives), 1762

> **Quick Check** High-Frequency Words, 1758

DAY 4

❓ Focus Question Today it is ____ and ____. What do you wear in this kind of weather?

Oral Vocabulary *clear, cozy, experience, hibernate, retreat,* 1764

Words That Compare, 1767

✔ **Phonemic Awareness**
Phoneme Blending, 1768

✔ **Phonics**
Picture Sort, 1768

Blend with -id, 1769

Activity Book, 29

Practice Book, 157–158

✔ **Review High-Frequency Words**, 1770

Interactive Read Aloud
Listening Comprehension, 1766

Read Aloud: "The Mitten"

Decodable Reader:
Pat and Tip, 1770

Read Aloud

Independent Writing
Revise and Edit Sentences, 1771

> **Quick Check** Phonics, 1769

DAY 5
Review and Assess

❓ Focus Question What do you think is the best thing we read this week?

Oral Vocabulary *clear, cozy, experience, hibernate, retreat,* 1772

Sound Words, 1774

✔ **Phonemic Awareness**
Phoneme Segmentation, 1775

✔ **Phonics**
Read Words, 1776

Dictation, 1776

Activity Book, 32

✔ **High-Frequency Words**
this, do, and, what, for, you, 1774

Read Across Texts
Strategy: Visualize, 1773

✔ Skill: Distinguish Between Fantasy and Reality, 1773

Activity Book, 31

Fluency Word Automaticity, 1774

Independent Writing
Publish and Present Sentences, 1777

✔ **Weekly Assessment, 1804–1805**

Differentiated Instruction

What do I do in small groups?

Teacher-Led Small Groups

Independent Activities

IF... children need additional instruction, practice, or extension based on your **Quick Check** observations for the following priority skills

✔ **Phonemic Awareness**
Phoneme Isolation, Blending, Segmentation

✔ **Phonics**
Bb, Ee, Ll

✔ **High-Frequency Words**
this, *do*, *and*, *what*

✔ **Comprehension**
Strategy: Visualize
Skill: Distinguish Between Fantasy and Reality

THEN... | **Approaching** | Preteach and
| **ELL** | Reteach Skills
| **On Level** | Practice
| **Beyond** | Enrich and Accelerate Learning

 Suggested Small Group Lesson Plan

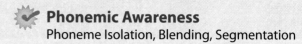

CD-ROM
TeacherWorks *Plus*
All-In-One Planner and Resource Center

	DAY 1	**DAY 2**
Approaching Level		

Tier 2 • **Preteach/Reteach** **Tier 2 Instruction**	• Oral Language, 1778
	• High-Frequency Words, 1778 **ELL**
	  High-Frequency Words Review, 1778
	• Phonemic Awareness, 1779
	• Phonics, 1779 **ELL**
	  Sound-Spellings Review, 1779
		• Oral Language, 1784
		• High-Frequency Words, 1784 **ELL**
		• Phonemic Awareness, 1785
		• Phonics, 1785

On Level		
• **Practice**	• High-Frequency Words, 1780 • Phonemic Awareness/Phonics, 1780 **ELL**	• Phonics, 1786
Beyond Level		
• **Extend/Accelerate** **Gifted and Talented**	• High-Frequency Words/Vocabulary, 1781 **ELL** Expand Oral Vocabulary, 1781 • Phonics, 1781	• Phonics, 1786
ELL		
• **Build English Language Proficiency** • See **ELL** in other levels.	• Oral Language Warm-Up, 1782 • Academic Language, 1782 • Vocabulary, 1783	• Access to Core Content, 1787

Focus on Leveled Readers

Levels A–G

Approaching

On Level

Beyond

ELL

Additional Leveled Readers

 Leveled Reader Database
www.macmillanmh.com

Search by

- Comprehension Skill
- Content Area
- Genre
- Text Feature
- Guided Reading Level
- Reading Recovery Level
- Lexile Score
- Benchmark Level

Subscription also available

Manipulatives

Sound-Spelling WorkBoards

Sound-Spelling Cards

Photo Cards

High-Frequency Word Cards

Visual Vocabulary Resources

DAY 3

- High-Frequency Words, 1788 **ELL**
- Phonemic Awareness, 1788
- Phonics, 1789
- Decodable Reader, 1789

- Decodable Reader, 1790

- Decodable Reader, 1790

- Access to Core Content, 1791
- Grammar, 1791

DAY 4

- Phonemic Awareness, 1792
- Phonics, 1792 **ELL**
- Leveled Reader Lesson 1, 1793

- Leveled Reader Lesson 1, 1794 **ELL**

- Leveled Reader Lesson 1, 1795
- Analyze, 1795

- Leveled Reader, 1796–1797

DAY 5

- Phonemic Awareness, 1798
- Phonics, 1798 **ELL**
- Leveled Reader Lesson 2, 1799
- High-Frequency Words, 1799

- Leveled Reader Lesson 2, 1800

- Leveled Reader Lesson 2, 1801
- Expand Vocabulary, 1801 **ELL**

- Fluency, 1802
- High-Frequency Words, 1803
- Writing, 1803

Managing the Class

What do I do with the rest of my class?

Teacher-Led Small Groups

Independent Activities

- Activity Book
- Practice Book
- ELL Practice Book
- Leveled Reader Activities
- Literacy Workstations
- Online Activities
- Buggles and Beezy

Classroom Management Tools

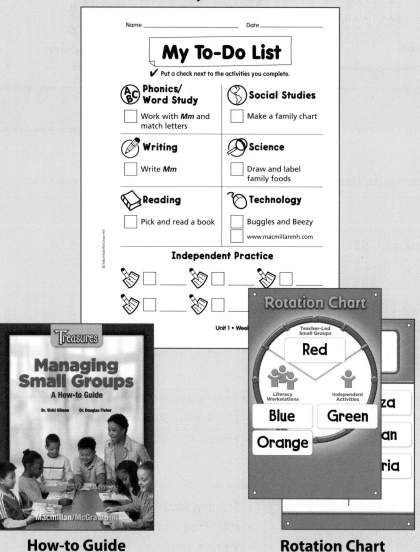

Weekly Contract

Name _____ Date _____

My To-Do List

✔ Put a check next to the activities you complete.

Phonics/Word Study
☐ Work with *Mm* and match letters

Social Studies
☐ Make a family chart

Writing
☐ Write *Mm*

Science
☐ Draw and label family foods

Reading
☐ Pick and read a book

Technology
☐ Buggles and Beezy
☐ www.macmillanmh.com

Independent Practice

Unit 1 • Week

Rotation Chart

Teacher-Led Small Groups

Red

Literacy Workstations

Independent Activities

Blue **Green**

Orange

How-to Guide

Treasures
Managing Small Groups
A How-to Guide
Dr. Vicki Gibson Dr. Douglas Fisher
Macmillan/McGraw-Hill

Rotation Chart

Digital Learning

Phonics Activities

- Match Letters
- Match Letters to Sounds
- Blend Words

Meet the Author/Illustrator

Karma Wilson

- Karma grew up an only child in Idaho.
- Reading was Karma's first love. By the age of 11, she read about one novel a day.
- Karma's books have been translated into dozens of languages.

Other books by Karma Wilson
- Wilson, Karma, and Jane Chapman. *Bear Snores On*. New York: Margaret K. McElderry, 2002.
- Wilson, Karma, and Douglas Cushman. *Never Ever Shout in a Zoo*. New York: Little, Brown Young Readers, 2004.

- Read Other Books by the Author or Illustrator

Practice

Activity Book

Practice Book **ELL Practice Book**

Independent Activities

ONLINE INSTRUCTION www.macmillanmh.com

Oral Language Activities

- Focus on Unit Vocabulary and Concepts
- English Language Learner Support

Vocabulary/Spelling Activities

- Differentiated Lists and Activities

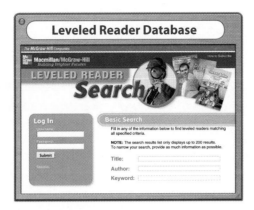

Leveled Reader Database

- Leveled Reader Database
- Search titles by level, skill, content area, and more

Available on CD

LISTENING LIBRARY
Recordings of selections
- Literature Big Books
- Read-Aloud Trade Books
- Leveled Readers
- ELL Readers

NEW ADVENTURES WITH BUGGLES AND BEEZY
Phonemic awareness and phonics activities

Leveled Reader Activities

Approaching

On Level

Beyond

ELL

See inside cover of all Leveled Readers.

Literacy Workstations

Reading

Phonics/Word Study

Writing

Science/Social Studies

See lessons on pages 1732–1733.

Managing the Class

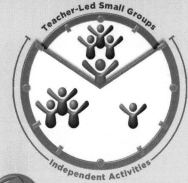

What do I do with the rest of my class?

Reading

Objectives
- Read and discuss a fantasy book with a partner
- Read a book and retell a story

Phonics/Word Study

Objectives
- Use Word-Building Cards to make and change words
- Identify different ways to sort words

Reading — **Buddy Reading** — 20 Minutes

Read a fantasy book with a partner.

❶ Read the book. ❷ Talk about it.

Do More
- What events in the story could not really happen?
- Draw something that happened in the book.

For more book titles, go to the Meet the Author/Illustrator page on www.macmillanmh.com

Mouse cooks food.

41

© Macmillan/McGraw-Hill

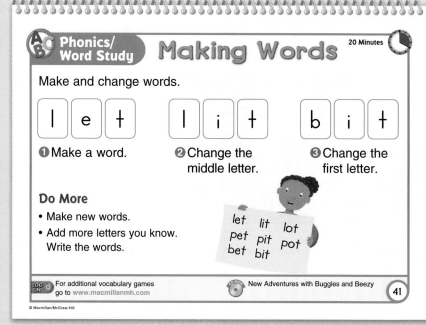

Phonics/Word Study — **Making Words** — 20 Minutes

Make and change words.

| l | e | t | | l | i | t | | b | i | t |

❶ Make a word. ❷ Change the middle letter. ❸ Change the first letter.

Do More
- Make new words.
- Add more letters you know. Write the words.

let lit lot
pet pit pot
bet bit

For additional vocabulary games go to www.macmillanmh.com

New Adventures with Buggles and Beezy

41

© Macmillan/McGraw-Hill

Reading — **Retell a Story** — 20 Minutes

Read and retell a story.

Bear Snores On What Can We Do? The Woodpecker

❶ Read a book. ❷ Retell it to a partner.

Do More
- Draw a picture of your favorite part of the story.
- Use the Retelling Cards to retell *Bear Snores On*.

For more book titles, go to the Meet the Author/Illustrator page on www.macmillanmh.com

Bear woke up!

42

© Macmillan/McGraw-Hill

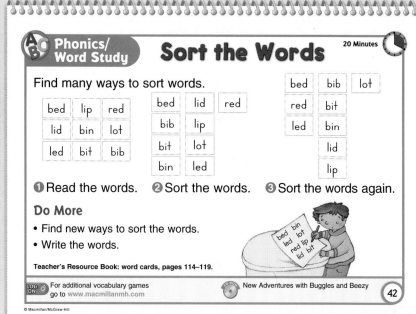

Phonics/Word Study — **Sort the Words** — 20 Minutes

Find many ways to sort words.

bed	lip	red
lid	bin	lot
led	bit	bib

bed	lid	red
bib	lip
bit	lot
bin	led

bed	bib	lot
red	bit
led	bin
	lid
	lip

❶ Read the words. ❷ Sort the words. ❸ Sort the words again.

Do More
- Find new ways to sort the words.
- Write the words.

Teacher's Resource Book: word cards, pages 114–119.

For additional vocabulary games go to www.macmillanmh.com

New Adventures with Buggles and Beezy

42

© Macmillan/McGraw-Hill

Literacy Workstations

Literacy Workstation Flip Charts

Writing

Objectives

- Write an invitation to a party
- Write a sentence about a winter activity

Content Literacy

Objectives

- Identify winter clothing that keeps people warm
- Make a chart to record the favorite seasons of classmates

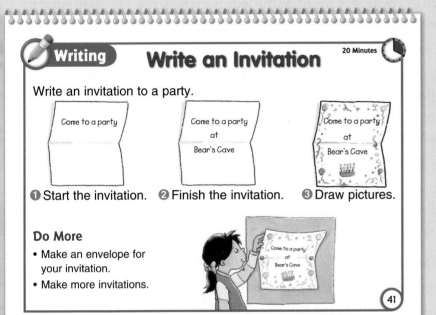

Writing — **Write an Invitation** — 20 Minutes

Write an invitation to a party.

Come to a party

Come to a party at Bear's Cave

Come to a party at Bear's Cave

❶ Start the invitation. ❷ Finish the invitation. ❸ Draw pictures.

Do More
- Make an envelope for your invitation.
- Make more invitations.

41

© Macmillan/McGraw-Hill

Science — **Keeping Warm** — 20 Minutes

How do you keep warm in winter?

hat scarf coat gloves boots

❶ Think about it. ❷ Draw a picture. ❸ Write labels.

Do More
- Write a sentence about what you wear to keep warm.
- Draw what you do to keep cool in summer. Label it.

I wear a coat, scarf, and mittens to keep warm.

LOG ON Internet Research and Inquiry Activity
www.macmillanmh.com

42

© Macmillan/McGraw-Hill

Writing — **Write About Winter** — 20 Minutes

Write about what you do in winter.

This is what I do in winter.

This is what I do in winter.

❶ Think about it. ❷ Write the sentence. ❸ Draw a picture.

Do More
- Write and draw what you do in the summer. Use punctuation at the end of the sentence.

This is what I do in summer.

42

© Macmillan/McGraw-Hill

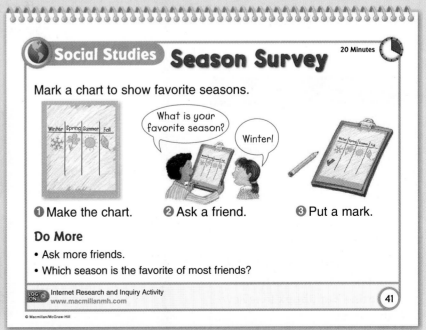

Social Studies — **Season Survey** — 20 Minutes

Mark a chart to show favorite seasons.

Winter Spring Summer Fall

What is your favorite season?

Winter!

❶ Make the chart. ❷ Ask a friend. ❸ Put a mark.

Do More
- Ask more friends.
- Which season is the favorite of most friends?

LOG ON Internet Research and Inquiry Activity
www.macmillanmh.com

41

© Macmillan/McGraw-Hill

Oral Language
- Build Background

✔ **Comprehension**
- Read *Bear Snores On*
- Strategy: Visualize
- Skill: Distinguish Between Fantasy and Reality

✔ **High-Frequency Words**
- Review *this, do, and, what*

✔ **Phonemic Awareness**
- Phoneme Isolation

✔ **Phonics**
- Review /l/l, /b/b, /e/e
- Handwriting: Review *Ll, Bb, Ee*

Grammar
- Describing Words (Adjectives)

Writing
- Shared Writing: A Chart

SMALL GROUP

- Differentiated Instruction, pages 1778–1803

Oral Vocabulary

Week 3

clear	cozy	experience
hibernate	retreat	

Review

mild	month	season
shiver	warning	

Use the **Define/Example/Ask** routine in the **Instructional Routine Handbook** to review the words.

Oral Language

 Build Background: *How Weather Affects Us*

INTRODUCE THE THEME

Tell children that this week they will be talking and reading about how weather affects people. Discuss what the weather is usually like at this time of year.

Write the following question on the board: *What do you like to do at this time of year?* Say: *I can point to the words in the message that I read.* Point to the word *What.* Say: *This is the word* What. *Who can point to the word* at? *Now let's count all the words in the sentence.* Then prompt children to answer the question.

ACCESS PRIOR KNOWLEDGE

- Have children share ideas and discuss their **experiences** outside in different types of weather, such as wind or snow. *Experience means "to do, see, or be a part of something." What do you experience in rainy weather?* Remind children to speak audibly and clearly.

Think Aloud Look at the photograph of the three running children. (Point to the children and count them.) They are holding spools of string, and I see kites behind them. (Point to the spools and kites.)

- *Have you flown a kite? What was it like? How did you get it in the air?*

DISCUSS THE PHOTOGRAPH

How can you tell what the weather is like in the photograph? Can you fly a kite if it isn't windy outside? Discuss other ways that the weather affects what we do. *What could you do in the winter to keep warm? Some animals* **hibernate***, or sleep all winter.*

Teaching Chart 48

Share the Trade Book
Listening Comprehension

PREVIEW Display the cover. *I see a mouse, raven, rabbit, mole, badger, gopher, and bear.* Point to each animal as you name it. *It looks like the bear is sleeping. Let's read about what happens while a bear hibernates.*

Read the title and names of the author and illustrator. *Will the animals wake the bear?*

GENRE: LITERARY TEXT: FICTION Tell children this story is **fantasy**. It could not really happen. The purpose of reading fantasy is to become involved in imagined characters and events and to enjoy language.

Trade Book

STRATEGY **Monitor Comprehension: Visualize**

EXPLAIN/MODEL Tell children that picturing the things described in a story can help them monitor and adjust their comprehension.

Think Aloud Sometimes the illustrations do not show everything that the words describe. I can try to picture what those things might look like and sound like in my mind. This helps me **experience** the story.

SKILL **Distinguish Between Fantasy and Reality**

EXPLAIN/MODEL Explain to children that some stories are fantasy, or make-believe, and cannot really happen. Display the cover.

Think Aloud Bears do sleep in caves, but I don't think that these animals would really be so close to a sleeping bear.

Read the Trade Book

SET PURPOSE Tell children to think about what could or could not really happen as they listen to the story. Use the **Define/Example/Ask** routine to teach the story words on the inside back cover.

Respond to Literature

MAKE CONNECTIONS Provide other books by the author and illustrator for children to read. Tell them to recognize similarities between the books.

Objectives

- Recognize that spoken words can be represented by print
- Discuss how weather affects people
- Use oral vocabulary words *experience* and *hibernate*
- Visualize/distinguish between fantasy and reality
- Recognize sensory details
- Make connections to ideas in other texts

Materials

- Teaching Chart 48
- Read-Aloud Trade Book: *Bear Snores On*

ELL

Use the Interactive Question-Response Guide for *Bear Snores On*, **ELL Resource Book** pages 196–203, to guide children through a reading of the book. As you read *Bear Snores On*, make meaning clear by pointing to the pictures, demonstrating word meanings, paraphrasing text, and asking children questions.

Digital Learning

Story on **Listening Library Audio CD**

Objectives

- Read the high-frequency words *this, do, and, what*
- Identify the words *this, do, and, what* in speech and text
- Review high-frequency words *for, you*
- Demonstrate one-to-one correspondence between spoken and printed words

Materials

- High-Frequency Word Cards: *this, do, and, what, for, you*
- Teaching Chart 49

ELL

Reinforce Vocabulary
Review the high-frequency words *this, do, and, what, for, you*. Display the High-Frequency Word Cards for *this, do, and, what, for, you* and ask individual children questions about classroom objects. For example: *What color is this crayon? What can you do with this crayon? Is this box for crayons? Are A and B letters?* After children answer, have them ask a partner the same question.

High-Frequency Words

 this, do, and, what

> this

REVIEW Display the **High-Frequency Word Card** for **this**. Use the **Read/Spell/Write** routine to teach the word.

- **Read** Point to and say *this*. This *pencil writes better than that one.*

- **Spell** *The word* this *is spelled* t-h-i-s. *What's the middle sound in* this? *That's right. The middle sound in* this *is /i/. That's why the middle letter is* i. *What's the ending sound in* this? *The ending sound in* this *is /s/. That's why the last letter is* s. *Let's read and spell* this *together.*

- **Write** *Now let's write the word* this *on our papers. Let's spell aloud the word as we write it:* this, t-h-i-s.

Repeat the routine with the words **do, and, what**.

 REVIEW *for, you* Display each High-Frequency Word Card and have children read the word.

READ THE RHYME AND CHIME
Ask children to point to the words *this, do, and,* and *what* each time they see them. Repeat the rhyme together for fluency.

Lemon, Eggs, and Butter
This bear can bake a lemon cake.
This lamb can make eggs and ham.
And what can this elephant do?
Make buns with butter and jam!

High-Frequency Words: this, do, and, what
Phonics: /e/e, /b/b, /f/f

Weather · Week 3 · 49

Teaching Chart 49

For Tier 2 instruction, see page 1778.

 **TIME TO MOVE!**

Play "Do This!" Have children take turns doing an action while other children copy it. For example, a child says, *Do this!* and hops or claps as he or she says the action word.

Phonemic Awareness

Phoneme Isolation

Model

Display the **Photo Card** for *bear*.

Repeat for *lemon* and *egg*.

This is a *bear*. Say the picture name with me: *bear*. Listen to the beginning sound in *bear*: /b/. *Bear* begins with /b/. Say the sound with me: /b/. What is the sound?

We'll touch our bellies when we hear a word that begins with /b/.

Read "Lemon, Eggs, and Butter." Have children touch their bellies every time they hear /b/. Repeat for *l* and *e*.

This bear can make a lemon cake. This lamb can make eggs and ham. And what can this elephant do? Make buns with butter and jam!

Display the Photo Card for *lamp*.

Repeat for *exit* and *bus*.

This is a lamp. The beginning sound in *lamp* is /l/. What is the sound?

Guided Practice/Practice

Display and name the remaining Photo Cards.

Children identify the initial sounds. Guide practice with the first card.

Each of you will choose a Photo Card. Name the picture and tell what sound is at the beginning of the word.

Quick Check

Can children identify the initial /b/, /l/, and /e/ sounds?

During **Small Group Instruction**

If No → | Approaching Level | Provide additional practice, page 1779.

If Yes → | On Level | Children blend words with /b/, /l/, and /e/, page 1780.

| Beyond Level | Children read words with /b/, /l/, and /e/, page 1781.

Objective

- Isolate the initial sound /b/, /l/, /e/ in words

Materials

- Photo Cards: *baby, balloon, banana, barn, bat, bear, berries, bike, bird, boat, boil, book, boot, bowl, box, boy, bus, butter, egg, elbow, elevator, exit, ladder, ladybug, lamp, leaf, lemon, light, lightning, lock*

ELL

Pronunciation Display and have children name Photo Cards from this and prior lessons to reinforce phonemic awareness and word meanings. Point to a card and ask: *What do you see?* (a bear) *What is the sound at the beginning of the word* bear? (/b/) Repeat using Photo Cards with words that begin with the /l/ and /e/ sounds.

Objectives

- Review sound-spellings for /l/l, /b/b, /e/e
- Recognize the difference between a letter and a word
- Handwriting: Review *Ll, Bb, Ee*

Materials

- Sound-Spelling Cards: *Bat, Egg, Lemon*
- Teaching Chart 49
- Word-Building Cards
- Handwriting
- Handwriting Teacher's Edition
- Activity Book, p. 24
- Practice Book, p. 153

Phonics

Review /l/l, /b/b, /e/e

Model

Display the *Lemon* **Sound-Spelling Card**.

Repeat the routine for *Bat* and *Egg*.

This is letter *l*. The letter *l* stands for the /l/ sound you hear in *lemon*. What is the letter? What does this letter stand for?

Reread the "Lemon, Eggs, and Butter" Rhyme and Chime. Reread the title. Point out that the word *Lemon* in the title begins with the letter *L*. Model placing a self-stick note under the *L* in *Lemon*. Encourage children to see the difference between a letter and a word.

Lemon, Eggs, and Butter

This bear can bake a lemon cake.
This lamb can make eggs and ham.
And what can this elephant do?
Make buns with butter and jam!

High-Frequency Words: this, do, and, what
Phonics: /e/e /b/b, /l/l

Unit 7 Rhyme and Chime

Weather Week 3 49

Teaching Chart 49

Guided Practice/Practice

Read the rest of the rhyme. Stop after each line. Children place self-stick notes below words that begin with *l*. Guide practice with *lemon* in line 1. Repeat with *b* and *e*.

Let's put a sticky note below the word in the line that begins with the letter *l*. The word *lemon* begins with the letter *l*. Which word in the next line begins with the letter *l*? Yes, *lamb* begins with the letter *l*.

Corrective Feedback

Blending Model blending sounds in words with /l/. Note the position of your teeth and tongue as you emphasize the sound. *This is the /l/ sound at the beginning of* lamb: /l/ /a/ /m/, /lllaaammm/, lamb.

Build Fluency: Sound-Spellings

 SPIRAL REVIEW Display the following **Word-Building Cards**: *a, b, c, d, e, f, h, i, l, m, n, o, p, r, s, t*. Have children chorally say each sound. Repeat and vary the pace.

Handwriting: Review *Ll, Bb,* and *Ee*

MODEL Model holding up your writing hand. Say the handwriting cues from **Handwriting Teacher's Edition** pages 62–64 as you write the capital and lowercase forms of *Ll, Bb,* and *Ee* on the board. Then trace the letters on the board and in the air as you say the sounds.

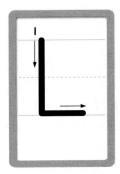 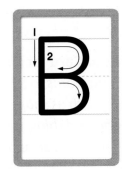 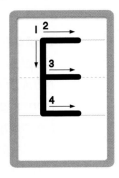

PRACTICE Ask children to hold up their writing hand.

- Say the cues together as children trace with their index finger the letters you wrote on the board.

- Have children write *L* and *l* in the air as they say /lll/. Have them write *B* and *b* in the air as they say /b/ multiple times. Have children write *E* and *e* in the air as they say /eee/.

- Distribute handwriting practice pages. Observe children's pencil grip and paper position, and correct as necessary. Have children say /lll/ as they write *L* and *l*. Have them say /b/ multiple times as they write *B* and *b*. Have children say /eee/ as they write *E* and *e*.

For Tier 2 instruction, see page 1779.

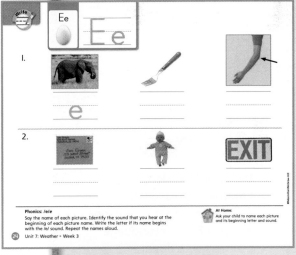

Activity Book, page 24
Practice Book, page 153

Objective

- Recognize describing words (adjectives)

Materials

- Read-Aloud Trade Book: *Bear Snores On*
- Photo Cards: *alligator, ant, bat, bear, bird, camel, deer, dog, dolphin, fish, fox, giraffe, goat, gorilla, hippo, horse, inchworm, kangaroo, kitten, koala, ladybug, moth, mouse, mule, octopus, ostrich, otter, owl, ox, penguin, pig, quail, rabbit, seal, sheep, tiger, turkey, turtle, walrus, whale, wolf, yak*

ELL

Basic and Academic Language Display the Photo Cards from the lesson and pair English Language Learners with fluent speakers. Have partners name their cards and then work together to dictate words that describe each animal. List the words and read them chorally. Then ask partners to make up sentences that describe the animals.

Grammar

Describing Words (Adjectives)

MODEL Use the **Trade Book** *Bear Snores On* to review describing words. Point to the cover as you read the title. *If I wanted to tell more about the bear, I could use the describing word* sleepy. *The* sleepy *bear snores on.* Ask: *What kind of bear is it?* Explain that the word *sleepy* is a describing word. It tells about the bear, who is ready to **hibernate**. Explain that describing words tell more about something.

- *What other describing words can we use to tell about the bear?* (*big, furry, sad, angry, happy*)

PRACTICE
Display the **Photo Card** for *ladybug*. Name the picture. *I want to think of describing words to tell more about the ladybug. I can use clues from the picture, such as shape and color. The ladybug is red and black. Her body is round and shiny. I can also use clues from what I know about ladybugs, such as their size and weight. The ladybug is small and light.* Write the descriptive sentences on the board.

> The ladybug is red *and* black.
>
> Her body is round *and* shiny.
>
> The ladybug is small *and* light.

- Put the *ladybug* card out of sight. *Which of these words help paint a picture of a ladybug in your mind?* (*red, black, round, shiny, small, light*) Read each sentence on the chart and have children name the words that tell more about the ladybug. Show the Photo Card for *ladybug* again. *What other words could we use to describe the ladybug?* (*spotted, friendly, quiet, smooth*)

- Distribute animal Photo Cards to children and tell each child to name his or her card. Ask each child to use describing words to talk about the animal. Then have children list the words that tell more about the animal. If they have difficulty, have them look at the picture. *What color is the animal? What size is it? What shape is it?*

Writing

Shared Writing: A Chart

BRAINSTORM

Remind children that in the **Trade Book** *Bear Snores On,* they read about a bear who was sleeping in a cave for the winter. Other animals began sneaking into the cave to escape the bad weather. *What other animals were in the book? What did they* **experience***?*

WRITE

Create a three-column chart as shown below. Read each column title aloud as you track the print. Have children repeat.

- Tell children that they will list the animals and two things that each one did. Model by reading pages 7–9. *Mouse creep-crawls in and lights wee twigs. I will write* Mouse *in the first column under* Character, creep-crawls *in the second column under* Does This, *and* lights wee twigs *in the third column under* and Does This. Have children share the pen to write the first letter in words, such as the *M* in *Mouse,* or to write words that they know, such as *this.*

- Continue by reading pages 12–13 and 16–17. After each group of pages, have children tell you what to write in each column.

Character	Does This	and Does This
Mouse	creep-crawls	lights wee twigs
Hare	pops white corn	brews black tea
Badger	brings honey-nuts	divvies them up

- Read the completed chart aloud as you track the print. Explain words that children do not understand or use a dictionary to determine the meanings of unknown words.

- Save the chart to refer to in other writing activities this week.

Write About It

Ask children to draw a picture of a sleeping bear in a cave and write a caption describing it under the picture.

Objectives

- Help to complete a chart
- Dictate or write information for lists and captions
- Identify the common sounds that letters represent

Materials

- Read-Aloud Trade Book: *Bear Snores On*

5-Day Writing	
Sentences	
DAY 1	Shared: A Chart
DAY 2	Interactive: Sentences
DAY 3	Independent: Prewrite and Draft Sentences
DAY 4	Independent: Revise and Edit Sentences
DAY 5	Independent: Publish and Present

ELL

Use New Language
Provide the Trade Book *Bear Snores On* for children to page through. Have them point to the animals, name them, and describe something each animal is doing in one of the illustrations.

Transitions That Teach

As children wait in line, have them talk about an **experience** they have had in kindergarten.

DAY 2
At a Glance

WHOLE GROUP

Oral Language
- Build Robust Vocabulary

✓ **Comprehension**
- Reread *Bear Snores On*
- Strategy: Visualize
- Skill: Distinguish Between Fantasy and Reality
- Fluency: Echo-Read

Vocabulary
- Sound Words
- Story Words: *cave, lair, den*

✓ **Phonemic Awareness**
- Phoneme Blending

✓ **Phonics**
- Review /b/b, /l/l, /e/e, /d/d
- Blend with -*in*
- Decodable Reader: *Pat and Tip*

Writing
- Interactive Writing: Sentences

SMALL GROUP

- Differentiated Instruction, pages 1778–1803

Oral Vocabulary

Week 3

clear	cozy	experience
hibernate	retreat	

Review

mild	month	season
shiver	warning	

Use the **Define/Example/Ask** routine in the **Instructional Routine Handbook** to review the words.

Oral Language

Talk About It

Build Robust Vocabulary

INTRODUCE WORDS

Tell children that today you are going to talk about the **Trade Book** *Bear Snores On* and why bears hibernate. *When animals hibernate, they spend the winter in a deep sleep. Why is Bear in* Bear Snores On *hibernating? How can you tell people do not hibernate? What are some other animals that hibernate?* Read and display pages 5–7.

Vocabulary Routine

Use the routine below to discuss the meaning of each word.

Define: When animals **hibernate**, they spend the winter in a deep sleep. Say the word with me.
Example: Animals hibernate to get through the winter without much food.
Ask: What are some animals that hibernate in winter?

Define: When you **experience** something, you do, see, or are a part of something. Say the word with me.
Example: Bears experience winter by hibernating in caves.
Ask: In winter, would you like to experience going sledding?

CREATE A WORD WEB

Draw a word web, or use **Teaching Chart G1**. Label the center circle as shown. Read the word aloud as you track the print. *Bear hibernates in the winter, so I will write* winter *on the web. When he hibernates, Bear sleeps. I will add* sleep *to the web. What other words can we add to the web to tell about the experience of hibernating?*

Guide children to use complete sentences when speaking. For example, recast children's responses using complete sentences. Add children's ideas to the word web. Read aloud the text on the completed web with children as you track the print.

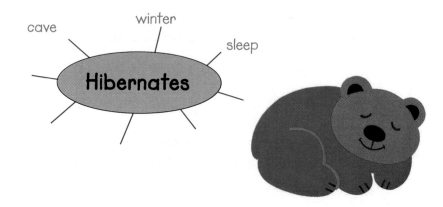

Listen for Rhythm

IDENTIFY RHYTHM

Tell children that rhythm in poetry means there is a regular beat to the poem. Explain that children can clap to hear the regular beat.

RHYME ABOUT WEATHER

Tell children they will learn a rhyme about how weather affects a dog. Play the rhyme "Little Dog," using the **Listening Library Audio CD**. Then teach children the words and recite the rhyme together.

Discuss the rhyme. *What kind of weather is described in the rhyme?* (fog) Ask children to describe what fog is like. If they are unfamiliar with fog, explain that fog looks similar to steam from a hot shower.

Point out the words *way* and *gray* and say that they end with the same sound /ay/. Ask children to generate other words that rhyme with *gray*.

Little Dog

Little Dog had lost his way
In a fog so thick and gray.

First, Dog bumped into a log.
Next, he sat upon a frog.

"Oh," Dog said in a ho-hum way.
"I guess this just is not my day!"

Objectives

- Discuss the theme
- Use oral vocabulary words *experience* and *hibernate*
- Discuss hibernating
- Complete a word web
- Respond to rhythm in poetry
- Orally generate rhymes in response to spoken words

Materials

- Read-Aloud Trade Book: *Bear Snores On*
- Listening Library Audio CD
- Graphic Organizer; Teaching Chart G1

Digital Learning

Rhyme on Listening Library Audio CD

ELL   ENGLISH LANGUAGE LEARNERS

Beginning	Intermediate	Advanced
Confirm Understanding Review oral vocabulary using the **Trade Book** *Bear Snores On.* Say, for example: *Show me the picture of the hare. Is the hare's fur brown or white? Repeat with other animals.*	**Enhance Understanding** Have children focus on how the animals get inside the bear's lair. For example, ask: *Which animal hops in?* Guide children to answer in complete sentences and act out being that animal.	**Describe Details** Have children describe details that make this story a fantasy. Write down their responses and elaborate. Ask children about other fantasy stories they might know.

Objectives

- Visualize
- Recognize sensory details
- Distinguish between fantasy and reality
- Respond to a story
- Retell a story
- Develop fluency

Materials

- Read-Aloud Trade Book: *Bear Snores On*
- Retelling Cards
- Activity Book, p. 25
- Practice Book, p. 154

Trade Book

Digital Learning

Story on **Listening Library Audio CD**

ELL

Use gestures and other strategies to help make the text comprehensible.

p. 5
sleeps, cold: Point to the illustration of Bear sleeping in his cave on a cold night. Dramatize *sleeps* and *cold* with children while saying the words.

p. 7
snores: Point to Bear and make a snoring sound. Say *snore.* Have children make the sound and name it.

Reread the Trade Book
Listening Comprehension

CONCEPTS ABOUT PRINT Display the cover and read the title aloud. Have children tell what they remember about the story.

 STRATEGY **Monitor Comprehension: Visualize**

Tell children that picturing the things described in a story can help them to understand it. *When we read the book, what did you picture in your mind? What sounds did you hear?*

 SKILL **Distinguish Between Fantasy and Reality**

Tell children that some stories are fantasy, or make-believe. Have them give examples of fantasy and reality from books and films.

Think Aloud I remember that the bear was hibernating in a cave. That is realistic. Then the animals have a party. That is fantasy.

Read the story and use the prompts on the inside cover.

page 5

RECOGNIZE RHYME AND ALLITERATION

- *Listen as I read the words on this page. Predict what the last word will be. How did you know?*

In a cave in the woods,
in his deep, dark lair,
through the long, cold winter
sleeps a great brown bear.

pages 6–7

 DISTINGUISH FANTASY/REALITY

Think Aloud I see the bear hibernating in the cave. That is realistic. There is a pot and tea kettle. Bears don't really have those things. That is not realistic.

Cuddled in a heap,
with his eyes shut tight,
he sleeps through the day,
he sleeps through the night.

The cold winds howl
and the night sounds growl.
But the bear snores on.

Develop Comprehension

pages 8–9

DISTINGUISH FANTASY/REALITY

- *The mouse is talking. Is that realistic or make-believe?* (make-believe)

pages 10–11

STORY STRUCTURE

- *This sentence will be repeated many times in the story. Let's say it together:* But the bear snores on.

pages 12–13

VISUALIZE

- *The illustrations do not show the hare hopping into the cave. Can you picture that in your mind?*

page 14

PHONEMIC AWARENESS

- *What are two words on this page that rhyme?* (slurps/burps)

Comprehension

Visualize
- (pages 12–13) The illustrations do not show the hare hopping into the cave. I will try to picture that in my mind.

Distinguish Between Fantasy and Reality
- (pages 6–7) I see the bear sleeping in the cave. That is realistic. The bear has a pot and a tea kettle. Bears don't really have those things.
- (pages 22–23) Do you think these animals could really have a party?

Story Words

(page 5) cave	(page 5) lair	(page 12) den

About the Illustrator: Karma Wilson
Karma Wilson likes to write stories with fun word play and rhythmic prose. When Karma isn't taking care of her family or writing, she enjoys visiting schools and libraries to share with children everywhere her love of reading and writing.

**Trade Book
Inside Back Cover**

ELL

p. 8
itty-bitty, tip-toe: Use your fingers and feet to gesture *itty-bitty* and *tip-toe.*

pp. 10–11
But the bear snores on: Point to the bear and make a snoring sound. Have children repeat this refrain.

pp. 12–13
mouse, hare: Point to the pictures of the mouse and hare on page 13. Have children repeat the animal names. Ask children to name the animal on page 12.

pp. 14–15
slurps: Point to the mouse and dramatize taking little slurps. Ask children to show you what they are doing when they slurp. Have them make a slurping sound and name it.

Develop Comprehension

Text Evidence

Fantasy and Reality

Explain Remind children that when they answer a question, they must support their answer with text evidence.

Discuss Have children look at and listen to pages 16–17. Ask them to point out what is not real. (The badger is talking.)

ELL

pp. 16–17
badger: Point to the badger on page 16 and name it. Ask children to point to and name the badger on page 17.

pp. 18–19
chew: Dramatize eating something and chewing. Say *chew.* Ask children to show you what it looks like when they chew food.

pp. 20–21
gopher: Point to the gopher on page 20 and name it. Ask children to point to and name the gopher on page 21.

pp. 22–23
party: Point to the animals having a party. Discuss any parties the class has had. Talk about what the class did at the party. For example, note whether they ate or played games. Tell children that the animals are holding a party, just as the class held a party.

pages 16–17

 DISTINGUISH FANTASY/REALITY

- *What is happening on these pages that tells you this is a fantasy?* (The badger is talking and handing a bag of honey-nuts to the hare.)

pages 18–19

PHONEMIC AWARENESS

- *What words start with the /b/ sound?* (*But, bear*)

pages 20–21

 VISUALIZE

- *The illustration does not show the gopher and the mole pushing up through the dirt. Can you picture that in your mind? How might that sound?*

pages 22–23

 IDENTIFY SETTING

- *Where does the story take place?* (a cave in a forest) *Which season is it? How can you tell?* (It is winter. The trees are bare, and it is snowy.)

pages 24–25

MAKE PREDICTIONS

- *What do you think the small pepper flake will make the bear do?* (Sneeze!)

pages 26–27

CONFIRM PREDICTIONS

- *How did you confirm your prediction? What do you think the bear is going to do next?*

pages 28–29

WRITER'S CRAFT

- *Why do you think the author uses all of those words to describe what bear does when he wakes up?* (The author uses many words to show us how angry bear is.)

pages 30–31

IDENTIFY CHARACTER

- *How does Bear feel?* (He is sad.) *Why does he feel different from the other animals?* (because the other animals had a party without him)

ELL

pp. 24–25

fire: Point to the fire on page 24, name it, and dramatize being hot. Turn to page 21 and have children point to and name the fire.

pp. 26–27

sneezes: Point to the picture of the bear sneezing. Dramatize sneezing and name it. Ask children to show you what a sneeze looks like.

pp. 28–29

growls: Point to the picture of the angry bear and make a growling sound. Ask children to growl.

pp. 30–31

whimpers: Point to the picture of the sad bear as he whimpers. Make a whimpering sound. Ask children to whimper.

pages 32–33

IDENTIFY CHARACTER

■ *What does Bear spend the night doing?* (telling tall tales) *What* **experiences** *do you think he tells about?*

page 34

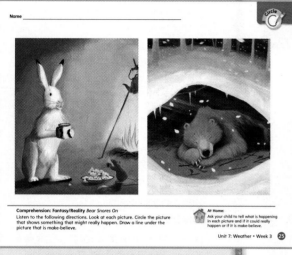

Activity Book, page 25
Practice Book, page 154

Retelling Rubric

4 Excellent

Retells the selection without prompting, in sequence, and using supporting details. Clearly describes the setting, main characters, and complete plot.

3 Good

Retells the selection with little guidance, in sequence, and using some details. Generally describes the setting, main characters, and plot.

2 Fair

Retells the selection with some guidance, mostly in sequence, and using limited details. Partially describes the setting, main characters, and plot.

1 Unsatisfactory

Retells the selection only when prompted, out of sequence, and using limited details. Does not describe the main characters or plot.

Respond to Literature

TALK ABOUT IT Have children discuss the book.

■ *Who snores throughout most of this story?* (Bear) LOCATE

■ *What animals have a party while Bear snores on?* (mouse, hare, badger, gopher, mole) COMBINE

■ *What is the main idea of this story?* (Bears hibernate or sleep during the winter, while the other animals don't.) CONNECT

Retell

GUIDED RETELLING

■ Display **Retelling Card 1**. Based on children's needs, use the Guided, Modeled, or ELL prompts. The Modeled prompts contain support for English Language Learners based on levels of language acquisition. Repeat with the rest of the Retelling Cards.

Retelling Cards

■ Have children retell a main event from the story.

Fluency: Echo-Read

MODEL Read page 28, using an angry voice and emphasizing the rhythm of the text. Reread and have children echo-read.

Quick Check

Can children tell apart reality and fantasy? Can children retell the story?

Vocabulary

Review Sound Words

Act out and chant the following jingle:

Drip, drop, splash, goes the rain.

Crack, bam, crash, goes the storm.

■ Repeat each line and ask children to raise their hands when they hear a word that names a sound.

NAME SOUND WORDS Reread pages 6–10 of the **Trade Book** *Bear Snores On*. Have children name the sound words that they hear. Ask them to create sentences with the sound words from the book. Display pictures of animals that make loud noises and soft noises. Have children sort the pictures into 'loud' and 'soft' sound categories.

Story Words: *cave, lair, den*

■ Display page 5 of *Bear Snores On* and point out the words *cave* and *lair*. *A cave is a hollow area in the earth with an opening to the outside.* Explain that a *lair* is the home of a wild animal. *Many animals **hibernate** in their lairs.*

■ Display page 12 and point out the word *den* and the picture of the rabbit peeking in. Explain that *cave, lair,* and *den* are three words that mean almost the same thing.

TIME TO MOVE!

Have children suppose they are bears by crawling around on all fours. Tell them to make sounds from *Bear Snores On*, for example: *Bears slurp some water.* Have children say a sentence about what they are doing. For example: *I growl at other bears.*

Objectives

- Use sound words
- Identify and sort pictures of objects into categories
- Learn story words *cave, lair, den*

Materials

- **Read-Aloud Trade Book:** *Bear Snores On*
- pictures of animals

Digital Learning

 LOG ON For children who need additional language support and oral vocabulary development, use the activities found at **www.macmillanmh.com**.

ELL

Develop Vocabulary
Display pages 6–10 of *Bear Snores On*. As you show each page, read the lines with a sound word and explain it. Have children repeat the sound words after you and make the sounds. Display **Photo Cards** and ask children what sounds those animals make. List them on the board.

Objectives

- Blend sounds to form words
- Review sound-spellings /b/b, /l/l, /e/e, /d/d
- Blend with the -in phonogram

Materials

- Puppet
- Word-Building Cards
- pocket chart
- Word-Building Cards; Teacher's Resource Book, pp. 95–102

Phonemic Awareness

✔ Phoneme Blending

Model

Use the **Puppet** to model how to blend the sounds in the word *bat*.
Repeat the routine with *Ben*.

Happy is going to say the sounds in a word. Listen to Happy as he says each sound: /b/ /a/ /t/. Happy can blend these sounds together: /baaat/, bat. Say the sounds with Happy: /b/ /a/ /t/. Now say the word with Happy: *bat*.

Guided Practice/Practice

Say the sounds. Children blend the sounds to form words.

Guide practice with the first word, using the same routine.

Happy is going to say the sounds in a word. Listen to Happy as he says each sound. Repeat the sounds and then blend them to say the word.

/l/ /o/ /t/	/b/ /i/ /t/	/n/ /e/ /t/
/l/ /i/ /p/	/r/ /ā/ /n/	/h/ /ī/ /d/

Phonics

✔ Review

b	d	e	l

Model

Say the word.

Hold up **Word-Building Card** *b*.

Repeat the routine for letters *l*, *e*, and *d*.

Listen as I say a word: *bear*. Say the word with me: *bear*. *Bear* begins with /b/. I will hold up the *b* card because *b* stands for the /b/ sound at the beginning of *bear*. What is the name of the letter? What sound does it stand for?

Guided Practice/Practice

Distribute copies of Word-Building Cards *b, d, e, l*. Say the words. Children hold up the card for the first sound. Guide practice with the first word.

I will say a word. Hold up the letter card that stands for the sound at the beginning of the word.

egg	door	book	ladder
damp	bus	lamp	edge
den	lair	ever	back

Build Fluency: Sound-Spellings

 Display the following **Word-Building Cards**: *a, b, c, d, e, f, h, i, l, m, n, o, p, r, s, t.* Have children chorally say each sound. Repeat and vary the pace.

 Blend with -in

Model

Place Word-Building Card *p* in the pocket chart. Point to the letter.

This letter is *p*. Letter *p* stands for the /p/ sound. Say /p/.

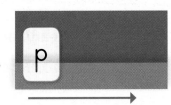

Place the letters *pin* in the pocket chart, leaving space after the *p*.

These are the letters *i* and *n*. The letters *i* and *n* stand for the sounds /i/ and /n/. Let's blend these two sounds together: /iiinnn/.

Place the letters *in* closer to the letter *p*. Move your hand from left to right.

Repeat the routine with *tin*.

The beginning sound in the word is /p/, and the rest of the word is /in/. Let's blend the beginning sound and the rest of the word together: /piiinnn/, *pin*.

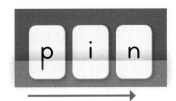

Guided Practice/Practice

Use the routine to blend the onset and rime in other words in the *-in* word family. Guide practice with the first word.

fin   bin   Min

din   tin   pin

What do you notice about the words *pin, tin, fin, bin, Min,* and *din*?

(They end with the letters *i* and *n*; they end with the sound /in/; they rhyme.)

For Tier 2 instruction, see page 1785.

Objectives

- Read decodable words with /b/b, /l/l, /e/e
- Read the words *do, this, and, what*
- Predict what will happen next based on cover, title, and illustrations
- Reread for fluency

Materials

- Decodable Reader: *Pat and Tip*
- High-Frequency Word Cards: *a, and, are, can, do, have, I, is, play, this, what, you*

Decodable Text

For additional decodable passages, see pages 31–34 of the **Teacher's Resource Book**.

Decodable Reader

Read *Pat and Tip*

Pat and Tip

 REVIEW HIGH-FREQUENCY WORDS Display **High-Frequency Word Cards** for **a**, **and**, **are**, **can**, **do**, **have**, **I**, **is**, **play**, **this**, **what**, and **you**. Review the words using the **Read/Spell/Write** routine.

MODEL CONCEPTS ABOUT PRINT
Guide children to follow along as you say: *I hold the book so that the cover faces me. I cannot see the back cover this way.*

PREDICT Tell children to say who they see on the cover and to read the title. Encourage them to ask questions, such as: *What is the girl holding? Where are they? What will this story be about?*

FIRST READ Point out the rebus and discuss what it stands for. Have children point to each word, sounding out decodable words and saying the high-frequency words quickly.

DEVELOP COMPREHENSION Ask the following: *What are the children in the story doing?* (They are playing a game.) *Why do they stop playing the game?* (It's raining.)

 SECOND READ Have partners reread the book together. Circulate, listen in, and provide corrective feedback.

I have a bat.
Can you play?

2

Ben can. Sam can.
Cam and Pam can.

3

Sam can bat.
Hit it Sam!

4

Can Ben bat?
Pop it Ben!

5

Pit, pat. It is ▨!
rain

6

Ben ran. Cam ran. Sam ran.
Pam, Pat, and Tip ran!

7

Pat and Tip are not sad.
Pat can sit. Tip can nap!

8

Decodable Reader

Writing

Interactive Writing: Sentences

REVIEW
Display and read aloud the chart children created for the Shared Writing activity.

WRITE
Today we will use and write complete sentences about the animals in Bear Snores On *and what they* **experienced** *while Bear was* **hibernating**.

■ Ask children to help you write the following sentence frames. For example, they can write words they know, such as *and* or *the*, and the first letters in words, such as the *M* in *Mouse*. Read the sentences aloud as you track the print.

> Mouse ____ into the cave and ____ wee twigs.
>
> Hare ____ white corn and ____ black tea.

■ Have children suggest words to complete each sentence, using the chart as a reference. Write the words in the frames to complete the sentences. Tell children to help by writing all of the letters that they know. Point out that each sentence begins with a capital letter and ends with a period.

■ Read the completed sentences together as you track the print.

■ Remind children that a sentence begins with a capital letter and ends with a period.

■ Save the sentences to use in other writing activities this week.

■ To extend the activity, ask children to write additional sentences about the characters in *Bear Snores On*.

Write About It
Ask children to draw a picture of a small animal and write a description of it using one of the following high-frequency words: *this, do, and, like.*

Objectives
- Write sentences
- Match sounds to letters to write letters in a word
- Capitalize the first letter in a sentence
- Use end punctuation

Materials
- Shared Writing chart from Day 1

5-Day Writing

Sentences	
DAY 1	Shared: A Chart
DAY 2	Interactive: Sentences
DAY 3	Independent: Prewrite and Draft Sentences
DAY 4	Independent: Revise and Edit Sentences
DAY 5	Independent: Publish and Present

ELL

Use New Language Ask children to dictate a sentence that describes a pet or a small animal they are familiar with.

Transitions That Teach

While lining up to go to lunch, have children tell about animals that **hibernate**.

WHOLE GROUP

Oral Language
- Build Robust Vocabulary
- Oral Vocabulary Cards: "Animals in Winter"

✔ **Comprehension**
- Read *Time For Kids:* "Let It Snow!"
- Text Features: Photographs

✔ **High-Frequency Words**
- Review *this*, *do*, *and*, *what*

✔ **Phonemic Awareness**
- Phoneme Segmentation

✔ **Phonics**
- Review
- Blend with *-ip*

Grammar
- Describing Words (Adjectives)

Writing
- Independent Writing: Prewrite and Draft Sentences

Additional Vocabulary

To provide 15–20 minutes of additional vocabulary instruction, see Oral Vocabulary Cards 5-Day Plan. The pre- and posttests can be found in the **Teacher's Resource Book**, pages 226–227.

Oral Language

 Talk About It

Build Robust Vocabulary

BUILD BACKGROUND

Introduce the selection "Animals in Winter" using **Oral Vocabulary Card 1** and read the title aloud. *What activities do you experience in winter? What can you do to stay warm and cozy?* Ask children to tell what they think is happening in the picture. Have them predict what this selection will be about.

- Read the selection on the back of the cards. Pause at each oral vocabulary word and read the definition. Check children's understanding using the Use Photographs, Main Idea and Details, and Generate Synonyms prompts.

Oral Vocabulary Cards

Vocabulary Routine

Use the routine below to discuss the meaning of each word.

Define: If something is **cozy**, it is warm, comfortable, and snug. Say the word with me.
Example: The kittens felt cozy in a little basket.
Ask: Where do you feel cozy?

Define: When the sky is **clear**, it is bright and not cloudy. Say the word with me.
Example: Flying a kite is fun on a clear day.
Ask: Is the sky cloudy or clear today?

Define: When you **retreat**, you go away from something. Say the word with me.
Example: When there's a thunderstorm, my dog retreats into the closet.
Ask: What kind of weather would make you retreat?

- Use the routine on Cards 2 and 4 to review the words **hibernate** and **experience**.

 SPIRAL REVIEW

- Review last week's words: *mild, month, season, shiver,* and *warning.*

Listen for Rhyme

IDENTIFY RHYME

Tell children that they will recite another rhyme. Play the rhyme and ask children to join in.

Listen to these pairs of words and tell which ones rhyme: square/air, here /there, air/there.

WEATHER TALK

Tell children that people often look out of their windows to see what the weather is like outside. *What would I see that would show me that the weather is rainy?* (falling rain, puddles, wet pavement, grey clouds, people carrying umbrellas) *How might I change what I wear if it is raining outside?* (I might put on a raincoat, boots, or rain hat.) *What would I see that would show me that the weather is windy?* (trees bending, flags waving in the wind)

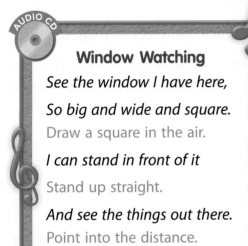

Window Watching

See the window I have here,

So big and wide and square.

Draw a square in the air.

I can stand in front of it

Stand up straight.

And see the things out there.

Point into the distance.

Objectives

- Listen and respond to an expository nonfiction selection
- Discuss cold weather activities
- Use oral vocabulary words *clear, cozy, experience, hibernate,* and *retreat*
- Recognize rhyming words

Materials

- Oral Vocabulary Cards: "Animals in Winter"
- Listening Library Audio CD

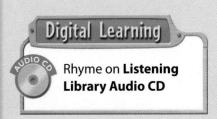

Digital Learning

Rhyme on **Listening Library Audio CD**

Objectives

- Retell and respond to expository text
- Analyze photographs
- Understand what snowy weather is like
- Identify ways that snow affects people

Material

- Big Book of Explorations, Vol. 2: "Let It Snow!" pp. 21–24
- old magazines (especially ski or travel magazines)

Content Vocabulary

storm a strong wind with heavy rain or snow

cloud tiny drops of water or bits of ice bunched together that float in the sky

Use a Picture Dictionary
Guide children to look up the words in a picture dictionary.

Informational Text

Genre

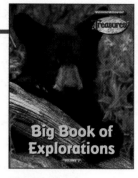

Big Book of Explorations

INFORMATIONAL TEXT: EXPOSITORY
Have children look at the photograph on page 21 and describe what the boy is doing. Tell children that in this nonfiction article is **expository text**. They will learn about snow and how snowy weather affects people.

READ "LET IT SNOW!"

- **Preview and Predict** Ask children to point to the title of the selection. Read the title as you track the print. Explain that *Time For Kids* is a magazine that writes articles for children. Preview the pages with children. *What will this article be about? How do you know?*

- **Content Vocabulary** Introduce and discuss the vocabulary words.

- **Text Feature: Photographs** Explain that this nonfiction selection uses photographs to give us a better understanding of what we are learning about.

CONTENT FOCUS
Read the selection aloud as you track the print. Tell children to use the photographs to help them understand what it is like when it snows.

Point to the clouds shown on page 22. Have children describe the clouds. (thick, dark) Explain that all clouds have water in them, but when there is enough water in clouds and it is cold, snow can fall. Mention that snowflakes are frozen crystals of ice and that no two are exactly the same. Nearly all snowflakes have six sides, but some are shaped like columns.

Ask children to tell what else may fall from dark clouds. (rain, sleet, hail)

As you read pages 22 and 23, mention that although snow can be difficult to walk in, drive in, or shovel, it can also be fun. Ask children to talk about ways that snow can be fun. List their ideas in a chart.

Use Photographs The photo on page 21 shows that it must be cold when it snows because the boy is dressed for cold weather.

Phonemic Awareness

Phoneme Segmentation

Model

Use the **Puppet** to say the sounds in *dad*.

Repeat with *did*.

Happy will say words sound by sound. Listen to Happy say the sounds in the word *dad*: /d/ /a/ /d/. There are three sounds. Say *dad* sound by sound with Happy. (/d/ /a/ /d/)

Guided Practice/Practice

Use the Puppet to say the words. Children repeat each word and then say it sound by sound. Guide practice with the first word.

Listen to Happy say a word. Say the word after Happy. Then say the word sound by sound.

can	had	hid	fed
fan	ran	fin	hen
led	cob	red	cab

For Tier 2 instruction, see page 1788.

Objective

• Segment the sounds in words

Materials

• Puppet

Objectives

- Review sound-spellings for /b/b, /e/e, /l/l
- Blend onsets and rimes to form simple words

Materials

- Word-Building Cards
- pocket chart
- Word-Building Cards; Teacher's Resource Book, pp. 95–102
- Sound Box
- WorkBoard Sound Boxes; Teacher's Resource Book, p. 136

Phonics

✔ Review

Model

Use the **Sound Box** and the **Word-Building Cards**.

Say the word. Place Word-Building Card *b* in the first box.

Place Word-Building Cards *e, d* in the middle and last boxes, using the routine.

Repeat the routine with *led*.

I will place cards in the Sound Box that stand for each sound in a word.

Listen to the word: *bed*. Say the word with me: *bed*. The /b/ sound is at the beginning of *bed*. I will place a *b* in the first box to show that /b/ is the first sound and *b* is the first letter in *bed*.

I will place an *e* in the middle box to show that /e/ is the middle sound and *e* is the middle letter in *bed*.

I will place a *d* in the last box to show that /d/ is the ending sound and *d* is the ending letter in *bed*.

Guided Practice/Practice

Distribute Sound Boxes and copies of the Word-Building Cards.

Say the words.

Children identify the letters in a word.

I will say a word. Say the word after me. Then put the cards in the Sound Box for each sound you hear.

can	had	hid	fed
fib	lid	fin	bad
lab	cab	lap	hen

Build Fluency: Sound-Spellings

Display the following Word-Building Cards: *a, b, c, d, e, f, h, l, m, n, o, p, r, s, t*. Have children chorally say each sound. Repeat and vary the pace.

For Tier 2 instruction, see page 1789.

Blend with *-ip*

Model

Place **Word-Building Card** *l* in the pocket chart.

This is the letter *l*. It stands for /l/. Say /l/.

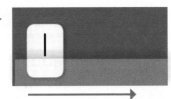

Place the letters *ip* in the pocket chart, leaving space after the *l*. Point to the letters *i* and *p*.

These are the letters *i* and *p*. The letters *i* and *p* stand for /i/ and /p/. Let's blend these two sounds together: /iiip/.

Place the letters *ip* next to the letter *l*. Move your hand from left to right below the letters.

Repeat the routine with *hip*.

The beginning sound in the word is /l/, and the sounds of the rest of the word are /ip/. Let's blend the beginning sound and the rest of the word together: /llliiip/, *lip*.

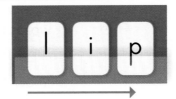

Guided Practice/Practice

Children blend the onset and rime in other words that end with *-ip*. Guide practice with *sip*, using the routine.

sip   tip   pip   rip   nip   dip

What do you notice about the words *lip*, *hip*, *sip*, *tip*, *pip*, *rip*, *nip*, and *dip*? (They all end with the letters *ip*; they end with the sounds /ip/; they rhyme.)

Corrective Feedback

Blending: Sound Error Model the sound that children missed, then have them repeat the sound. For example, for the word *lip*, say: *My turn*. Tap under the letter *p* in the word *lip* and say: *Sound? What's the sound?* Then return to the beginning of the word. Say: *Let's start over*. Blend the word with children again.

ELL

Pronunciation Because there is no direct sound-symbol match for /i/ in Spanish, Cantonese, Vietnamese, and other languages, provide extra practice in pronouncing and blending /i/. Additionally, some Spanish speakers may have difficulty perceiving and pronouncing final /p/. Use the Approaching Level phonics lessons for additional pronunciation and decoding practice.

Objectives

- Recognize describing words (adjectives)
- Recognize sensory details

Materials

- Oral Vocabulary Cards: "Animals in Winter"
- Photo Cards: *apple, ball, balloon, banana, box, butter, carrots, celery, cherry, corn, dime, dog, egg, envelope, feather, grapes, hair, jar, kitten, leaf, lemon, lock, nail, newspaper, pea, peach, pear, penny, pie, pillow, pizza, plate, pumpkin, quarter, rose, shell, soap, strawberry, toothbrush, watch, watermelon*

ELL

Basic and Academic Vocabulary Display the **Photo Cards** from the lesson and pair English Language Learners with fluent speakers. Have partners make up sentences that describe the pictured items. Encourage them to use more than one descriptive word. Write children's sentences, read them chorally, and ask: *What descriptive words did you use in your sentence? What are other descriptive words you can use?*

Grammar

Describing Words (Adjectives)

MODEL Use the **Oral Vocabulary Cards** for "Animals in Winter" to review describing words. Remind children that describing words tell more about something.

- Write the first line below the ellipse on Card 1 on the board and then read it aloud: *When snow falls and cold winds blow, people stay warm and cozy inside their homes.*

- *What are the describing words in this sentence?* (cold, warm, cozy) Explain that the word *cold* is a describing word. *Wind can be cool and refreshing on a hot day. The describing word* cold *tells us what type of wind is happening in this selection.* Explain that describing words help listeners or readers paint a picture of something in their minds.

- Show children the photograph on Card 4. *What are some describing words we can use to talk about snow?* (cold, white, wet, soft)

PRACTICE Display the **Photo Card** for *pumpkin*. Name the card. Tell children that you will say some words to describe the pumpkin and then you will say a complete sentence about the pumpkin.

- *First I look at the picture. I see that the pumpkin is orange. It has a round shape. There are lines in the pumpkin with bumps between them, which are called ridges or ribs. I carved a pumpkin before, so I know pumpkins have smooth skin. The words to describe the pumpkin are* orange, round, ribbed, *and* smooth. *I can make a sentence from those words. My sentence is:* The pumpkin has smooth, orange skin.

- Distribute Photo Cards to children. Have each child name his or her card, list words to describe the pictured item, and say a complete sentence to describe the item on the card. After each sentence, ask other children to list more words to describe the object. If children have difficulty, ask them to tell you the shape, color, taste, or texture of the object.

Writing

Independent Writing: Sentences

Display the chart children created in the Shared Writing activity.

BRAINSTORM

WRITING TRAIT: WORD CHOICE Explain that children will write about what they might do if they visited Bear's cave. First they need to select the right words to express their ideas.

Think Aloud Good writers use clear and interesting words so the reader can understand what they wrote. I'll think about what I'd do if I visited Bear's cave. It would be a good place to curl up and **hibernate**. So I'll use the words *rests* and *sleeps*.

Ask children to think of things they would do if they visited Bear's cave. List their ideas on chart paper to use as a reference.

PREWRITE

Write the following sentence frame on the board.

_____ _____ _____and_____.

- Complete the sentence by writing your name in the first frame and the words *will rest* and *sleep* in the second, third, and fourth frames. Read the completed sentence aloud as you track the print.

- Have children select two things that they will do if they visit Bear's cave using the chart paper list and Word Wall.

DRAFT

- Have children write their names in the first frames and what they might do in Bear's cave in the other frames.

- Ask children to add a drawing to illustrate their sentence. Collect and save children's work to use tomorrow.

Write About It
Ask children to draw a picture of a small animal in the snow and label it.

Objectives

- Write sentences
- Begin to understand writing trait: word choice
- Use letter knowledge to write words in a sentence
- Understand and use future tense when speaking

Materials

- Shared Writing chart from Day 1

5-Day Writing

	Sentences
DAY 1	Shared: A Chart
DAY 2	Interactive: Sentences
DAY 3	Independent: Prewrite and Draft Sentences
DAY 4	Independent: Revise and Edit Sentences
DAY 5	Independent: Publish and Present

ELL

Use New Language Display the bear cave on page 7 of the **Trade Book**. Have children describe what they would do if they were in the cave with the bear. Record their responses and ask children to illustrate them.

Transitions That Teach

While children are packing up, have them tell about what they like to do on a **clear** day, when the skies are sunny.

DAY 4
At a Glance

WHOLE GROUP

Oral Language
- Build Robust Vocabulary

Comprehension ✓
- Read Aloud: "The Mitten"

Vocabulary
- Words That Compare
- Story Words: *cave, lair, den*

Phonemic Awareness ✓
- Phoneme Blending

Phonics ✓
- Picture Sort
- Blend with *-id*
- Decodable Reader: *Pat and Tip*

Writing
- Independent Writing: Revise and Edit Sentences

SMALL GROUP
- Differentiated Instruction, pages 1778–1803

Oral Language

 Talk About It ## Build Robust Vocabulary

WHAT WE WEAR IN COLD WEATHER
Talk with children about how people dress in response to weather. *What clothes might you wear in cold weather to keep warm? What would you wear on your head? What would you wear on your hands?*

CREATE A CHART
Draw a figure as shown, or use **Teaching Chart G3**. Write the title and read the words as you track the print from left to right.

Think Aloud Let's dress this boy so he can **experience** the cold weather on a **clear** day. In cold weather we wear hats to keep our heads warm. I will draw a hat on the boy and write *hat* next to it. What else should the boy wear in the cold weather?

Add children's ideas, drawing and labeling each item of clothing they suggest. Read the words with children as you track the print.

Dressed for Cold Weather — scarf, hat, coat, boots

ELL
ENGLISH LANGUAGE LEARNERS

Beginning

Confirm Understanding
Use the clothed figure to review vocabulary. For example, say: *We wear a hat when it's cold. A hat keeps our head warm.* Point to the hat and ask: *What is this?* (a hat) Repeat with other clothing items.

Intermediate

Enhance Understanding
Ask children questions such as: *What do we wear in winter to keep our feet dry? What do we wear around our necks when it's cold outside?* Guide children to answer in complete sentences.

Advanced

Compare and Contrast
Have children dictate sentences that describe clothes worn in winter and clothes worn in summer. Then encourage children to compare how the two types of clothing are alike and different.

Listen for Rhythm

IDENTIFY RHYTHM

Remind children that some poems have a rhythm or a regular beat. Tell children that they can clap to the beat of the poem as it is read.

Theme: *How Weather Affects Us*

FOGGY WEATHER RHYME

Tell children that they will recite "Little Dog," the rhyme they learned this week about how weather affects a dog. Play the rhyme and have children join in.

Have children listen to the beginning sound in the words *dog, sat,* and *day.* Explain that *sat* doesn't belong because it doesn't begin with /d/. Repeat with *so, sat,* and *log.* (*log*) Provide children with other sets of words and ask children to say which word doesn't belong: *gray, say, sell; bump, job, jump.*

Ask children to name and describe the type of weather featured in the rhyme. *How does the weather affect Little Dog?* (He gets lost, bumps into a log, and sits on a frog because he can't see well in the fog.)

Have children list other types of weather and identify how Little Dog would be affected by the weather. For example, Little Dog might not be able to find a favorite toy that is buried in snow.

How does weather affect your pets or animals you see outside? (Dogs pant in hot weather. Birds bathe in water in hot weather. Cats lie in sunlight in cool weather.)

Little Dog

Little Dog had lost his way

In a fog so thick and gray.

First, Dog bumped into a log.

Next, he sat upon a frog.

"Oh," Dog said in a ho-hum way.

"I guess this just is not my day!"

Objectives

- Discuss winter clothing and complete a diagram
- Use oral vocabulary words *clear, cozy, experience, hibernate,* and *retreat*
- Categorize phonemes
- Respond to rhythm and rhyme in poetry
- Dictate or write information for lists

Materials

- Graphic Organizer; Teaching Chart G3
- Listening Library Audio CD

Oral Vocabulary

Have children use each word in a sentence about this week's stories.

clear	cozy
experience	hibernate
retreat	

Review Work with children to review last week's words. Ask children to list *months* in which they experience *mild* temperatures. *In which season are you likely to wear a coat? Show me what it looks like when you* shiver. *Why is it important to listen to a warning?*

mild	month
season	shiver
warning	

Digital Learning

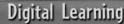

Rhyme on **Listening Library Audio CD**

Objectives

- Listen and respond to a folktale
- Visualize to help understand a story

Materials

- Read-Aloud Anthology: "The Mitten," pp. 105–108
- Story Patterns; Teacher's Resource Book, pp. 171–198

ELL

Reinforce Understanding

Distribute copies of the Story Patterns. As you read the story, point to each animal and have children name it. Move each animal to the mitten. Have children repeat sentences such as: *The mouse is in the mitten.*

Readers Theater

BUILDING LISTENING AND SPEAKING SKILLS

Distribute copies of "So Long as There's Weather," Read-Aloud Anthology pages 185–186. Have children practice performing the play throughout the unit. Assign parts and have children present the play or perform it as a dramatic reading at the end of the unit.

Interactive
Read Aloud
Listening Comprehension

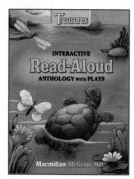

Read Aloud

GENRE: FOLKTALE

Explain that "The Mitten" is a **folktale**, a story told by parents to children and passed down from family to family. Remind children of the other folktales you have read, such as "The Gingerbread Man" and "The Little Red Hen." See the information about this folktale in the **Read-Aloud Anthology** lesson.

CULTURAL PERSPECTIVES

Tell children that "The Mitten" folktale is from the Ukraine, a country in eastern Europe that has very long, cold winters.

READ "THE MITTEN"

- **MODEL ASKING QUESTIONS ABOUT VISUALIZING** Use the Think Alouds provided at point of use in the folktale for the strategy.

- **MODEL FLUENT READING** Read aloud the folktale with fluent expression. Stop occasionally so that children can picture the story events in their mind.

- **EXPAND VOCABULARY** See page 105 of the Read-Aloud Anthology to teach new words using the **Define/Example/Ask** routine.

Respond to Literature

TALK ABOUT IT Ask children to discuss the big idea of this folktale.

- *How do you know a mouse could really fit in a boy's mitten? Could a bear and other creatures also fit in? How do you know? Would a mitten be a good place to* **hibernate**?

- *Was the ending of the story realistic or make-believe? What did you picture in your mind as you listened?* Have children draw a picture.

Write About It

Ask children to write a new ending to the story and illustrate it.

Vocabulary

Words That Compare

REVIEW WORDS THAT COMPARE
Ask three children to help you. Give each child one paper strip. Have children hold the strips vertically, making sure the bottom edges of the paper strips are evenly matched. Model pointing to each strip and saying which is tall, taller, and tallest. *Each time I say the word* tall, taller, *or* tallest, *point to the child holding the strip of paper that matches the word.* Read the following story:

> *Three sisters, Nicky, Vicky, and Micky went out to play. Nicky climbed a* tall *tree. Then Vicky climbed a* taller *tree. Micky climbed the* tallest *tree of all.*

Have children turn the strips of paper horizontally. Point to each strip and say which is long, longer, and longest.

Each time I say the word long, longer, *or* longest, *point to the child holding the strip of paper that matches the word.* Continue reading the story:

> *Then the three sisters decided to go running. Nicky ran down a* long *road before she got tired. Vicky ran down an even* longer *road before she got tired. And Micky ran down the* longest *road of all.*

Display pictures of the same item in three different sizes. Encourage children to sort the items into 3 categories — big, bigger, biggest.

Story Words: *cave, lair, den*

Display pages 12–13 of *Bear Snores On*. Explain that wild animals live in dens. Remind children that *cave, lair,* and *den* mean almost the same thing. Ask if children have ever been to a house that had a cozy room called a *den*.

If you could have your very own lair in which to **hibernate**, *what would it be like?* Tell children to illustrate and label pictures of their lairs.

TIME TO MOVE!

Have children hum a song for a *long* time, a *longer* time, and the *longest* time. After humming, ask them to say in a complete sentence how long they hummed. For example: *I hummed longer than I did before.*

Objectives

- Use words that compare
- Identify and sort pictures of objects into conceptual categories
- Review story words *cave, lair, den*

Materials

- 3 strips of paper in three sizes
- pictures of the same item in different sizes
- Read-Aloud Trade Book: *Bear Snores On*

ELL

Reinforce Understanding
Cut paper rectangles in three different sizes and ask children to paste them on a sheet of paper from tall to tallest and and from long to longest.

Objectives

- Blend sounds to form one-syllable words
- Review sound-spellings for /b/b, /l/ll, /e/e, /h/h
- Blend onsets and rimes to form simple words

Materials

- Photo Cards: *fan, hat, mop, net; book, bike, exit, elbow, horse, hat, lock, lamp*
- Word-Building Cards
- pocket chart
- Activity Book, p. 29
- Practice Book, pp. 157–158

ELL

Pronunciation Display and have children name Photo Cards from this and prior lessons to reinforce sound-letter relationships and word meanings. Point to a card and ask: *What do you see?* (a book) *What is the sound at the beginning of the word* book? (/b/). *What is the letter at the beginnig of the word* book? (b). Repeat using Photo Cards with words that begin with the sounds /l/, /e/, and /h/.

Phonemic Awareness

✔ Phoneme Blending

Model

Display **Photo Cards** for *hat, mop, net, fan.*

Repeat the routine using the Photo Cards for *hat, net, fan.*

I'm thinking of something I use to clean the floor. It is a /m/ /o/ /p/. Listen as I say each sound again: /m/ /o/ /p/. I can blend these sounds: *mop.* Say the sounds with me: /m/ /o/ /p/. Now say the word with me: *mop.*

Guided Practice/Practice

Say each riddle. Children blend the sounds to solve the riddle. Guide practice with the first one. Create riddles with children.

Use the clues to solve each riddle.

I'm thinking of something in which food is cooked. It is a /p/ /o/ /t/. What is it? (pot)

I'm thinking of something you use to hit a baseball. It is a /b/ /a/ /t/. What is it? (bat)

Phonics

✔ Picture Sort

Model

Place **Word-Building Card** b in the pocket chart.

Repeat for *e, h,* and *l.*

This is letter *b.* Letter *b* stands for the /b/ sound.

Hold up the Photo Card for *book.*

This is a *book. Book* begins with /b/. I will place *book* under the letter *b,* because the letter *b* stands for /b/.

Guided Practice/Practice

Children sort the Photo Cards by initial letter. Guide practice with the first card.

Build Fluency: Sound-Spellings

 Display the following **Word-Building Cards**: *a, b, c, d, e, f, h, i, l, m, n, o, p, r, s, t*. Have children chorally say each sound. Repeat and vary the pace.

✓ Blend with *-id*

Model

Place Word-Building Card *l* in the pocket chart.	This is letter *l*. It stands for /l/. Say /l/. 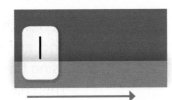
Place the letters *id* in the pocket chart, leaving space after the *l*. Point to the letters *i* and *d*.	These are the letters *i* and *d*. The letters *i* and *d* stand for /i/ and /d/. Let's blend these two sounds together: /iiid/. 
Place the letters *id* next to letter *l*. Move your hand from left to right below the letters. Repeat the routine with *hid*.	The beginning sound in the word is /l/ and the rest of the word is /id/. Let's blend the beginning sound and the rest of the word together: /lllliiid/, *lid*. 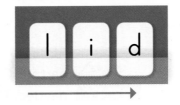

Guided Practice/Practice

Children blend the onset and rime in other words that end with *-id*. Guide practice with *bid*, using the routine.	bid did rid Sid
	What do you notice about the words *lid, hid, bid, did, rid,* and *Sid*?
	(They all end with the letters *id*; they end with the sounds /id/; they rhyme.)

For Tier 2 instruction, see page 1792.

Corrective Feedback

Blending: Sound Error Model the sound that children missed, then have them repeat the sound. For example, for the word *lid*, say: *My turn.* Tap under the letter *d* in the word *lid* and say: *Sound? What's the sound?* Then return to the beginning of the word. Say: *Let's start over.* Blend the word with children again.

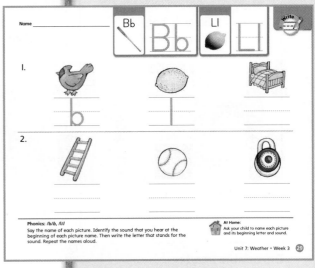

Activity Book, page 29
Practice Book, pages 157–158

Objectives

- Read decodable words with /b/b, /l/l, /e/e
- Read the words *a, and, are, have, I, is, play, you*
- Reread for fluency

Materials

- Decodable Reader: *Pat and Tip*
- Sound-Spelling Cards: *Egg, Bat, Lemon*

Decodable Text

For additional decodable passages, see pages 31–34 of the **Teacher's Resource Book**.

Decodable Reader

Read *Pat and Tip*

Pat and Tip

 REVIEW Review this week's high-frequency words and phonics skills using the word lists on the inside back cover of *Pat and Tip*.

Review the high-frequency words **a**, **and**, **are**, **have**, **I**, **is**, **play**, and **you** using the **Read/Spell/Write** routine. Then have children chorally read the high-frequency word list.

Review the phonics skills /e/e, /b/b, and /l/l using the *Egg, Bat,* and *Lemon* **Sound-Spelling Cards**. Then have children chorally read the decodable word list. Model blending as needed and note children who struggle while reading these words in a list and in text. Provide additional instruction and practice during Small Group time.

MODEL CONCEPTS ABOUT PRINT Guide children to follow along. *I open the book by turning the cover. Then I turn each page as I read it, starting with the first page and ending with the last page.*

REREAD FOR FLUENCY Have children reread the book with a partner. Circulate and listen in, providing corrective feedback as needed. Then have children reread the book independently.

I have a bat.
Can you play?

2

Ben can. Sam can.
Cam and Pam can.

3

Sam can bat.
Hit it Sam!

4

Can Ben bat?
Pop it Ben!

5

Pit, pat. It is rain!

6

Ben ran. Cam ran. Sam ran.
Pam, Pat, and Tip ran!

7

Pat and Tip are not sad.
Pat can sit. Tip can nap!

8

Decodable Reader

Writing

Independent Writing: Sentences

REVISE AND EDIT

Distribute children's sentences. Have them reread them and check for the following:

- Did I write my name at the top of my paper?

- Did I write a complete sentence on my paper?

- Did I use words that told clearly what I might do in Bear's cave?

- Did I draw a picture to illustrate my sentence?

- Did I begin my sentence with a capital letter and end with a period?

Circulate and help children as they review and revise their sentences. Check to make sure that sentences are grammatically correct. Have children use their phonetic knowledge and understanding of spelling conventions to self-correct any errors in their work. Tell them to add any details to their sentences to describe their ideas more. Have them share and discuss their sentences with a partner.

Ana

bear

Ana draws and writes.

Write About It

Ask children to draw and label a picture of themselves dancing with a bear.

Objectives

- **Capitalize the first letter in a sentence**
- **Use end punctuation**
- **Revise drafts by adding details**
- **Use letter knowledge to write words in a sentence**

Materials

- children's sentences from Day 3
- Writer's Checklist; Teacher's Resource Book, p. 205

5-Day Writing

Sentences	
DAY 1	Shared: A Chart
DAY 2	Interactive: Sentences
DAY 3	Independent: Prewrite and Draft Sentences
DAY 4	Independent: Revise and Edit Sentences
DAY 5	Independent: Publish and Present

ELL

Use New Language Ask children to help you list things that the bear in *Bear Snores On* does. Then have children draw the bear doing one of the listed things. Help children write a caption to go with their drawing.

Transitions That Teach

While they line up, have children describe a **cozy** place at home.

DAY 5
At a Glance

WHOLE GROUP

Oral Language
- Build Robust Vocabulary

Comprehension
- Strategy: Visualize
- Skill: Distinguish Between Fantasy and Reality
- Read Across Texts

Vocabulary
- Review High-Frequency Words
- Build Fluency
- Review Sound Words

Phonemic Awareness
- Phoneme Segmentation

Phonics
- Build Fluency
- Read Words
- Dictation

Writing
- Independent Writing: Publish and Present

SMALL GROUP

- Differentiated Instruction, pages 1778–1803

Review and Assess
Oral Language
Build Robust Vocabulary

REVIEW WORDS

Review this week's oral vocabulary words with children. Explain that all of the words will be used to discuss the life of a bear. Use the following questions to check children's understanding:

- What does a bear do when it **hibernates**?

- What kind of place can be a bear **retreat**?

- What types of things would help a bear be **cozy** in its retreat?

- Why would a bear want to find a **clear** river to catch fish?

- What kinds of things would you **experience** if you were a bear?

REVIEW A RHYME ABOUT WEATHER

Recite the rhyme "Little Dog" and ask children to join you. Have children name other words that rhyme with *way*. (*bay, clay, day, gray, hay, lay, may, pay, ray, say, stay*) List the rhyming words on chart paper.

Have children identify the type of weather mentioned in the rhyme and describe it. Ask them to name another type of weather and alter the rhyme to describe what would happen in that weather. For example: *Little Dog wants to stay. In the sun he likes to play.* Tell children to use their list of rhyming words to help them change the rhyme.

Review and Assess
Comprehension

STRATEGY Visualize

REFLECT ON THE STRATEGY Remind children that they have learned how to create pictures in their mind as they read some parts of a story. Creating these pictures can help them better **experience** and enjoy the story.

Think Aloud I can use the pictures of the story that I paint in my mind to help me decide which parts of a story are realistic and could happen in real life and which are fantasy.

SKILL Distinguish Between Fantasy and Reality

Review with children *Bear Snores On* and "The Mitten" to help them recall each selection. Then use the following questions to have children distinguish between fantasy and reality.

■ *What parts of* Bear Snores On *tell how bears really* **hibernate**?

■ *What parts of "The Mitten" tell what a child might really do?*

■ *What parts in* Bear Snores On *could not really happen? What parts in "The Mitten" could not really happen?*

Reading Across Texts

Create a Venn diagram to compare and contrast the fantasy story *Bear Snores On* and the expository selection "Let It Snow!" Have children talk about how the folktale "The Mitten" compares with the other two selections.

Bear Snores On
- fantasy story
- could not really happen
- illustrations
- lines that rhyme
- animals having fun in winter

Both
take place in winter

Let It Snow!
- nonfiction article
- about real people and things
- photographs
- does not rhyme
- people having fun in winter

Objectives

- Review visualizing
- Review fantasy and reality
- Compare and contrast genres, stories, and characters
- Listen to and share information

Materials

- Read-Aloud Trade Book: *Bear Snores On*
- Big Book of Explorations, Vol. 2: "Let It Snow!"
- Read-Aloud Anthology: "The Mitten"
- Activity Book, p. 31

Activity Book, page 31

Objectives

- Review the high-frequency words *this, do, and, what, for, you*
- Review sound words *bam, crack, crash, drip, drop, splash*
- Dictate or write information for lists

Materials

- High-Frequency Word Cards: *this, do, what, and, for, you*
- sound words on index cards: *bam, crack, crash, drip, drop, splash*

Fluency

Connected Text Have children reread this week's **Decodable Reader** with a partner. Circulate, listen in, and note those children who need additional instruction and practice reading this week's decodable and sight words.

Review and Assess

Vocabulary

High-Frequency Words

Distribute one of the following **High-Frequency Word Cards** to children: **this**, **do**, **and**, **what**, **for**, **you**. *When you hear the word that is on your card, stand and hold up your Word Card.*

- What do you *want to* do *today?*
- *Mike* and *Maria want to* do this for you.
- *The girls* and *boys are running around.*
- This *ball is* for you.
- Do *we have recess* this *afternoon?*

Build Fluency: Word Automaticity

Display the High-Frequency Word Cards. Point quickly to each card, at random, and have children read the word as fast as they can.

this	do	and
what	for	you

Sound Words

Ask children to list things that can make the following sounds: *drip, drop, splash, crack, bam,* and *crash*. Have children take turns creating sentences using one or more of the sound words.

Rapid Naming Display the sound words on index cards and have children read the words as quickly as they can.

TIME TO MOVE!

Have children create sentences using sound words and then act them out.

Review and Assess
Phonemic Awareness

Phoneme Segmentation

Objective
- Segment words into sounds

Materials
- Photo Cards: *man, mop, net*

Guided Practice

Display the **Photo Card** for *man*.

Repeat the routine with *mop* and *net*.

This is a *man*. Say *man* sound by sound with me: /m/ /a/ /n/. There are three sounds in *man*: /m/ /a/ /n/.

Practice

Say each word. Children repeat the word and then say the word sound by sound.

I will say a word. Repeat the word after me. Then say the word sound by sound.

pet	same	bet	sit
tape	pot	light	Tom
job	cake	fate	late

Objectives

- Read simple one-syllable words
- Write simple one-syllable words

Materials

- Word-Building Cards
- 7 index cards with: *Ben, did, do, for, Ted, What*, question mark
- 8 index cards with: *and, are, bib, cob, for, Lin, This*, period mark
- Sound Box
- markers
- WorkBoard Sound Boxes; Teacher's Resource Book, p. 136
- Activity Book, p. 32

Review and Assess
Phonics

Build Fluency: Sound-Spellings

Rapid Naming Display the following **Word-Building Cards**: *a, b, c, d, e, f, h, i, l, m, n, o, p, r, s, t*. Have children chorally say each sound as quickly as they can.

 ## Read Words

Apply

Distribute the first set of cards.	Let's read the sentence together.
	What did Ben do for Ted?
Have children stand in sequence.	
Repeat, using the other set of cards.	Let's read the sentence together.
	This cob and bib are for Lin.

 ## Dictation

Apply

Dictate sounds for children to spell.

Listen as I say a sound. Repeat the sound, then write the letter that stands for the sound.

/b/   /a/   /l/   /o/   /f/

/h/   /d/   /i/   /r/   /e/

Then dictate words for children to spell. Model for children how to use the **Sound Boxes** to segment the sounds in the word. Have them repeat.

Write the letters and words on the board for children to self-correct.

Now let's write some words. I will say a word. I want you to repeat the word, then think about how many sounds are in the word. Use your Sound Boxes to count the sounds. Then write one letter for each sound you hear.

pet   red   lap   den

bit   lot   bib   met

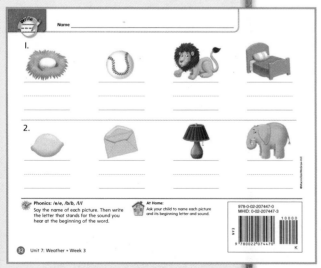

Activity Book, page 32

Review and Assess
Writing

Independent Writing: Sentences

PUBLISH

Gather children's sentences to make a class book.

- Brainstorm ideas for a title, such as "Bear Has Visitors."

- Have a few children create a book cover and write the title.

- Make holes along the edges of the cover and each page.

- Bind the pages together with yarn.

PRESENT

Have children read their sentences to the class. Ask them to act out their sentences.

SPEAKING, LISTENING, AND VIEWING

- Remind children to speak clearly and audibly, to listen to and share information with classmates, and to applaud one another's presentation.

- Place the finished book on a section of the Big Question Board.

- Have children select favorite samples of their work from their Writing Portfolios to share with classmates and family members. Have children discuss and dictate sentences about how they have changed as writers.

Write About It

Ask children to draw and label a picture of themselves at the party in Bear's cave.

Objectives

- Publish and present sentences
- Speak audibly and clearly

Materials

- children's sentences from Day 4

5-Day Writing

Sentences	
DAY 1	Shared: A Chart
DAY 2	Interactive: Sentences
DAY 3	Independent: Prewrite and Draft Sentences
DAY 4	Independence: Revise and Edit Sentences
DAY 5	Independent: Publish and Present

Transitions That Teach

While children pack up, have them describe places at home where they **retreat** for some quiet time.

An Outside Experience

Have children draw a picture of something they have done outdoors in sunny weather. Ask them to write the following caption on their drawing: *This is what I do in sunny weather.*

ELL

Partners When pairing children to make up sentences, pair English Language Learners with children who are more proficient. Write their sentences, read them together, and point out the high-frequency words.

Approaching Level

Oral Language

Objective	Preteach oral vocabulary
Materials	• none

THEME WORDS: *experience, hibernate*

- Have children talk about **experiences** they have had in different types of weather. *To experience means "to do, see, or be part of something." What did you* experience *when the weather was windy? Rainy? Snowy?* Guide children to respond in complete sentences. For example, remind them that sentences tell who and what. Recast their response in complete sentences.

- Point out that animals have different experiences than people. *Some animals* **hibernate***, or sleep all winter. What would it be like to* hibernate *in the winter?*

- Have children use the following sentence frames to generate complete oral sentences using the vocabulary words: *I would like to experience _____. When a bear hibernates, it _____.*

High-Frequency Words

Objective	Review high-frequency words
Materials	• **High-Frequency Word Cards:** *this, do, and, what*

REVIEW *this, do, and, what*

- Display the **High-Frequency Word Card** for **this**.

- **Read** Point to and say the word *this. This is the word* this. *It is a word we use when we talk about a person, place, or thing. This is my house.*

- **Spell** *The word* this *is spelled* t-h-i-s. Have children read and spell *this.*

- **Write** Finally, have children write the word *this*. Repeat the routine using the words **do**, **and**, and **what**.

- Have children work with a partner to make up sentences using the words. Ask them to talk about a fun school experience they have had.

HIGH-FREQUENCY WORDS REVIEW

Display the High-Frequency Word Cards for words previously taught, one card at a time, as children chorally read and spell the word. Mix and repeat. Note words children need to review.

Tier 2

Approaching Level

Phonemic Awareness

Objective Identify initial sounds /b/, /e/, /l/

Materials
- **Photo Cards:** *banana, bike, book, butter, egg, elbow, elevator, exit, lamp, light, lightning, lock*

PHONEME ISOLATION

Model

- Display the **Photo Card** for *bike. This is a* bike. *Listen to the beginning sound:* /b/. Bike *begins with* /b/. Repeat with *egg* and *lock.*

Guided Practice/Practice

- Display the Photo Cards. Have children take turns selecting a picture, naming it, and saying the initial sound. Guide practice with the first card.

- Have children note the position of their mouths and tongues as they say /b/, /e/, and /l/.

Phonics

Objective Recognize words with initial /b/b, /e/e, and /l/l

Materials
- **Sound-Spelling Cards:** *Bat, Egg, Lemon* • **Word-Building Cards**
- **Photo Cards:** *balloon, banana, bat, bike, book, bus, egg, elbow, elevator, envelope, exit, ladder, ladybug, lamp, lemon, lock*

PRETEACH: RECOGNIZE /b/b, /e/e, /l/l

Model

- Display the Photo Card for *bus* and the *Bat* **Sound-Spelling Card.** *This letter is* b. B *stands for the* /b/ *sound. I'll put* b *on* bus *because* bus *begins with* /b/. Repeat with *elbow* and *ladder.*

- Say each letter sound as you trace the letter on the small **Word-Building Card.**

Guided Practice/Practice

- Display the Photo Cards. Point to a card and have children say the name, repeat the initial sound, and identify the letter. Continue with the remaining cards.

- Have children trace *b, e,* and *l* on small Word-Building Cards.

- Identify classroom objects with names that begin with *b, e,* or *l.*

SOUND-SPELLINGS REVIEW

Tier 2

Display Word-Building Cards *m, a, s, p, t, i, n, c, o, f, h, d, r, e, b,* and *l,* one at a time. Have children chorally say the sound. Repeat and vary the pace.

Corrective Feedback

Mnemonic Error Display the *Egg, Bat,* and *Lemon* Sound-Spelling Cards. Say: *These are the letters* e, b, *and* l. E *stands for the* /e/ *sound. Let's say it together:* /eee/. B *stands for the* /b/ *sound. Let's say it together:* /b/. L *stands for the* /l/ *sound. Let's say it together:* /lll/. What words can help us remember the e, b, and l sounds? What are the sounds? What are the letters?

ELL

Extra Practice Provide additional practice in recognizing and naming letters for children whose native languages do not use the symbols of the Latin alphabet.

Weather Experiences

Have children draw a picture of a weather experience, such as playing in the rain or snow. Ask them to write a sentence telling about the experience, using high-frequency words.

Puppet

ELL

Sound-Letter Relationships Provide additional practice in pronouncing and blending the initial /b/, /e/, /l/, /t/ sounds and naming the corresponding letters as children point to them.

On Level

High-Frequency Words

Objective Review high-frequency words *this, do, and, what, you, for*
Materials • **High-Frequency Word Cards:** *this, do, and, what, you, for*

REVIEW

- Display the **High-Frequency Word Card** for **this**.
- **Read** Point to and say the word *this. This is the word* this. *It is a word we use when we talk about a person, place, or thing. This is my brother.*
- **Spell** *The word* this *is spelled* t-h-i-s. Have children read and spell *this.*
- **Write** Finally, have children write the word *this.*
- Repeat with **do, and, what, you,** and **for**. Then have partners make up sentences using the words.

Phonemic Awareness/Phonics

Objective Review blending sounds to form words and recognizing and blending initial /b/b, /e/e, /l/l, and /t/t
Materials • **Word-Building Cards** • pocket chart • **Puppet**

PHONEME BLENDING

Model

- *Listen as Happy says the sounds in the word* Ben: /b/ /e/ /n/. *Now Happy will blend the sounds: /beeennn/,* Ben. *Happy blended /b/ /e/ /n/ together to say the word* Ben.

Practice

- Have the **Puppet** say /r/ /a/ /n/. Ask children to repeat the sounds. *Now you blend the sounds and say the word: /rrraaannn/, ran.* Continue with the following:

| /r/ /e/ /d/ | /e/ /d/ | /b/ /e/ /d/ |
| /b/ /e/ /t/ | /r/ /i/ /p/ | /b/ /i/ /l/ |

REVIEW /b/*b*, /e/*e*, /l/*l*

- Display **Word-Building Card** *b. The name of this letter is* b. B *stands for the /b/ sound we hear at the beginning of* bet. *I'll hold up the* b *card because* bet *begins with /b/.* Repeat with *e* and *edge,* and *l* and *leg.*
- Say: *bed, elbow, bit, lot, end, bet, lit, led, bat, echo, lip, edge.* Have children hold up the Word-Building Card that corresponds to the beginning sound. Guide practice with the first two words.

Beyond Level

High-Frequency Words/Vocabulary

Objective Review high-frequency words
Materials • none

✔ ACCELERATE

- Write *kind* and *every* on the board.

- **Read** Point to and say the word *kind*. *This is the word* kind. *It means "caring and sweet." I like to be around kind people.*

- **Spell** *The word* kind *is spelled* k-i-n-d. *What's the first sound in* kind? *The first sound is /k/. That's why the first letter is* k. Continue with /ī/i, /n/n, and /d/d. Have children read and spell *kind*.

- **Write** Have children write the word *kind*. Repeat with *every*.

- Have children work with a partner to make up oral sentences using the words *kind* and *every*.

EXPAND ORAL VOCABULARY

- **Multiple-Meaning Words** Review the meaning of the oral vocabulary word *clear* with children. Explain that a *multiple-meaning word* is a word that has more than one meaning.

- Say: *Another meaning of the word* clear *is "easy to see through." Most windows are easy to see through because glass is* clear. *A cardboard box is not* clear, *so you cannot see through it.*

- Have children take turns using the new meaning of *clear* in a sentence. Then tell children that they will work with a partner to come up with a question using the word *clear*.

Phonics

Objective Read words with /l/l, /b/b, and /e/e
Materials • **Word-Building Cards**

✔ ENRICH

- Have children listen as you blend these sounds together: /b/ /e/ /d/, /beeed/. Ask: *What word did I say?* (bed) Repeat with *elf*.

- Write the following words on the board for children to blend and read: *below, mob, ball, end, bath, lunch, will, elf*.

- Display **Word-Building Cards** *a, b, c, d, e, h, i, l, m, n, o, p, r, s, t,* and *w*. Have partners use the letters to build as many words as they can. Ask them to list the words and share their lists.

ELL ENGLISH LANGUAGE LEARNERS

Oral Language Warm-Up

Content Objective Learn theme vocabulary
Language Objective Repeat and say a poem to demonstrate understanding
Materials • **Listening Library Audio CD** • **Trade Book:** *Bear Snores On*

BUILD BACKGROUND KNOWLEDGE

All Language Levels

Window Watching
See the window I have here,
So big and wide and square.
Draw a square in the air.
I can stand in front of it
Stand up straight.
And see the things out there.
Point into the distance.

- Continue developing vocabulary around the unit theme "Weather" using "Window Watching." Display a picture of a snow storm. Teach the word *snowstorm* as you point to the snow falling down. Have children repeat the word three times.

- Play "Window Watching" on the **Listening Library Audio CD**. Display the picture of the snow. Explain that in a snowstorm snow covers the ground, trees, and houses. Use the pictures in *Bear Snores On* to show the effects of a snowstorm.

- Then teach children the poem by playing it several times and having them act out the motions. Emphasize the key words that describe what the children are doing, such as *see* and *stand*.

- Ask children to tell about what they might see if they look out of a window during a snowstorm. Build on their responses. For example: *You see snowflakes falling. The snow covers the ground.*

Academic Language

Language Objective Use academic language in classroom conversations

All Language Levels

- This week's academic words are **boldfaced** throughout the lesson. Define the word in context and provide a clear example from the selection. Then ask children to generate an example or a word with a similar meaning.

Academic Language Used in Whole Group Instruction

Oral Vocabulary Words	Vocabulary and Grammar Concepts	Strategy and Skill Words
clear cozy experience hibernate retreat	sound words describing words	visualize fantasy reality; realistic describing

Cognates

Help children identify similarities and differences in pronunciation and spelling between English words and Spanish cognates:

Cognates

experience	*experiencia*
hibernate	*hibernar*
reality	*realidad*
fantasy	*fantasía*

ELL ENGLISH LANGUAGE LEARNERS

Vocabulary

Language Objective Demonstrate understanding and use of key words by describing how the weather affects what people and animals do

Materials • **Visual Vocabulary Resources**

✔ PRETEACH KEY VOCABULARY

All Language Levels

Use the **Visual Vocabulary Resources** to preteach the weekly oral vocabulary words *clear, cozy, experience, hibernate,* and *retreat.* Focus on one or two words per day. Use the routine on the cards.

- Define the word in English and provide the example given.

- Define the word in Spanish, if appropriate, and indicate if the word is a cognate.

- Display the picture and explain how it illustrates or demonstrates the word.

- Then engage children in structured partner-talk about the image, using the key word.

- Ask children to chorally say the word three times.

- Point out any known sound-spellings or focus on a key aspect of phonemic awareness related to the word.

PRETEACH FUNCTION WORDS AND PHRASES

All Language Levels

Use the Visual Vocabulary Resources to preteach the function words *all* and *none.* Focus on one word per day. Use the detailed routine on the cards.

- Define the word in English and, if appropriate, in Spanish. Point out if the word is a cognate.

- Refer to the picture and engage children in talk about the word. For example, children will partner-talk using sentence frames, or they will listen to sentences and replace a word or phrase with the new function word.

- Ask children to chorally repeat the word three times.

TEACH BASIC WORDS

Beginning/Intermediate

Use the Visual Vocabulary Resources to teach the basic words *squeak, chomp, groan, sneeze, snore,* and *tweet.* Teach these "ways animals make noise" words using the routine provided on the card.

Visual Vocabulary Resources

What We Do

Have children pick a type of weather and draw a picture of what they like to do outside during that type of weather. Ask them to write the following sentence frame on their picture: *I do this in _____ weather.* Help them complete the sentence.

ELL

Partners When pairing children to make up sentences, pair English Language Learners with children who are more proficient. Write their sentences, read them together, and point out the high-frequency words.

Approaching Level

Oral Language

Objective   Reinforce oral vocabulary
Materials   • none

THEME WORDS: *experience, hibernate*

- *We have talked about different **experiences** we have had in different types of weather. Would it be a better experience to make a snowman with a friend or to watch it snow on television? Why?*

- *Some animals **hibernate** during the winter season. Would you like to hibernate during the winter? Why or why not?*

- *Which experience would you most like to try—hibernating like bears or shedding your skin like a snake? Why?* Have children answer questions in complete sentences.

High-Frequency Words

Objective   Review high-frequency words
Materials   • **High-Frequency Word Cards:** *this, do, and, what*
                • **Sound-Spelling WorkBoards**

Tier 2

RETEACH WORDS: *this, do, and, what*

- Distribute a **WorkBoard** to each child. Then display the **High-Frequency Word Card** for **do**.

- Use the **Read/Spell/Write** routine to reteach the word. Point to and say the word. *This is the word* do. *We use this word when we want to participate in something: I want to* do *that.* Do *is spelled* d-o. Have children read and spell *do*. Then have them write the word on their WorkBoards.

- Repeat the routine with the words **this**, **and**, and **what**.

- Have children work with a partner to make up sentences using the words *this, do, and,* and *what*. Ask them to talk about what they would like to experience when they grow up.

CUMULATIVE REVIEW

Display the High-Frequency Word Cards for words previously taught, one card at a time, as children chorally read and spell the word. Mix and repeat. Note words children need to review.

Approaching Level

Phonemic Awareness

Objective Blend sounds to form words
Materials • **Puppet**

Puppet

PHONEME BLENDING

Tier 2

Model

- *Listen as Happy says the sounds in the word* Ben: /b/ /e/ /n/.
  Now Happy will blend the sounds: /beeennn/, Ben. *Happy blended*
  /b/ /e/ /n/ *together to say the word* Ben. *Repeat with* den.

Practice

- Have the **Puppet** segment *sell:* /s/ /e/ /l/. Ask children to repeat.
  Now blend the sounds and say the word: /ssseeelll/, sell. *Repeat*
  with the following:

  /r/ /e/ /d/   /l/ /e/ /d/   /b/ /e/ /d/   /b/ /e/ /t/

Phonics

Objective Reinforce letter-sound correspondence for /b/b, /e/e, /l/l, /d/d, /r/r
Materials • **Sound-Spelling Cards:** *Bat, Egg, Lemon, Dolphin, Rose*
• **Sound-Spelling WorkBoards** • **Word-Building Cards**
• **Decodable Reader:** *Pat and Tip*

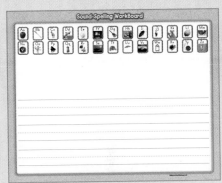

Sound-Spelling WorkBoard

RECOGNIZE /b/*b*, /e/*e*, /l/*l*, /d/*d*, /r/*r*

Model

- Display the *Bat* **Sound-Spelling Card.** *The letter* b *stands for the* /b/ *sound as in* bat. *Let's say the word and sound together.* Repeat with *d, e, l,* and *r.*

- Trace *b* on a **Word-Building Card.** *We will trace* b *on the cards when we hear* /b/. *Say:* Barry bought blueberries. *Repeat using* Diana the dinosaur dines *for* /d/; Ellen enjoys an egg *for* /e/; Lee lives on Lime Lane *for* /l/; *and* Rose rides on red roads *for* /r/.

Decodable Reader

Guided Practice/Practice

- Distribute **WorkBoards.** *Say:* bike, read, den, lion, butter, rip, egg, leg, roof, elbow, butterfly, *and* dish. Have children write the letter that stands for the initial sound in each word. Guide them with the first two words.

- **Read the Decodable Reader** Read *Pat and Tip* with children. Have them echo-read each page. Chorally reread the story.

CUMULATIVE REVIEW

Display Word-Building Cards *m, a, s, p, t, i, n, c, o, f, h, d, r, e, b, l,* one at a time. Point to the letters in a random order. Have children chorally say the sound. Repeat and vary the pace.

Corrective Feedback

Blending: Sound Error
Model the sound that children missed, then have them repeat the sound. For example, for the word *sell,* say: *My turn.* Tap under the letter *e* in the word *sell* and say: *Sound? What's the sound?* Then return to the beginning of the word. Say: *Let's start over.* Blend the word with children again.

Sound-Spelling WorkBoard

Decodable Reader

On Level

Phonics

Objective	Review recognizing and blending initial /b/b, /e/e, /l/l, and /t/t
Materials	• **Word-Building Cards** • pocket chart
	• **Sound-Spelling WorkBoards** • **Decodable Reader:** *Pat and Tip*

REVIEW /b/b, /e/e, /l/l, /t/t

- Display **Word-Building Card** b. *The name of this letter is* b. B *stands for the /b/ sound we hear at the beginning of* bed. *I'll hold up the* b *card because* bed *begins with /b/.* Repeat with e and *exit*, l and *lemon*, t and *table*.

- Distribute small Word-Building Cards. Say: *bag, tuna, bat, egg, tiger, leg, love, belt, edge, end, laugh, little, buckle, toast.* Have children repeat the initial sound of each word and hold up the corresponding card. Guide practice with the first two words.

- **Blend Words** Place Word-Building Cards b, e, and t in the pocket chart. Have children identify each letter. Move your hand from left to right below the letters as children blend the sounds to say the word. Continue with *let, bell, tell,* and *ebb*.

- Have children write b, e, and t on their **WorkBoards** as they say /b/, /e/, and /t/. Repeat with l, e, t.

- **Read the Decodable Reader** Read *Pat and Tip* with children. Have them reread each page. Then chorally reread the story.

Beyond Level

Phonics

Objective	Read words with /o/o, /ō/o_e, /i/i, /ī/i_e, /a/a, /ā/a_e
Materials	• **Word-Building Cards** • pocket chart

ACCELERATE

- Display Word-Building Cards r, o, d in a pocket chart. Review the letter-sound associations and blend the word with children. Then add an e and review how a final silent e changes the vowel sound.

- Write the following word pairs on the board for children to blend and read: *rod/rode, ton/tone, dim/dime, cod/code, rid/ride, Tam/tame.*

ELL   ENGLISH LANGUAGE LEARNERS

Access to Core Content

Content Objective Develop listening comprehension

Language Objective Discuss text using key words and sentence frames

Materials • **ELL Resource Book**, pp. 196–203

PRETEACH TRADE BOOK

All Language Levels

Use the Interactive Question-Response Guide on **ELL Resource Book** pages 196–203 to introduce children to *Bear Snores On*. Preteach half of the selection on Day 1 and half on Day 2.

■ Use the prompts provided in the guide to develop meaning and vocabulary. Use the partner-talk and whole-class responses to engage children and increase student talk.

■ When completed, revisit the selection and prompt children to talk about the illustrations. Provide sentence starters as needed and build on children's responses to develop language.

ELL Resource Book

Trade Book

Beginning	Intermediate	Advanced
Use Visuals During the Interactive Reading, select several pictures. Describe them and have children summarize what you said.	**Summarize** During the Interactive Reading, select a few lines of text. After you read them and explain them, have children summarize the text.	**Expand** During the Interactive Reading, select a larger portion of text. After you read it and explain it, have children summarize the text.

Approaching Level

High-Frequency Words

Objective Recognize high-frequency words *this, do, and, what*

Materials
- **High-Frequency Word Cards:** *this, do, and, what*
- **Word-Building Cards**

REVIEW WORDS: *this, do, and, what*

- Display the **High-Frequency Word Card** for **this**. Say the word and have children repeat it. Point to each letter and have children name it.

- Distribute small **Word-Building Cards** *t, h, i, s*. Model putting the letters together to form the word *this*. Then have children form *this*.

- Repeat the above routines with **do**, **and**, and **what**.

- Have children create cloze sentences for the high-frequency words *this, do, and,* and *what*. For example: *I like peanut butter _____ jelly sandwiches.* Ask children to point to and say the word that completes each sentence.

CUMULATIVE REVIEW

Display the High-Frequency Word Cards for words previously taught, one card at a time, as children chorally read and spell the word. Mix and repeat. Note words children need to review.

Phonemic Awareness

Objective Segment words into separate sounds

Materials • **Puppet**

PHONEME SEGMENTATION

Tier 2

Model
- Have the **Puppet** say the word *fan* and segment it. *Listen as Happy segments the word* fan: /f/ /a/ /n/. *Let's count the number of sounds in the word:* /f/, /a/, /n/. Fan *has three sounds.* Repeat with the word *ban.*

Guided Practice/Practice
- *Listen as Happy says a word:* hid. *Let's segment Happy's word into sounds:* hid, /h/ /i/ /d/. *How many sounds do you hear?*

- Have children segment each of the following words and count the number of sounds.

can	rid	let	bin	den	tell
late	bake	sell	elk	pan	set

Puppet

Approaching Level

Phonics

Objective Blend sounds to form words and build fluency
Materials • **Word-Building Cards** • pocket chart

REVIEW

Tier 2

Model

■ Place **Word-Building Card** *b* in the pocket chart. *The name of this letter is* b. *The letter* b *stands for the /b/ sound. Say /b/. What is the letter? What is the sound?*

■ Repeat with the letters *e* and *d*, forming the word *bed*. *Listen as I blend the three sounds together: /beeed/, bed. What is the word? Let's say the sounds and blend the word together.*

Guided Practice/Practice

■ Give *l*, *i*, and *p* cards to three children. Have them name their letters and say the sounds: /l/ /i/ /p/. *Now blend the sounds together and say the word: /llliiip/, lip.* Have children blend the sounds to say these words: *rip, hip, sip, lap, map, tap.*

Build Fluency

■ Have children blend *bed, lip, rip, hip, sip, lap, map,* and *tap* as quickly as they can.

Decodable Reader

Objective Preteach Decodable Reader *Pat and Tip*
Materials • **Decodable Reader:** *Pat and Tip*

PRETEACH *Pat and Tip*

■ **Preview** Display the cover of the book and read the title. Open to the title page and point to the title. Have children sound out each word as you run your finger under it. *Who is in the picture? What are they doing? What do you think this story is about?*

■ Page through the book. Ask children what they see in each picture. Point out and name the rebus. Ask children to find and point to the words *and, I, have, a, you, play,* and *are.*

■ **Read the Book** Read the book chorally with children. Have them point to each word as they read it. Tell them to blend the sounds in the words together as they read. Provide corrective feedback as needed.

■ **Check Comprehension** Ask children to use the high-frequency words to talk about the pictures. *What are Pat and Tip doing? What else are children doing in the pictures?*

Decodable Reader

ON YOUR OWN

What Will Pat and Tip Do Next?

Have children draw pictures to show what the weather might be like the next day and what Pat and Tip might do. Have them write sentences about their pictures.

On Level

Decodable Reader

Objective Reread *Pat and Tip* to develop fluency
Materials • **Decodable Reader:** *Pat and Tip*

REREAD FOR FLUENCY

- Ask children to page through the illustrations in *Pat and Tip* and use their own words to retell what the book was about.

- Have children reread a page or two of the story to monitor and adjust their comprehension. Model reading with accuracy and expression. Point out how you used your voice to say the words as someone in the story would say them: *When I read, "Can Ben bat?" my voice went up at the end of the sentence. I wanted to show that it was a question.*

- Provide time to listen as children read. Comment on their accuracy and expression and provide corrective feedback.

Decodable Reader

Beyond Level

Decodable Reader

Objective Reread *Pat and Tip* to reinforce fluency
Materials • **Decodable Reader:** *Pat and Tip*

REREAD FOR FLUENCY

- Have partners reread *Pat and Tip*.

- Provide time to listen as children read. Comment on their accuracy and expression, and provide corrective feedback by modeling proper fluency. Encourage children to reread a portion to help monitor and adjust their comprehension.

INNOVATE

- Discuss children's experiences in the rain. Then ask children to talk about things Pat and Tip could do in the rain. Have children fold a sheet of paper in half and make a booklet titled *Pat and Tip in the Rain*. Ask them to draw two pictures on the inside showing Pat and Tip playing in the rain and write a sentence about each picture.

ELL ENGLISH LANGUAGE LEARNERS

Access to Core Content

Content Objective Develop listening comprehension
Language Objective Discuss text using key words and sentence frames
Materials • **ELL Resource Book**, pp. 204–205

PRETEACH BIG BOOK OF EXPLORATIONS

All Language Levels

Use the Interactive Question-Response Guide on **ELL Resource Book** pages 204–205 to preview the **Big Book Of Explorations** selection "Let It Snow!" Preteach half of the selection on Day 3 and half on Day 4.

Grammar

Content Objective Identify describing words
Language Objective Speak in complete sentences, using sentence frames
Materials • **Listening Library Audio CD** • **Photo Cards**

DESCRIBING WORDS (ADJECTIVES)

All Language Levels

- Review describing words (adjectives). Tell children that describing words tell about naming words. Say: *I see the bright sun. What kind of sun does the sentence tell about?* (bright) Ask for other words that describe the sun. (yellow) Have children repeat the phrase *yellow sun.*

Little Dog
*Little Dog had lost his way
In a fog so thick and gray.*

*First, Dog bumped into a log.
Next, he sat upon a frog.*

*"Oh," Dog said in a ho-hum way.
"I guess this just is not my day!"*

- Play "Little Dog" from the **Listening Library Audio CD**. Tell children to listen for describing words.

- Point out the describing words *thick* and *gray*. Ask children what these words describe. (*Thick* and *gray* describe *fog.*) Display the **Photo Cards** for *ladybug, moon, turtle.* Point to each and have children name a word to describe the picture. Then have them say the describing word and naming word in a sentence.

PEER DISCUSSION STARTERS

All Language Levels

- Distribute animal-related Photo Cards such as *rabbit* and *mouse.*

- Pair children and have them complete the sentence frame *This is a _____.* Ask them to expand on their sentences by providing details. For example: *This is a _____ _____.* Circulate, listen in, and provide feedback.

Big Book of Explorations

Puppet

Corrective Feedback

Sound Error If children miss making the sound-letter correspondence, say: *My turn: led, /llleeed/. I hear /d/ at the end of led, /llleeed/. I'll hold up my d card because /llleeed/ ends with /d/. What is the sound? What letter stands for that sound? Let's start again.*

ELL

Extra Practice Provide additional practice in recognizing and naming letters for children whose native languages do not use the symbols of the Latin alphabet.

Approaching Level

Phonemic Awareness

Objective   Blend sounds to form words
Materials   • **Photo Cards:** *bike, bus, dog, fan, hat, jet, lamp, mop, net, nut, pig*
                • **Puppet**

PHONEME BLENDING

Tier **2**

Model

- Display the **Photo Cards.** *Happy is going to say the sounds in a word: /m/ /o/ /p/. Happy can blend these sounds together: /mmmooop/. Now you blend the sounds to say the word with Happy:* mop. Then point to the *mop* Photo Card.

- Repeat with *lamp.*

Guided Practice/Practice

- *Happy will say some sounds: /n/ /e/ /t/. Repeat the sounds Happy said. Now blend the sounds together to make a word: /nnneeet/,* net. Point to the Photo Card for *net.*

- Continue with *pig, bike, bus, dog, fan, hat, jet,* and *nut.*

Phonics

Objective   Blend with /b/b, /e/e, /l/l, /h/h, /i/i, and /d/d to read words
Materials   • **Word-Building Cards**   • pocket chart

REVIEW SKILLS: BLEND SOUNDS

Tier **2**

Model

- Place **Word-Building Cards** *l, e, d* in the pocket chart. Point to the letter *l. What is this letter? What sound does it stand for?* Continue with *e* and *d.*

- *Now let's put these three sounds together to say the word. /llleeed/,* led. *We blended /l/ /e/ /d/ together to say the word* led. Children repeat and say the word *led. Listen as I blend another word.* Repeat the blending routine with the word *bed: /b/ /e/ /d/, /bed/, bed.*

Guided Practice/Practice

- Display the cards for *h, i, d.* Have children point under the cards and say the sound each letter stands for. Have them repeat, quickly saying the sounds one after the other: */hiiid/, hid.* Repeat with the words *bid, lid, bell, bill, dill.*

Approaching Level

Leveled Reader Lesson 1

Objective Read *What Can We Do?* to apply skills and strategies
Materials • **Leveled Reader:** *What Can We Do?*

BEFORE READING

- **Preview and Predict** Read the title and the name of the author. *Who do you see on the cover? What is happening? Where are they? What are they wearing? What time of year is it? How can you tell?* Turn to the title page and point out that it also has the title and the name of the author. *What do you think the book is about?*

- **Model Concepts About Print** *I can point to words in the title.* Point to the word *What. This is the word* What. *Who can point to the word* Can? *Now let's count all the words in the title.*

- **Review High-Frequency Words** Write **what**, **and**, **I**, **do**, **we**, and **this**. Read the words. Guide children to name the letters in each word. Have children find each word in the book and point to and read it.

- **Page Through the Book** Name unfamiliar terms with children.

- **Set a Purpose for Reading** *Let's find out what the bunnies can do in different kinds of weather.*

DURING READING

- Remind children to use the illustrations to gain information and to look for the high-frequency words they know.

- Model how to self-correct if a word doesn't sound right or doesn't make sense in the sentence. *On page 2, I look at the sentence and reread "What can Den and I do?" That doesn't make sense. I look at the picture and see two bunnies playing. I look at the word again and see that the word actually begins with a b. I read, "What can Ben and I do?" That makes sense.*

- Monitor children's reading and provide help as needed.

AFTER READING

- Ask children to point out words that they had trouble reading and to share strategies they used to help figure them out. Reinforce good behaviors. For example: *Dylan, I see that you sounded out the words* can *and* Ben.

- Ask children to retell the story and to share personal responses. *What do you like to do in different kinds of weather? Which activities described in the book have you done?*

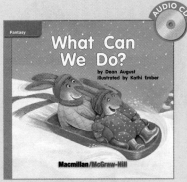

Leveled Reader

ON YOUR OWN

Write What They Will Do

Have children draw pictures to show what the bunny and its mother might do together in the rain. Help children write sentences about their pictures.

We can read.

Leveled Reader

ELL

Retell Use the Interactive Question-Response Guide Technique to help English Language Learners understand *In the Snow*. As you read, make meaning clear by pointing to pictures, demonstrating word meaning, paraphrasing text, and asking children questions.

What Can You Do?

After reading *In the Snow*, have children draw a picture of what they would like to do in snow. Ask them to write a sentence to describe their drawing.

On Level

Leveled Reader Lesson 1

Objective Read *In the Snow* to apply skills and strategies
Materials • **Leveled Reader:** *In the Snow*

BEFORE READING

- **Preview and Predict** Read the title and the name of the author. *Who do you see on the cover? What are they wearing? What are they doing? What season is it? How can you tell?* Open and page through the book. *What do you think will happen in the story?*

- **Model Concepts About Print** *I can point to the words in the title.* Point to *In. The first word is* In. *What is the second word? What is the next word? Let's count the words in the title.*

- **Review High-Frequency Words** Write **go**, **and**, **what**, **do**, **you**, **have**, **a**, and **this** on chart paper. Have children find each word in the book and point to the word as they read it.

- **Set a Purpose for Reading** *Let's find out what the children do in the snow.*

DURING READING

- Have children turn to page 2 and begin by whisper-reading the first two pages.

- Remind children to look for the high-frequency words and to use the illustrations.

- Monitor children's reading and provide help. Stop during the reading and ask open-ended questions to facilitate discussion, such as: *What is the author telling us about snow? What does the book show you about winter?* Build on children's responses to develop deeper understanding of the text.

AFTER READING

- Ask children to point out words they had trouble reading and to share strategies they used to figure them out. Reinforce good behaviors. For example: *Mia, I noticed you sounded out* Ted *and* Lil.

- **Retell** Ask children to retell a main event from the story. Help them make a personal connection. *Have you played in snow? What activity do you like to do in snow? What activity would you like to do in snow? Is it shown in this story?*

Beyond Level

Leveled Reader Lesson 1

Objective   Read *The Woodpecker* to apply skills and strategies
Materials   • **Leveled Reader:** *The Woodpecker*

BEFORE READING

- **Preview and Predict** Read the title and the name of the author. *Who do you see on the cover? Where are they? What time of year is it? How can you tell? What do you think the book is going to be about?* Turn to the title page and point out that it also has the title and the name of the author. Page through the book with children and pause to name unfamiliar items.

- **Introduce Story Words** Point to the word *woodpecker* on page 3. Read the sentence and ask children to use the picture to tell what a *woodpecker* is.

- **Set a Purpose for Reading** Discuss purpose for reading. *Let's find out how a woodpecker's life changes as the weather changes.*

DURING READING

- Remind children that when they come to an unfamiliar word, they can look for familiar chunks in the word, break the word into syllables and sound out each part, or think about what the word might mean. If the word does not sound right or make sense in the sentence, children can self-correct.

AFTER READING

- Ask children to point out words they had trouble reading and to share the strategies they used.

- Tell children to retell the story and to share personal responses. *Where do birds build nests? Have you ever seen a bird building a nest? What was the nest made of? Where and when did you see it? Why do birds build nests?*

- **Analyze** *Why was the woodpecker tapping the tree? Explain what the woodpecker ate and how it got its food. Do you think all birds eat the same food in the same way? Why or why not?*

- On the board, list a variety of birds, such as blackbirds, starlings, sparrow, robins, and hummingbirds. Assign two birds per pair. Have pairs use a children's encyclopedia to research what and how these birds eat.

- **Model** Tell children they will write a short monologue using their research results. Write an example on the board: *I am a pelican. I scoop up fish with my long bill.* Have children make bird masks, memorize their monologues, and perform for the class.

Leveled Reader

ON YOUR OWN

Predict What Will Happen

Have children write and draw what they predict will happen to the five eggs that Bob sees in his woodpecker's nest.

Baby birds come out of the eggs.

Leveled Reader

Vocabulary

Preteach Vocabulary Use the routine in the **Visual Vocabulary Resources**, pages 341–342, to preteach the ELL Vocabulary listed on the inside front cover of the Leveled Reader.

ELL ENGLISH LANGUAGE LEARNERS

Leveled Reader

Content Objective Read to apply skills and strategies
Language Objective Retell information using complete sentences
Materials • **Leveled Reader:** *Snow*

BEFORE READING

All Language Levels

- **Preview** Read the title *Snow*. Ask: *What's the title? Say it again.* Repeat with the author's name. Point to the cover illustration and say: *I see a snowman.* Point to the snowman as you name it. *It has a hat and a carrot nose. Now turn to a partner and tell about this picture.*

- **Page Through the Book** Use simple language to tell about the illustration on each page. Immediately follow up with questions, such as: *Is this a sled? Are they skating or jumping?*

- **Review Skills** Use the inside front cover to review the phonics skill and high-frequency words.

- **Set a Purpose** Say: *Let's read to find out about fun in the snow.*

DURING READING

All Language Levels

- Have children whisper-read each page, or use the differentiated suggestions below. Circulate, listen in, and provide corrective feedback, such as modeling how to read questions.

- **Retell** Stop after every two pages and ask children to state what they have learned so far. Reinforce language by restating children's comments when they have difficulty using story-specific words. Provide differentiated sentence frames to support children's responses and engage children in partner-talk where appropriate.

Beginning	Intermediate	Advanced
Echo-Read Have children echo-read after you.	**Choral-Read** Have children choral-read with you.	**Choral-Read** Have children choral-read.
Check Comprehension Point to pictures and ask questions such as: *Do you see a tree? Point to the ice skates.*	**Check Comprehension** Ask questions/prompts such as: *What do Lil and Ted do here? Where are Lil and Ted?*	**Check Comprehension** Ask: *Look at the dog. Could this happen in real life? What could really happen in this picture?*

ELL ENGLISH LANGUAGE LEARNERS

AFTER READING

All Language Levels

Book Talk Children will work with peers of varying language abilities to discuss their books for this week. Display the four **Leveled Readers** read this week: *The Woodpecker* (Beyond Level), *In the Snow* (On Level), *What Can We Do?* (Approaching Level), and *Snow* (English Language Learners).

Ask the questions and provide the prompts below. Call on children who read each book to answer the questions or respond to the prompt. If appropriate, ask children to find the pages in the book that illustrate their answers.

- What kind of weather did you read about?
- What did the characters do?
- What did you read about that could happen in real life?
- What can you do that you read about?
- Which part of the book did you like best? Tell about it.

Develop Listening and Speaking Skills Tell children to remember the following:

- Share information in cooperative learning interactions. Remind children to work with their partners to retell the story and complete any activities. Ask: *What happened next in the story?*

- Employ self-corrective techniques and monitor their own and other children's language production. Children should ask themselves: *What parts of this passage were confusing to me? Can my classmates help me clarify a word or sentence that I don't understand?*

- Use high-frequency English words to describe people, places, and objects.

- Narrate, describe, and explain with specificity and detail. Ask: *Where did the story take place? Can you describe the setting? What else did you notice?*

- Express opinions, ideas, and feelings on a variety of social and academic topics. Ask: *What do you think about the characters in the story?*

Approaching Level

Phonemic Awareness

Objective Segment words into sounds
Materials • **Photo Cards:** *man, mop, net*

PHONEME SEGMENTATION

Tier 2

Model

■ Display the **Photo Card** for *man*. Say: *This is a man. Listen as I say the sounds in* man: */m/ /a/ /n/. There are three sounds in the word* man. *I'll say them again:* /m/ /a/ /n/. Repeat the routine with the Photo Cards for *mop* and *net*.

Guided Practice/Practice

■ Have children segment the words below. *I will say a word. Repeat the word after me and then say the sounds in the word.*

| net | pet | same | pot | Tom |
| bet | sit | tape | light | neck |

Phonics

Objective Identify initial sounds /b/b, /d/d, /e/e, /l/l and build fluency
Materials • **Photo Cards:** *balloon, banana, bat, bike, book, bus, deer, doctor, dog, doll, door, dolphin, egg, elbow, elevator, envelope, exit, ladder, ladybug, lamp, lemon, lock* • **Word-Building Cards**
• **Sound-Spelling WorkBoards** • pocket chart

BUILD FLUENCY

Tier 2

Model

■ Place **Word-Building Cards** *b, d, e, l* in the top row of the pocket chart. Have children name the letters and review the sound each letter stands for. Stack the Photo Cards facedown.

■ Choose a card. Say the name of the picture, repeat the initial sound, and place the card under the letter that stands for the initial sound. For example: *This is a dog. Dog begins with /d/. I'll place* dog *under the* d *card because* d *stands for the /d/ sound.*

Guided Practice/Practice

■ Have each child choose a Photo Card, say the name of the picture, repeat the initial sound, and place the card under the appropriate letter. Guide practice with the first Photo Card.

Build Fluency

■ Display the Word-Building Cards. Have children say each letter name as quickly as they can. Then ask them to write the letters *b, d, e,* and *l* on their **WorkBoards** several times as they say the sound for each letter.

Approaching Level

Leveled Reader Lesson 2

Objective Reread *What Can We Do?* to reinforce fluency and to distinguish between fantasy and reality

Materials • **Leveled Reader:** *What Can We Do?*

FOCUS ON FLUENCY

■ Tell children that you will read one page of the book and they should read that page right after you. They should follow along in their books and try to read at the same speed and with the same expression that you use.

✔ SKILL DISTINGUISH BETWEEN FANTASY AND REALITY

■ *Look at the pictures. Are the bunnies in this book like real bunnies, or are they make-believe? How do you know? What can these bunnies do that real bunnies can't do?*

REREAD BOOKS

■ Distribute copies of the past six **Leveled Readers**. Tell children that rereading books will help them develop their reading skills and enjoy language.

■ Circulate and listen in as children read. Stop them periodically and ask them how they are figuring out words or checking their understanding. Ask them if they are using sensory images to help monitor their comprehension. Have children reread other Leveled Readers during independent reading time.

High-Frequency Words

Objective Review high-frequency words *this, do, and, what, you, for*

Materials • **High-Frequency Word Cards:** *this, do, and, what, you, for*

✔ BUILD WORD AUTOMATICITY: *this, do, and, what, you, for*

■ Distribute **High-Frequency Word Cards** for **this**. Say the word and have children repeat it. Have children name the letters in the word. Repeat with the words **do**, **and**, **what**, **you**, and **for**.

■ **Build Fluency** Use the High-Frequency Word Cards to review previously taught words. Repeat, guiding children to read more rapidly.

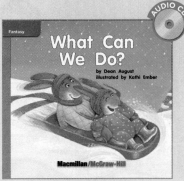

Leveled Reader

ON YOUR OWN

If I Were a Bunny

Ask children to suppose they are little bunnies, like the one in the book. Have them draw what they would do with their moms and write about their pictures.

Meet Grade-Level Expectations

As an alternative to this day's lesson, guide children through a reading of the On Level Leveled Reader. See page 1794. Because both books contain the same vocabulary, phonics, and comprehension skills, the scaffolding you provided will help most children gain access to this more challenging text.

Leveled Reader

Change the Season

Have children choose scenes from the book and change them to another season. For example, they could draw pictures showing what the characters might do in the fall. Tell children to write about their drawings.

Ben and Lin in the leaves.

On Level

Leveled Reader Lesson 2

Leveled Reader Library

Objective Reread to apply skills and strategies to retell a story
Materials • **Leveled Reader:** *In the Snow*

BEFORE READING

- Ask children to look through *In the Snow* and recall what the book is about. Reinforce vocabulary by repeating children's sentences, using more sophisticated language. For example: *The children experience many snow activities.*

DURING READING

- Have children join you in a choral-reading of the story. Model reading with expression. *When I read page 3, I emphasized* What can Ben do? What can Lin do? *by saying the questions a little stronger. I used the same emphasis on every other page when the words formed questions. I wanted to show that the author wanted the reader to answer the questions.* Ask children to use the same kind of expression when they read. Discuss how reading a variety of texts with expression can help them enjoy language.

- Assign each child a page. Have children practice by whisper-reading. *Follow along as other children read, and be ready to come in when it is your turn. Remember, use lots of expression.*

AFTER READING

- Have children retell the selection in their own words. *What happened at the beginning of the story? What happened in the middle of the story? What happened at the end of the story?*

- *Look at the pictures. Do the characters act like real children? What happens in the story that could really happen? What happens that could not really happen?*

- Have children make connections to other texts. *What other stories have we read that take place in winter? Did they have people or animals in them? Could the events in those stories have really happened?*

- To extend this lesson, encourage children to use puppets, toys, and/or other props as they retell and dramatize the story.

Beyond Level

Leveled Reader Lesson 2

Objective   Reread to apply skills and strategies to retell a story

Materials   • **Leveled Reader:** *The Woodpecker*

BEFORE READING

- Ask children to page through *The Woodpecker* and recall what the book is about. Point out that this story is make-believe. However, parts of the story are real. *What in the story could really happen? What could not really happen? How can you tell which things can or cannot really happen?*

DURING READING

- Assign each child a page of the book to read aloud. Have children practice by whisper-reading. *Follow along as each child reads, and be ready to come in when it is your turn. Remember, use lots of expression.* Have children then work with a partner and ask each other questions about the text. Encourage children to respond in complete sentences.

AFTER READING

- Explain that readers can better understand a story if they create sensory images in their minds. Model the strategy: *As I read, I picture the woodpecker tapping on the tree in summer. Then I imagine how the tree changes and how the bird builds its nest. What do you picture about the woodpecker?*

Expand Vocabulary

Objective   Discuss the words *birds* and *tap* and brainstorm other things birds can do

Materials   • **Leveled Reader:** *The Woodpecker*

ENRICH: *birds, tap*

- Write the words *birds* and *tap* on cards. Display the cards and have children find the words in the story (*birds*, page 2; *tap*, page 4). Ask children to demonstrate birds tapping on a tree.

- Have children find other words in the book that tell what birds can do and record them in a web called "What Birds Can Do." (*come, go, bring sticks, make nests, eat*) Have children demonstrate the actions and use the words in complete sentences to tell about birds. Then ask children to brainstorm other things that birds can do. (*fly, sing, sleep, see*) Add these words to the web.

Leveled Reader

Write About Woodpeckers

Discuss what the woodpecker does in the story. Have children draw one thing the woodpecker does and write a sentence about it.

ELL

Partners When children create their webs about birds, pair English Language Learners with children who are more proficient.

ELL ENGLISH LANGUAGE LEARNERS

Fluency

Content Objectives Reread the Decodable Reader to develop fluency; develop speaking skills

Language Objective Tell a partner what a selection is about

Materials • **Decodable Reader:** *Pat and Tip*

REREAD FOR FLUENCY

Beginning

- Review the high-frequency words **this**, **do**, **and**, **what**, **for**, and **you** using the **Read/Spell/Write** routine.

Intermediate/Advanced

- Use each word in a sentence that illustrates its use, such as: *What do you do with this?* Show a book or pencil. Have children answer the question.

- Then provide sentence starters for children to complete. Where appropriate, act out children's responses. For example: *I can sit and stand.*

All Language Levels

- Guide children through a choral-reading of *Pat and Tip*. Point to the question mark at the end of the second sentence on page 2. Tell children that when a sentence ends in a question mark, we make our voices go up at the end of the sentence to show that this is a question. Model reading the page again and have children chorally repeat.

DEVELOP SPEAKING/LISTENING SKILLS

All Language Levels

- Have children reread *Pat and Tip* to a partner. Remind them to listen carefully and follow along in their book as their partner is reading. Work with children to read with accuracy and expression.

- Ask children to tell their partner about the pictures on each page. Then have the other partner describe the pictures. Circulate, listen in, and provide additional language as needed.

Beginning	Intermediate	Advanced
Confirm Understanding Point to the pictures for partners to identify. Ask: *What do you see?* Restate the correct answer in a complete sentence.	**Express Opinions** Ask partners to tell you which is their favorite picture in the book. Prompt them to explain why it is their favorite picture.	**Compare and Contrast** Have partners compare two different pictures and describe them. Prompt them to explain how they are alike and different.

ELL ENGLISH LANGUAGE LEARNERS

High-Frequency Words

Content Objective Spell high-frequency words correctly
Language Objective Write in complete sentences, using sentence frames
Materials • **Sound-Spelling WorkBoards** • **Sound-Spelling Cards** • **Photo Cards**

Beginning/Intermediate

- Write the high-frequency words **this**, **and**, **do**, and **what** on the board. Have children copy the words on their **WorkBoards**. Help them say the words, then write a sentence for each word. Provide the sentence starters *This is a _____. I see _____ and _____. What do you _____?*

Advanced

- Children should first orally state their sentence. Correct as needed. Then they can draw a picture to complete the sentence. For children who are ready, help them spell words using their growing knowledge of English sound-spelling relationships. Model how to segment the word children are trying to spell and attach a spelling to each sound. Use the **Sound-Spelling Cards** to reinforce the spellings for each English sound.

Writing

All Language Levels

- Dictate the following words and ask children to write the words: *bed, let.* Have them write each word five times as they say *bed* and then *let.* Demonstrate correct letter formation, as needed.

- Then display a set of **Photo Cards**. Select at least five cards whose picture names begin with /b/ (balloon, banana, bike, book, bus), five whose picture names begin with /e/ (egg, elbow, elevator, envelope, exit), and five whose picture names begin with /l/ (leaf, light, ladybug, lemon, lock).

- Say the name of each card, stretching or reiterating the initial sound to emphasize it. You may also need to reinforce the meaning of the word and model correct mouth formation when forming the sound. Use the articulation pictures and prompts on the back of the small Sound-Spelling Cards for support. Tell children to write the first letter of each picture name on their WorkBoards.

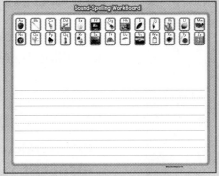

Sound-Spelling WorkBoard

Phonemic Awareness/ Phonics

For English Language Learners who need more practice with this week's phonemic awareness and phonics skills, see the Approaching Level lessons. Focus on minimal contrasts, articulation, and those sounds that do not transfer from the child's first language to English. For a complete listing of transfer sounds, see pages T10–T31.

Weekly Assessment

Use your Quick Check observations and the assessment opportunities identified below to evaluate children's progress in key skill areas.

Skills	Quick Check Observations	Pencil and Paper Assessment
PHONEMIC AWARENESS/ PHONICS /e/e, /b/b, /l/l e b	1737	Activity Book, pp. 24, 29, 32 Practice Book, pp. 153, 157–158
HIGH-FREQUENCY WORDS *this, do, and, what* what	1758	Activity Book, pp. 27–28 Practice Book, pp. 155–156
COMPREHENSION Distinguish Between Fantasy and Reality	1748	Activity Book, pp. 25, 31 Practice Book, p. 154

Quick Check Rubric

Skills	1	2	3
PHONEMIC AWARENESS/ PHONICS	Does not connect the /e/, /b/, /l/ sounds with the letters *Ee, Bb, Ll* and has difficulty blending the CVC words *Bob, bib, tab, bed, bet, lap, led, lid, pen, den, set, Ned.*	Usually connects the /e/, /b/, /l/ sounds with the letters *Ee, Bb, Ll* and blends the CVC words *Bob, bib, tab, bed, bet, lap, led, lid, pen, den, set, Ned* with only occasional support.	Consistently connects the /e/, /b/, /l/ sounds with the letters *Ee, Bb, Ll* and blends the CVC words *Bob, bib, tab, bed, bet, lap, led, lid, pen, den, set, Ned.*
HIGH-FREQUENCY WORDS	Does not identify the high-frequency words.	Usually recognizes the high-frequency words with accuracy, but not speed.	Consistently recognizes the high-frequency words with speed and accuracy.
COMPREHENSION	Does not distinguish between fantasy and reality using the pictures and text.	Usually distinguishes between fantasy and reality using the pictures and text.	Consistently distinguishes between fantasy and reality using the pictures and text.

DIBELS LINK

PROGRESS MONITORING

Use your DIBELS results to inform instruction.

IF...

Initial Sound Fluency (**ISF**)   0–34

THEN...

Evaluate for Intervention

TPRI LINK

PROGRESS MONITORING

Use your TPRI scores to inform instruction.

IF...

Phonemic Awareness	Still Developing
Graphophonemic Knowledge	Still Developing
Listening Comprehension	Still Developing

THEN...

Evaluate for Intervention

Diagnose		Prescribe
Review the assessment answers with children. Have them correct their errors. Then provide additional instruction as needed.		
PHONEMIC AWARENESS/ PHONICS /e/e, /b/b, /l/l	**IF...** **Quick Check Rubric:** Children consistently score 1 or **Pencil and Paper Assessment:** Children get 0–2 items correct	**THEN...** Reteach Phonemic Awareness and Phonics Skills using the **Phonemic Awareness** and **Phonics Intervention Intervention Teacher's Editions**. *SPIRAL REVIEW* Use the Build Fluency lesson in upcoming weeks to provide children practice reading words with /e/e, /b/b, and /l/l.
HIGH-FREQUENCY WORDS *this, do, and, what*	**Quick Check Rubric:** Children consistently score 1 or **Pencil and Paper Assessment:** Children get 0–2 items correct	Reteach High-Frequency Words using the **Phonics Intervention Teacher's Edition**. *SPIRAL REVIEW* Use the High-Frequency Words lesson in upcoming weeks to provide children practice reading the words *this, do, and, what*.
COMPREHENSION Skill: Distinguish Between Fantasy and Reality	**Quick Check Rubric:** Children consistently score 1 or **Pencil and Paper Assessment:** Children get 0–2 items correct	Reteach Comprehension Skill using the **Comprehension Intervention Teacher's Edition**.

Response to Intervention

To place children in Tier 2 or Tier 3 Intervention use the *Diagnostic Assessment*.

- Phonemic Awareness
- Phonics
- Vocabulary
- Comprehension
- Fluency

Use this page to record lessons that work well or need to be adapted for future reference.

Lessons that work well

Lessons that need adjustments

Use this page to record lessons that work well or need to be adapted for future reference.

Lessons that work well

Lessons that need adjustments

Unit 7 Computer Literacy

Objectives

- Learn that the Internet gives information
- Learn how to perform a key word search

Materials

- www.macmillanmh.com

Vocabulary

online connected to the Internet

World Wide Web a system of Internet servers that supports specially formatted documents containing links

Web page a page on the Internet that gives information

link an electronic connection from one place on the Web to another place on the Web

search engine a program that looks for word matches based on key words

key word a word used to help find information on a topic

Computer Literacy
Focus on Keyboard and Internet Skills and Media Literacy
www.macmillanmh.com

Remind children not to give personal information to anyone over the Internet.

Internet Readiness
The World Wide Web

ACCESS PRIOR KNOWLEDGE

Discuss with children:

- *What are some things you want to learn about?*

- *Where can we go to get information about these things?*

EXPLAIN

- When on a computer, you must be **online** to look at information on the **World Wide Web**.

- The Web contains many **Web pages** that give people information.

MODEL

- Show children the Internet icon on the desktop. Demonstrate how to connect to the Web.

- Show children a Web page. Point out the title of the Web page and other parts, such as the URL.

- Point out what a **link** looks like on the Web page and what it does. Tell children that links are usually blue and underlined. Click on the link to demonstrate how it jumps to another place on the page or to another Web page.

Technology Makes a Difference

Explain that:

▶ When on the Web, people can do a search to look for Web pages that contain information on different topics.

▶ Open a **search engine**. Demonstrate how to type a **key word** in the search box and press *Search* or *Go*.

▶ Show children the results. Click on one of the links to show children how to go to a Web page.

▶ Brainstorm different topics to search. Choose a topic as a class and perform a key word search.

Media Literacy
Sounding Off!

ACCESS PRIOR KNOWLEDGE

Discuss with children:

- *What are some sounds that get your attention?* (bells, whistles, sirens, horns, alarms)

- *Why are these sounds effective in getting your attention? How are they different than normal, everyday sounds?* (These sounds are usually loud, high-pitched and shrill. They also tend to signify something specific, such as the bell that sounds at the end of the school day.)

- With children, make the sounds listed in response to the first question aloud.

EXPLAIN

Introduce the lesson vocabulary by discussing each word and its definition with children.

- Sounds are all around us: cars honking, phones ringing, friends talking, and dogs barking are all sounds. People who create media use **sound** to attract attention and to entertain an **audience**.

- Television and radio advertisements often use music to encourage their audience to buy their **product**. Do you like music? Most people do. This is why using music is a good media **technique**.

- A song used in an advertisement is called a **jingle**. A jingle is a short saying that is easy to remember set to a catchy **melody**. Jingles are designed to stick in the mind of the listener.

MODEL

- Play some examples of popular television or radio jingles for children. Ask children to identify any sound techniques they hear being used in the jingles.

- Prompt students to talk about why they like or dislike the jingle, whether it is catchy, and whether they think it was successful in persuading an audience to buy a particular product.

- With children, create a class jingle. Brainstorm words that describe the class that could be used in the jingle. Provide children with a simple melody and have them create a short saying in jingle form. Have the class perform the final jingle together.

- Have children identify the message after listening to the jingle.

Objectives

- Identify sound techniques used in media
- Explore the function of advertising jingles and create a class jingle

Materials

- Examples of television or radio jingles

LOG ON ▶ FIND OUT

Media Literacy Activities
Lessons that help children explore and identify the use of sound in different forms of media

Theme Project Wrap-Up
Research/Organizing and Presenting Ideas

After children complete their projects, they can have a Weather Day to present their findings.

Step 3 **Review and Evaluate**

How do I share what I have learned?

The following checklists and Scoring Rubric will help you and children assess their projects.

cold   hot

Teacher's Checklist

Assess the Research Project

Plan the Project

✔ Used describing words to discuss various kinds of weather.

✔ Identified sources or people that could answer questions.

✔ Gathered evidence from provided text sources.

Do the Project

✔ Used pictures and words to record information.

✔ Chose an appropriate format for presentation.

✔ Identified essential information.

Assess the Presentation

Speaking

✔ Spoke clearly and to the point.

✔ Shared information and ideas by speaking audibly.

✔ Demonstrated courteous responses to audience.

Representing

✔ Contained a clear beginning, middle, and end.

✔ Visuals added details and interest to the presentation.

✔ Met goals of presentation successfully.

Assess the Listener

Listening

✔ Developed and applied effective listening skills.

✔ Listened attentively by facing speakers.

✔ Asked questions to clarify information.

Children's Checklist

Research Process

✔ Did you choose a topic that would interest your classmates?

✔ Did you choose sources that could answer your questions?

✔ What was your favorite part of the project?

Presenting

Speaking

✔ Did you speak in a clear, confident voice?

✔ Did you pause after each part of your report?

✔ Did you speak loudly in complete sentences?

Representing

✔ Were your visuals necessary?

✔ Did you use writing with your visuals?

✔ Did you give the audience time to ask questions?

SCORING RUBRIC FOR THEME PROJECT			
4 Excellent	**3** Good	**2** Fair	**1** Unsatisfactory
The child	The child	The child	The child
• presents the main idea with supporting details; • may make sophisticated observations; • presents accurate, well-produced visuals that enhance the topic.	• clearly fulfills all the steps of the project; • provides adequate details; • makes several relevant observations.	• attempts to present some of the required steps; • demonstrates some difficulty with research; • may make somewhat unclear observations.	• does not appear to grasp the task in its entirety; • has great difficulty with organizational skills; • presents unnecessary or inaccurate information.

 Home-School Connection

Weather Day provides an excellent opportunity for home and community involvement.

■ Invite family members, other children, and members of the community to come to school to view children's presentations.

Big Question Wrap-Up

Review the Big Question for this unit with children. Discuss what they learned about weather.

Help children respond to the following questions: *What are the four seasons? What types of weather occur in each season?* Remind children to take turns when speaking.

End-of-Unit Assessment

Administer the Test

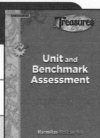

Unit 7 TEST

TESTED SKILLS AND STRATEGIES

COMPREHENSION STRATEGIES AND SKILLS

- Strategy: Visualize
- Skills: Identify main ideas and detail, identify setting, distinguish between fantasy and reality

HIGH-FREQUENCY WORDS

- *this, do, and, what*

PHONEMIC AWARENESS

- Phoneme isolation
- Phoneme blending
- Phoneme segmentation

PHONICS

- *e, b, l*
- Review *-it, -ip* phonograms

CONCEPT WORDS

- Words that compare

Use Multiple Assessments for Instructional Planning

To create instructional profiles for your children, look for patterns in the results from any of the following assessments.

Running Records

Use the instructional reading level determined by the Running Record calculations for regrouping decisions.

Benchmark Assessments

Administer tests three times a year as an additional measure of both children's progress and the effectiveness of the instructional program.

Analyze the Data

Use information from a variety of informal and formal assessments, as well as your own judgment, to assist in your instructional planning. Children who consistently score at the lowest end of each range should be evaluated for Intervention. Use the **Diagnostic Assessment** for guidelines in the **Intervention Teacher's Editions**.

Diagnose		Prescribe
ASSESSMENTS	**IF...**	**THEN...**
UNIT TEST	0–15 Correct	Reteach skills using the **Intervention Teacher's Editions**.
RUNNING RECORDS	Rebus	Reteach skills using the **Intervention Teacher's Editions**.

For users of DIBELS

Use the results from the DIBELS Progress Monitoring tests to confirm instructional decisions.

DIBELS LINK

PROGRESS MONITORING

Use your DIBELS results to inform instruction.

IF...
Initial Sound Fluency (ISF)   0–7
Phoneme Segmentation Fluency (PSF) Start midyear

THEN...
Evaluate for Intervention

For users of TPRI

Use the scores from the TPRI as a progress monitoring tool to confirm instructional decisions.

TPRI LINK

PROGRESS MONITORING

Use your TPRI scores to inform instruction.

IF...
Phonemic Awareness   Still Developing
Graphophonemic Knowledge   Still Developing
Listening Comprehension   Still Developing

THEN...
Evaluate for Intervention

Response to Intervention

To place children in Tier 2 or Tier 3 Intervention use the *Diagnostic Assessment*.

- Phonemic Awareness
- Phonics
- Vocabulary
- Comprehension
- Fluency

Instructional Routines

Professional Development

- Read the routine prior to using *Treasures*. Use the Routine QuickNotes as a reminder of key routine steps throughout Unit 1, or as needed.

- View the online classroom video clip through **TeacherWorks Plus**. Watch master teachers use these routines.

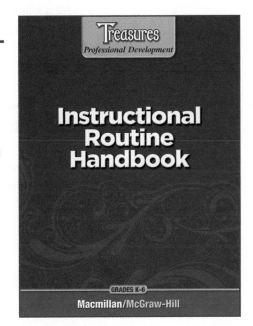

1. **Phonological Awareness/ Phonemic Awareness**
   Rhyme
   Oddity Tasks
   Sound Categorization
   Oral Blending
   Oral Segmentation
   Manipulation

2. **Phonics**
   Blending
   Introducing Sound-Spelling Cards
   Letter Recognition
   Building Words
   Building Fluency
   Reading Decodables
   Multisyllabic Words Routine

3. **Fluency**
   Strategies

4. **Vocabulary**
   Define/Example/Ask Routine
   Strategies

5. **High-Frequency Words**
   Read/Spell/Write Routine
   Reading Pre-decodables

6. **Spelling**
   Dictation

7. **Comprehension**
   Strategies
   Skills
   Reading Big Books
   Reading Student Book

8. **Writing**
   Conferences
   Revision Assignments
   Writing Process
   Using Rubrics
   Using Anchor Papers
   Writers' Express Sequence

9. **Research Process**
   Big Question Board

10. **Classroom Management**
    Workstation Flip Charts
    Contracts
    Centers
    Small Groups

11. **Listening/Speaking/Viewing**

12. **Assessment**

Additional Readings

By the Authors and Illustrators

For additional information on authors, illustrators, and selection content, go to www.macmillanmh.com.

Nelson, Robin. *A Snowy Day.* **First Avenue Editions, 2001.** A good companion piece to *A Rainy Day*, this book introduces children to weather as it describes the essence of different days, beginning with snow.

Related to the Theme

Use these and other classroom or library resources to provide additional read alouds to build academic language.

Burton, Virginia Lee. *Katy and the Big Snow.* **Houghton Mifflin, 1974.** The story of one little snowplow's determination in the face of a small town blizzard.

Carle, Eric. *Little Cloud.* **Putnam, 2001.** A cloud changes itself into a series of shapes, such as a lamb, a shark, and a clown.

Halpern, Julie. *Toby and the Snowflakes.* **Houghton Mifflin, 2004.** Toby, lonely since his best friend moved away, makes friends with the falling snowflakes.

Hutchins, Hazel. *One Dark Night.* **Viking, 2001.** Jonathan helps his grandparents rescue a stray cat and her new little kittens on a stormy night.

Hutchins, Pat. *The Wind Blew.* **Simon & Schuster, 1993.** Here is a rhyming tale about the capricious nature of the wind.

Stojic, Manya. *Rain.* **Crown, 2001.** The animals of the African savanna use their senses to predict a change in the weather and the approach of rain.

Rau, Dana Meachen. *Explore in a Cave.* **Rourke Publishing, 2001.** Explore a cave and enjoy the natural world as you watch for hanging bats and cave paintings, and follow a trickling stream.

Wilson, Karma. *Bear Wants More.* **Margaret K. McElderry, 2003.** This sweet story follows Bear as he wakes up from a winter of hibernation and discovers he is very, very hungry.

Borden, Louise W. *Caps, Hats, Socks, and Mittens.* **Scholastic, 1992.** Children learn about the four seasons through repetition and rhyme.

Bancroft, Henrietta. *Animals in Winter.* **HarperTrophy, 1997.** Different animals and the ways they prepare for winter are discussed.

Crew, Nina. *One Hot Summer Day.* **Greenwillow, 1995.** A young African American girl describes her hot summer day in an urban setting.

Chapman, Cheryl. *Snow on Snow on Snow.* **Dial Books, 1994.** A young boy wakes up to snow, goes sledding, and then loses, but eventually finds, his beloved dog.

Deady, Kathleen. *All Year Long.* **Carolrhoda, 2004.** Each season is briefly described in rhyme as a young girl finds activities she enjoys with her mother and father.

Fleming, Denise. *Time to Sleep.* **Henry Holt, 2001.** Autumn turns into winter, and the various hibernation habits of different animals are described.

Florian, Douglas. *A Winter Day.* **Greenwillow, 1987.** A family has fun and enjoys a relaxing winter day.

Poole, Amy Lowry. *The Ant and the Grasshopper.* **Holiday House, 2000.** A retelling of the well-known fable of how an ant and a grasshopper approach the winter season in different ways.

Hoberman, Mary Ann. *Right Outside My Window.* **Mondo, 2002.** There's something special happening outside during each season of the year. One sentence on each colorful page describes a scene, ending with "right outside my window," each time.

Shannon, David. *The Rain Came Down.* **Blue Sky Press, 2000.** An unexpected rain shower causes a chain of misunderstandings in a neighborhood.

Spinelli, Eileen. *I Know It's Autumn.* **HarperCollins, 2004.** All of the ways your senses tell you that it's autumn are shown in simple text and appealing illustrations.

Stojic, Manya. *Snow.* **Alfred A. Knopf, 2002.** As the snow begins to fall, each animal prepares in a different way.

Theme Bibliography

Selection Honors, Prizes, and Awards

Bear Snores On

by *Karma Wilson*

Illustrated by *Jane Chapman*

National Parenting Publications Awards (NAPPA) Children's Resource Gold Award Winner, Oppenheim Toy Portfolio Platinum Book Award (2002); ALA Notable Children's Book (2003); Great Lakes' Great Books Award (2004)

Resources

Audio Bookshelf
44 Ocean View Drive
Middletown, RI 02842
800-234-1713
www.audiobookshelf.com

Discovery Communications
4540 Preslyn Drive
Raleigh, NC 27616
888-892-3484

Dorling Kindersley
375 Hudson Street
New York, NY 10014
Tel: 800-631-8571
Fax: 201-256-0000
http://us.dk.com

Great Plains National Instructional Television Library
GPN Educational Media
1407 Fleet Street
Baltimore, MD 21231
800-228-4630
http://shopgpn.com

Innovative Educators
P.O. Box 520
Montezuma, GA 31063
888-252-KIDS
Fax: 888-536-8553
www.innovative-educators.com

Library Video Co.
P.O. Box 580
Wynnewood, PA 19096
800-843-3620
www.libraryvideo.com

Listening Library
400 Hahn Road
Westminster, MD 21157
800-243-4504

Live Oak Media
P.O. Box 652
Pine Plains, NY 12567
800-788-1121
www.liveoakmedia.com

Macmillan/McGraw-Hill
220 East Danieldale Road
DeSoto, TX 75115-9960
Tel: 800-442-9685
Fax: 972-228-1982
www.macmillanmh.com

MCA Video
MCA Records/Universal Studios
100 Universal City Plaza
Universal City, CA 91608
818-777-1000

Microsoft Corp.
One Microsoft Way
Redmond, WA 98052
800-426-9000
www.microsoft.com

National Geographic Society
1145 17th Street N.W.
Washington, DC 20036
800-647-5463
www.nationalgeographic.com

Recorded Books
270 Skipjack Road
Prince Frederick, MD 20678
800-636-3399
www.recordedbooks.com

Sunburst Communications
Sunburst Technology
1550 Executive Drive
Elgin, IL 60123
888-492-8817
www.sunburst.com

SVE & Churchill Media
6465 North Avondale Avenue
Chicago, IL 60631
800-253-2788

Tom Snyder Productions
100 Talcott Avenue
Watertown, MA 02472
800-342-0236
www.tomsnyder.com

Weston Woods
143 Main Street
Norwalk, CT 06851
800-243-5020
www.teacher.scholastic.com/products/westonwoods/

Web Sites

Go to www.macmillanmh.com.
Use the zip code finder to locate other resources in your area.

The Academy of Natural Sciences
http://www.ansp.org/

Acadia National Park
http://www.nps.gov/acad

Agriculture in the Classroom
http://www.agclassroom.org/

Arches National Park
http://www.nps.gov/arch

Asian American History Resources Online - CET
http://www.cetel.org/res.html

Association of Zoos and Aquariums
http://www.aza.org/

Bronx Zoo
http://www.bronxzoo.com/

Cincinnati Zoo
http://www.cincinnatizoo.org/

Colonial Williamsburg
http://www.history.org/

Denali National Park and Preserve
http://www.nps.gov/dena

Ellis Island
http://www.ellisisland.org/

Glacier National Park
http://www.nps.gov/glac

Grand Canyon National Park
http://www.nps.gov/grca

Grand Teton National Park
http://www.nps.gov/grte

High Museum of Art, Atlanta
http://www.high.org/

International Civil Rights Center and Museum
http://www.sitinmovement.org/

Japanese American National Museum
http://www.janm.org/

K12Station – Library of K–12 Education Links
http://www.k12station.com/k12link_library.html

Kids.gov
http://www.kids.gov/

KidsHealth in the Classroom
http://classroom.kidshealth.org/

Meteorology
http://www.wxdude.com/

The Metropolitan Museum of Art, New York
http://www.metmuseum.org/

Minneapolis Institute of Arts
http://www.artsmia.org/

Minnesota Zoo
http://www.mnzoo.com/

MoMA | The Museum of Modern Art
http://www.moma.org/

Monterey Bay Aquarium
www.montereybayaquarium.org

Mount Rushmore National Memorial
http://www.nps.gov/moru

Museum of Fine Arts, Boston
http://www.mfa.org/

Museum of Science, Boston
http://www.mos.org/

Museum of Science and Industry, Chicago
http://www.msichicago.org/

NASA
http://www.nasa.gov/

NASA Kids' Club
http://www.nasa.gov/audience/forkids/kidsclub/flash/index.html

National Air and Space Museum
http://www.nasm.si.edu/

National Civil Rights Museum
http://www.civilrightsmuseum.org/home.htm

National Museum of African American History and Culture
http://nmaahc.si.edu/

National Museum of American History
http://americanhistory.si.edu/

National Museum of the American Indian
http://www.nmai.si.edu/

National Museum of Women in the Arts
http://www.nmwa.org/

National Music Museum
http://www.usd.edu/smm/

National Park Service
http://www.nps.gov/

National Weather Service Education Resources
http://www.nws.noaa.gov/om/edures.shtml

National Women's History Museum
http://www.nwhm.org/

National Zoo
http://nationalzoo.si.edu/

Native American Facts for Kids: Resources on American Indians for Children and Teachers
http://www.native-languages.org/kids.htm

New England Aquarium
http://www.neaq.org/index.php

New York Aquarium
http://www.nyaquarium.com/

Newseum
http://www.newseum.org/

Omaha's Henry Doorly Zoo
http://www.omahazoo.com/

Philadelphia Museum of Art
http://www.philamuseum.org/

Philadelphia Zoo
http://www2.philadelphiazoo.org/

Plimoth Plantation
http://www.plimoth.org/

Redwood National and State Parks
http://www.nps.gov/redw

Rocky Mountain National Park
http://www.nps.gov/romo

Saint Louis Art Museum
http://www.slam.org/

San Diego Zoo
http://www.sandiegozoo.com/

San Francisco Museum of Modern Art
http://www.sfmoma.org/

Shedd Aquarium
http://www.sheddaquarium.org/

Smithsonian Education
http://www.smithsonianeducation.org/

Smithsonian: Science and Technology
http://www.si.edu/Encyclopedia_SI/science_and_technology/

Space Center Houston
http://www.spacecenter.org/

Tennessee Aquarium
http://www.tennis.org/

United States Holocaust Memorial Museum
http://www.ushmm.org/

University of California Museum of Paleontology
http://www.ucmp.berkeley.edu/

The White House Historical Association
http://www.whitehousehistory.org/

Yellowstone National Park
http://www.nps.gov/yell

Yosemite National Park
http://www.nps.gov/yose

Zion National Park
http://www.nps.gov/zion

High-Frequency Words

High-Frequency Words	UNIT/WEEK
I	Start Smart Week 1
can	Start Smart Week 2
we	Unit 1 Week 1
the	Unit 1 Week 2
like	Unit 2 Week 1
a	Unit 2 Week 2
see	Unit 3 Week 1
go	Unit 3 Week 2
to	Unit 4 Week 1
have	Unit 4 Week 2
is	Unit 5 Week 1
play	Unit 5 Week 2
are	Unit 6 Week 1
for	Unit 6 Week 2
you	Unit 6 Week 2
this	Unit 7 Week 1
do	Unit 7 Week 1
and	Unit 7 Week 2
what	Unit 7 Week 2
little	Unit 8 Week 1
said	Unit 8 Week 1
here	Unit 8 Week 2
was	Unit 8 Week 2
she	Unit 9 Week 1
he	Unit 9 Week 1
has	Unit 9 Week 2
look	Unit 9 Week 2
with	Unit 10 Week 1
my	Unit 10 Week 1
me	Unit 10 Week 2
where	Unit 10 Week 2

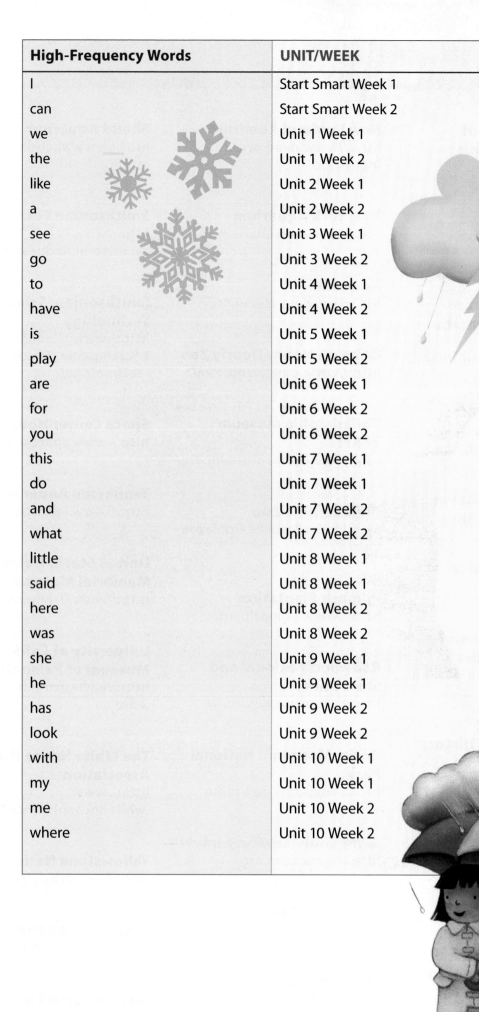

Oral Vocabulary

Week		Theme Words	Oral Vocabulary Card Words	
1	**A Rainy Day**	weather cloud	drizzle blustery chilly	weather cloud
2	**In the Yard**	season month	shiver mild warning	month season
3	**Bear Snores On**	experience hibernate	cozy clear retreat	hibernate experience

Language Transfers:

The Interaction Between English and Students' Primary Languages

Dr. Jana Echevarria
California State University, Long Beach

Dr. Donald Bear
University of Nevada, Reno

It is important for teachers to understand why English Language Learners (ELLs) use alternative pronunciations for some English words. Many English sounds do not exist or transfer to other languages, so English Language Learners may lack the auditory acuity to "hear" these English sounds and have difficulty pronouncing them. These students are not accustomed to positioning their mouth in a way the sound requires. The charts that appear on the following pages show that there is variation among languages, with some languages having more sounds in common and thus greater transfer to English than others.

For example, an English speaker may be able to pronounce the /r/ in the Spanish word *pero* ("but"), but not the /rr/ trill in *perro* ("dog"). The English speaker may also lack the auditory acuity to detect and the ability to replicate the tonal sounds of some Chinese words. Similarly, a Vietnamese speaker may have difficulty pronouncing /th/ in words such as *thin* or *thanks*.

Further, English Language Learners make grammatical errors due to interference from their native languages. In Spanish, the adjective follows the noun, so often English Language Learners say "the girl pretty" instead of "the pretty girl." While English changes the verb form with a change of subject (*I walk. She walks.*), some Asian languages keep the verb form constant across subjects. Adding /s/ to the third person may be difficult for some English Language Learners. Students may know the grammatical rule, but applying it consistently may be difficult, especially in spoken English.

When working with English Language Learners, you should also be aware of sociocultural factors that affect pronunciation. Students may retain an accent because it marks their social identity. Speakers of other languages may feel at a social distance from members of the dominant English-speaking culture.

English Language Learners improve their pronunciation in a nonthreatening atmosphere in which participation is encouraged. Opportunities to interact with native English speakers provide easy access to language models and give English Language Learners practice using English. However, students should not be forced to participate. Pressure to perform—or to perform in a certain way—can inhibit participation. In any classroom, teacher sensitivity to pronunciation differences contributes to a more productive learning environment.

Phonics, word recognition, and spelling are influenced by what students know about the sounds, word structure, and spelling in their primary languages. For example, beginning readers who speak Spanish and are familiar with its spelling will often spell short *o* with an *a*, a letter that in Spanish makes the short *o* sound. Similarly, English Language Learners who are unaccustomed to English consonant digraphs and blends (e.g., /ch/ and *s*-blends) spell /ch/ as *sh* because /sh/ is the sound they know that is closest to /ch/. Students learn about the way pronunciation influences their reading and spelling, beginning with large contrasts among sounds, then they study the finer discriminations. As vocabulary advances, the meaning of words leads students to the sound contrasts. For example, *shoe* and *chew* may sound alike initially, but meaning indicates otherwise. Students' reading and discussions of what they read advances their word knowledge as well as their knowledge in all language and literacy systems, including phonics, pronunciation, grammar, and vocabulary.

Phonics Transfers:
Sound Transfers

This chart indicates areas where a positive transfer of sounds and symbols occurs for English Language Learners from their native languages into English. This symbol (✔) identifies a positive transfer. "Approximate" indicates that the sound is similar.

Sound Transfers	Spanish	Cantonese	Vietnamese	Hmong	Korean	Khmer
Consonants						
/b/ as in bat	✔	approximate	approximate	approximate	approximate	✔
/k/ as in cake, kitten, peck	✔	✔	✔	✔	✔	✔
/d/ as in dog	✔	approximate	approximate	✔	approximate	✔
/f/ as in farm	✔	✔	✔	✔		
/g/ as in girl	✔	approximate	✔	approximate	approximate	
/h/ as in ham	✔	✔	✔	✔	✔	approximate
/j/ as in jet, page, ledge		approximate	approximate		approximate	
/l/ as in lion	✔	✔	✔	✔	✔	
/m/ as in mat	✔	✔	✔	✔	✔	✔
/n/ as in night	✔	✔	✔	✔	✔	✔
/p/ as in pen	✔	✔	✔	approximate	✔	✔
/kw/ as in queen	✔	approximate	✔		✔	✔
/r/ as in rope	approximate					✔
/s/ as in sink, city	✔	✔	✔	✔	✔	approximate
/t/ as in ton	✔	✔	approximate	approximate	✔	✔
/v/ as in vine	✔		✔	✔		
/w/ as in wind	✔	✔			✔	✔
/ks/ as in six	✔				✔	✔
/y/ as in yak	✔	✔		✔	✔	✔
/z/ as in zebra			✔			
Digraphs						
/ch/ as in cheek, patch	✔	approximate		✔	✔	✔
/sh/ as in shadow			✔	✔	✔	
/hw/ as in whistle					✔	✔
/th/ as in path	approximate		approximate			
/TH/ as in that	approximate					
/ng/ as in sting	✔	✔	✔	✔	✔	approximate

Sound Transfers	Spanish	Cantonese	Vietnamese	Hmong	Korean	Khmer
Short Vowels						
/a/ as in cat	approximate		approximate	✔	✔	
/e/ as in net	✔	approximate	approximate		✔	
/i/ as in kid	approximate	approximate			✔	
/o/ as in spot	approximate	approximate	approximate	approximate	approximate	✔
/u/ as in cup	approximate	approximate	✔		✔	✔
Long Vowels						
/ā/ as in lake, nail, bay	✔	approximate	approximate	approximate	✔	✔
/ē/ as in bee, meat, cranky	✔	approximate	✔	✔	✔	✔
/ī/ as in kite, tie, light, dry	✔	approximate	✔	✔	✔	✔
/ō/ as in home, road, row	✔	approximate	approximate		✔	
/ū/ as in dune, fruit, blue	✔	approximate	✔	✔	✔	✔
/yü/ as in mule, cue	✔	approximate			✔	
r-Controlled Vowels						
/är/ as in far	approximate	approximate				
/ôr/ as in corn	approximate	approximate				
/ûr/ as in stern, bird, suburb	approximate	approximate				
/âr/ as in air, bear						
/îr/ as in deer, ear						
Variant Vowels						
/oi/ as in boil, toy	✔	approximate	approximate		✔	✔
/ou/ as in loud, down	✔	approximate	✔	approximate	✔	✔
/ô/ as in law	approximate	✔	✔	approximate	approximate	✔
/ô/ as in laundry	approximate	approximate	✔	approximate	approximate	✔
/ôl/ as in salt, call	approximate	approximate			approximate	✔
/ü/ as in moon, drew	✔	approximate	approximate	✔	✔	✔
/ů/ as in look		approximate	approximate		approximate	✔
/ə/ as in askew			approximate		✔	

Phonics Transfers:
Sound-Symbol Match

Sound-Symbol Match	Spanish	Cantonese	Vietnamese	Hmong	Korean	Khmer
Consonants						
/b/ as in bat	✔		✔			
/k/ as in cake	✔		✔			
/k/ as in kitten	✔		✔	✔		
/k/ as in peck						
/d/ as in dog	✔		✔	✔		
/f/ as in farm	✔			✔		
/g/ as in girl	✔		✔			
/h/ as in ham			✔	✔		
/j/ as in jet, page, ledge						
/l/ as in lion	✔		✔	✔		
/m/ as in mat	✔		✔	✔		
/n/ as in night	✔		✔	✔		
/p/ as in pen	✔		✔	✔		
/kw/ as in queen			✔			
/r/ as in rope	approximate					
/s/ as in sink, city	✔		✔			
/t/ as in ton	✔		✔	✔		
/v/ as in vine	✔		✔	✔		
/w/ as in wind	✔					
/ks/ as in six	✔					
/y/ as in yak	✔			✔		
/z/ as in zebra						
Digraphs						
/ch/ as in cheek, patch	✔					
/sh/ as in shadow						
/hw/ as in whistle						
/th/ as in path			✔			
/TH/ as in that						
/ng/ as in sting	✔		✔			
Short Vowels						
/a/ as in cat			✔	✔		
/e/ as in net	✔		✔			
/i/ as in kid						
/o/ as in spot			✔	✔		
/u/ as in cup						

Sound-Symbol Match	Spanish	Cantonese	Vietnamese	Hmong	Korean	Khmer
Long Vowels						
/ā/ as in lake						
/ā/ as in nail						
/ā/ as in bay						
/ē/ as in bee						
/ē/ as in meat						
/ē/ as in cranky						
/ī/ as in kite, tie, light, dry						
/ō/ as in home, road, row						
/ū/ as in dune			✔	✔		
/ū/ as in fruit, blue						
/yü/ as in mule, cue						
r-Controlled Vowels						
/är/ as in far	✔					
/ôr/ as in corn	✔					
/ûr/ as in stern	✔					
/ûr/ as in bird, suburb						
/âr/ as in air, bear						
/îr/ as in deer, ear						
Variant Vowels						
/oi/ as in boil	✔		✔			
/oi/ as in toy	✔					
/ou/ as in loud						
/ou/ as in down						
/ô/ as in law						
/ô/ as in laundry						
/ôl/ as in salt	✔					
/ôl/ as in call						
/ü/ as in moon, drew						
/ u̇/ as in look						
/ə/ as in askew						

How to Use the Phonics Transfer Charts

To read and speak fluently in English, English Language Learners need to master a wide range of phonemic awareness, phonics, and word study skills. The Phonics Transfer Charts are designed to help you anticipate and understand possible student errors in pronouncing or perceiving English sounds.

1. **Highlight Transferrable Skills** If the phonics skill transfers from the student's primary language to English, state that during the lesson. In most lessons an English Language Learner feature will indicate which sounds do and do not transfer in specific languages.

2. **Preteach Non-Transferrable Skills** Prior to teaching a phonics lesson, check the chart to determine if the sound and/or spelling transfers from the student's primary language into English. If it does not, preteach the sound and spelling during Small Group time. Focus on articulation, using the backs of the small **Sound-Spelling Cards**, and the minimal contrast activities provided.

3. **Provide Additional Practice and Time** If the skill does NOT transfer from the student's primary language into English, the student will require more time and practice mastering the sound and spellings. Continue to review the phonics skill during Small Group time in upcoming weeks until the student has mastered it. Use the additional resources, such as the extra decodable stories in the **Teacher's Resource Book**, to provide oral and silent reading practice.

Teaching Supports for Students Transitioning from Spanish to English

The **Sound-Spelling Cards** have been created to assist you in working with English Language Learners. For example:

1. The dotted border on many of the cards indicates that the sound transfers from Spanish to English. On these cards, the same image is used in both English and Spanish (e.g., *camel/camello*). Therefore, students learning the sound in Spanish can easily transfer that knowledge to English.

2. Students whose primary language is not English will need additional articulation support to pronounce and perceive non-transferrable English sounds. Use the articulation photos on the backs of the Sound-Spelling Cards and the student-friendly descriptions of how to form these sounds during phonics lessons.

Sound-Spelling Cards

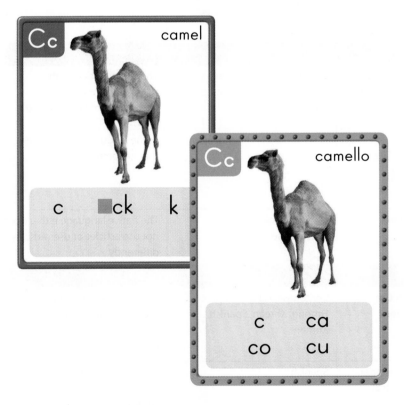

Transfer Skill Support

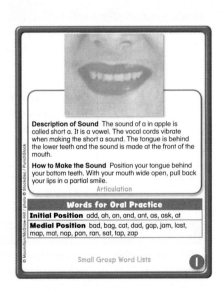

Description of Sound The sound of a in apple is called short a. It is a vowel. The vocal cords vibrate when making the short a sound. The tongue is behind the lower teeth and the sound is made at the front of the mouth.

How to Make the Sound Position your tongue behind your bottom teeth. With your mouth wide open, pull back your lips in a partial smile.

Articulation

Words for Oral Practice		
Initial Position add, ah, an, and, ant, as, ask, at		
Medial Position bad, bag, cat, dad, gap, jam, last, map, mat, nap, pan, ran, sat, tap, zap		

Small Group Word Lists

Articulation Support

Grammar Transfers:
Grammatical Form

This chart can be used to address common mistakes that some English Language Learners make when they transfer grammatical forms from their native languages into English.

Grammatical Form	Transfer Mistakes in English	Native Language	Cause of Difficulty
Nouns			
Plural Marker -s	**Forgets plural marker -s** *I have 3 sister.*	Cantonese, Haitian Creole, Hmong, Korean, Vietnamese, Khmer	Native language does not use a plural marker.
Countable and Uncountable Nouns	**Confuses countable and uncountable nouns** *the homeworks* or *the informations*	Haitian Creole, Spanish	Countable and uncountable nouns are different in English and native language.
Possessives	**Uses prepositions to describe possessives** *the book of my brother* as opposed to *my brother's book*	Haitian Creole, Hmong, Spanish, Vietnamese	Possession is often described using a prepositional phrase.
	Avoids using 's *dog my father* as opposed to *my father's dog*	Haitian Creole, Vietnamese, Khmer	A noun follows the object in the native language.
Articles			
	Consistently omits articles *He has book. They want dog not cat.*	Cantonese, Haitian Creole, Hmong, Korean, Vietnamese, Khmer	There is no article in the native language or no difference between *the* and *a*.
	Overuses articles *The English is difficult. The soccer is popular in the Europe.*	Haitian Creole, Hmong, Spanish	Some languages use articles that are omitted in English.
a/an	**Mistakes one for a/an** *She is one nurse.*	Haitian Creole, Hmong, Vietnamese	The native language either does not use articles or uses articles differently.
Pronouns			
Gender-Specific Pronouns	**Uses pronouns with the inappropriate gender** *He is my sister.*	Cantonese, Haitian Creole, Hmong, Korean, Spanish, Khmer	The third person pronoun in the native language is gender free, or the personal pronoun is omitted.
	Uses inappropriate gender, particularly with neutral nouns *The day is sunny. She is beautiful.*	Spanish	Nouns have feminine or masculine gender in the native language, and the gender may be carried over into English.

Grammatical Form	Transfer Mistakes in English	Native Language	Cause of Difficulty
Pronouns			
Object Pronouns	**Confuses subject and object pronouns** *Her talks to me.*	Cantonese, Hmong, Khmer	The same pronoun form is used for subject and object in the native language.
	Omits object pronouns *That girl is very rude, so nobody likes.*	Korean, Vietnamese	The native language does not use direct objects.
Pronoun and Number Agreement	**Uses the wrong number for pronouns** *I saw many red birds. It was pretty.*	Cantonese, Korean	The native language does not require number agreement.
Subject Pronouns	**Omits subject pronouns** *Mom isn't home. Is at work.*	Korean, Spanish	Subject pronouns may be dropped because in the native language the verb ending gives information about the number and/or gender.
Pronouns in Clauses	**Omits pronouns in clauses** *If don't do homework, they will not learn.*	Cantonese, Vietnamese	The native language does not need a subject in the subordinate clause.
Pronouns and Nouns	**Overuses pronouns with nouns** *This school, it very good.*	Hmong, Vietnamese	This is popular in speech in some languages. The speaker mentions a topic, then makes a comment about it.
	Avoids pronouns and repeats nouns *Carla visits her sister every Sunday, and Carla makes a meal.*	Korean, Vietnamese	In the native language, the speaker repeats nouns and does not use pronouns.
Pronoun *one*	**Omits the pronoun *one*** *I saw two dogs, and I like the small.*	Spanish	Adjectives can stand alone in the native language, but English requires a noun or *one*.
Possessive Forms	**Confuses possessive forms** *The book is my.*	Cantonese, Hmong, Vietnamese	Cantonese and Hmong speakers tend to omit the final *n* sound, which may create confusion between *my* and *mine*.

Grammar Transfers:
Grammatical Form

Grammatical Form	Transfer Mistakes in English	Native Language	Cause of Difficulty
Verbs			
Present Tense	**Omits -s in present tense, third person agreement** *He like pizza.*	Cantonese, Haitian Creole, Hmong, Korean, Vietnamese, Khmer	Subject-verb agreement is not used in the native language.
Irregular Verbs	**Has problems with irregular subject-verb agreement** *Tom and Sue has a new car.*	Cantonese, Hmong, Korean, Khmer	Verbs' forms do not change to show the number of the subject in the native language.
Inflectional Endings	**Omits tense markers** *I study English yesterday.*	Cantonese, Haitian Creole, Hmong, Korean, Vietnamese, Khmer	The native language does not use inflectional endings to change verb tense.
Present and Future Tenses	**Incorrectly uses the present tense for the future tense** *I go next week.*	Cantonese, Korean	The native language may use the present tense to imply the future tense.
Negative Statements	**Omits helping verbs in negative statements** *Sue no coming to school.*	Cantonese, Korean, Spanish	The native language does not use helping verbs in negative statements.
Present-Perfect Tense	**Avoids the present-perfect tense** *Marcos live here for three months.*	Haitian Creole, Vietnamese	The native language does not use the present-perfect verb form.
Past-Continuous Tense	**Uses the past-continuous tense for recurring action in the past** *When I was young, I was talking a lot.*	Korean, Spanish	In the native language, the past-continuous tense is used but in English the expression *used to* or the simple past tense is used.
Main Verb	**Omits the main verb** *Talk in class not good.*	Cantonese	Cantonese does not require an infinitive marker when using a verb as a noun. Speakers may confuse the infinitive for the main verb.
Main Verbs in Clauses	**Uses two or more main verbs in one clause without any connectors** *I took a book went studied at the library.*	Hmong	In Hmong, verbs can be used consecutively without conjunctions or punctuation.
Linking Verbs	**Omits the linking verb** *He hungry.*	Cantonese, Haitian Creole, Hmong, Vietnamese, Khmer	In some languages, *be* is implied in the adjective form. In other languages, the concept is expressed with a verb.
Helping Verb in Passive Voice	**Omits the helping verb in the passive voice** *The homework done.*	Cantonese, Vietnamese	In Cantonese and Vietnamese, the passive voice does not require a helping verb.

Grammatical Form	Transfer Mistakes in English	Native Language	Cause of Difficulty
Verbs			
Passive Voice	**Avoids the passive voice** *They speak English here.* *One speaks English here.* *English is spoken here.*	Haitian Creole	The passive voice does not exist in the native language.
Transitive Verbs	**Confuses transitive and intransitive verbs** *The child broke.* *The child broke <u>the plate</u>.*	Cantonese, Korean, Spanish	Verbs that require a direct object differ between English and the native language.
Phrasal Verbs	**Confuses related phrasal verbs** *I ate at the apple.* *I ate up the apple.*	Korean, Spanish	Phrasal verbs are not used in the native language, and there is often confusion over their meaning.
Have* and *be	**Uses *have* instead of *be*** *I have thirst.* *He has right.*	Spanish	Spanish and English have different uses for *have* and *be*.
Adjectives			
Word Order	**Places adjectives after nouns** *I saw a car red.*	Haitian Creole, Hmong, Spanish, Vietnamese, Khmer	Nouns often precede adjectives in the native language.
	Consistently places adjectives after nouns *This is a lesson new.*	Cantonese, Korean	Adjectives always follow nouns in the native language.
-er and -est Endings	**Avoids -er and -est endings** *I am more old than you.*	Hmong, Korean, Spanish, Khmer	The native language shows comparative and superlative forms with separate words.
-ing and -ed Endings	**Confuses -ing and -ed forms** *Math is bored.*	Cantonese, Korean, Spanish, Khmer	Adjectives in the native language do not have active and passive meanings.
Adverbs			
Adjectives and Adverbs	**Uses an adjective where an adverb is needed** *Talk quiet.*	Haitian Creole, Hmong, Khmer	Adjectives and adverb forms are interchangeable in the native language.
Word Order	**Places adverbs before verbs** *He quickly ran.* *He ran quickly.*	Cantonese, Korean	Adverbs usually come before verbs in the native language, and this tendency is carried over into English.
Prepositions			
	Omits prepositions *I like come school.*	Cantonese	Cantonese does not use prepositions the way that English does.

How to Use the Grammar Transfer Charts

The grammar of many languages differs widely from English. For example, a student's primary language may use a different word order than English, may not use parts of speech in the same way, or may use different verb tenses. The Grammar Transfer Charts are designed to help you anticipate and understand possible student errors in speaking and writing standard English. With all grammar exercises, the emphasis is on oral communication, both as a speaker and listener.

1. **Highlight Transferrable Skills** If the grammar skill transfers from the student's primary language to English, state that during the lesson. In many lessons an English Language Learner feature will indicate which skills do and do not transfer.

2. **Preteach Non-Transferrable Skills** Prior to teaching a grammar lesson, check the chart to determine if the skill transfers from the student's primary language into English. If it does not, preteach the skill during Small Group time. Provide sentence frames and ample structured opportunities to use the skill in spoken English. Students need to talk, talk, and talk some more to master these skills.

3. **Provide Additional Practice and Time** If the skill does NOT transfer from the student's primary language into English, the student will require more time and practice mastering it. Continue to review the skill during Small Group time. Use the additional resources, such as the grammar lessons in the **Intervention Kit** (K–3) or review lessons, in upcoming weeks.

4. **Use Contrastive Analysis** Tell students when a skill does not transfer and include contrastive analysis work to make the student aware of how to correct their speaking and writing for standard English. For example, when a student uses an incorrect grammatical form, write the student sentence on a **WorkBoard**. Then write the correct English form underneath. Explain the difference between the student's primary language and English. Have the student correct several other sentences using this skill, such as sentences in their Writer's Notebooks.

5. **Increase Writing and Speaking Opportunities** Increase the amount of structured writing and speaking opportunities for students needing work on specific grammatical forms. Sentence starters and paragraph frames, such as those found in the lessons, are ideal for both written and oral exercises.

6. **Focus on Meaning** Always focus on the meanings of sentences in all exercises. As they improve and fine-tune their English speaking and writing skills, work with students on basic comprehension of spoken and written English.

To help students move to the next level of language acquisition and master English grammatical forms, recast their responses during classroom discussions or provide additional language for them to use as they respond further. Provide leveled-language sentence frames orally or in writing for students to use as they respond to questions and prompts. Below are samples.

English Language Learner Response Chart

Beginning (will respond by pointing or saying one word answers)	**Sample Frames** (simple, short sentences) *I see a _____.* *This is a _____.* *I like the _____.*
Early Intermediate (will respond with phrases or simple sentences)	**Sample Frames** (simple sentences with adjectives and adverbs added, and compound subjects or predicates) *I see a _____ _____.* *The _____ animal is _____.* *There are _____ and _____.*
Intermediate (will respond with simple sentences and limited academic language)	**Sample Frames** (harder sentences with simple phrases in consistent patterns; some academic language included) *The animal's prey is _____ because _____.* *The main idea is _____ because _____.* *He roamed the park so that _____.*
Early Advanced (will begin to use more sophisticated sentences and some academic language)	**Sample Frames** (complex sentences with increased academic language, beginning phrases and clauses, and multiple-meaning words) *When the violent storm hit, _____.* *As a result of the revolution, the army_____.* *Since most endangered animals are _____, they _____.*
Advanced (will have mastered some more complex sentence structures and is increasing the amount of academic language used)	Use the questions and prompts provided in the lessons for the whole group. Provide additional support learning and using academic language. These words are boldfaced throughout the lessons and sentence starters are often provided.

Cognates

Cognates are words in two languages that look alike and have the same or similar meaning (e.g., *school/escuela*, *telephone/teléfono*) and can be helpful resources for English Language Learners. This list identifies some Spanish cognates for the academic language used during the lessons.

Students must also be aware of false cognates—words that look similar in two languages, but have different meanings, such as *soap* in English and *sopa* (meaning *soup*) in Spanish.

accent	*acento*	**context**	*contexto*
action	*acción*	**contrast**	*contrastar*
action verb	*verbo de acción*	**definition**	*definición*
adjective	*adjetivo*	**demonstrative**	*demostrativo*
adverb	*adverbio*	**denotation**	*denotación*
alphabetical order	*orden alfabético*	**description**	*descripción*
analogy	*analogía*	**dialogue**	*diálogo*
analyze	*analizar*	**dictionary**	*diccionario*
antecedent	*antecedente*	**direct**	*directo*
antonym	*antónimo*	**effect**	*efecto*
apostrophe	*apóstrofe*	**evaluate**	*evaluar*
article	*artículo*	**event**	*evento*
author	*autor*	**example**	*ejemplo*
cause	*causa*	**exclamation**	*exclamación*
classify	*clasificar*	**family**	*familia*
combine	*combinar*	**fantasy**	*fantasía*
compare	*comparar*	**figurative**	*figurativo*
complex	*complejo*	**fragment**	*fragmento*
comprehension	*comprensión*	**future**	*futuro*
conclusion	*conclusión*	**generalization**	*generalización*
confirm	*confirmar*	**generalize**	*generalizar*
conjunction	*conjunción*	**glossary**	*glosario*
connotation	*connotación*	**Greek**	*Griego*
consonant	*consonante*	**homophone**	*homófono*

idea	*idea*	**prefix**	*prefijo*
identify	*identificar*	**preposition**	*preposición*
illustration	*ilustración*	**prepositional**	*preposicional*
indirect	*indirecto*	**present**	*presente*
introduction	*introducción*	**problem**	*problema*
irregular	*irregular*	**pronunciation**	*pronunciación*
language	*lenguaje*	**punctuation**	*puntuación*
Latin	*Latín*	**reality**	*realidad*
myth	*mito*	**relationship**	*relación*
negative	*negativo*	**sequence**	*secuencia*
object	*objeto*	**singular**	*singular*
opinion	*opinión*	**solution**	*solución*
order	*orden*	**structure**	*estructura*
origin	*orígen*	**subject**	*sujeto*
paragraph	*párrafo*	**suffix**	*sufijo*
part	*parte*	**syllable**	*sílaba*
perspective	*perspectiva*	**synonym**	*sinónimo*
persuasion	*persuasión*	**technique**	*técnica*
phrase	*frase*	**text**	*texto*
plural	*plural*	**theme**	*tema*
possessive adjective	*adjetivo posesivo*	**verb**	*verbo*
predicate	*predicado*	**visualize**	*visualizar*
prediction	*predicción*	**vowel**	*vocal*

ELL ENGLISH LANGUAGE LEARNERS

The **English Language Learners** in your classroom have a variety of backgrounds. An increasing proportion of English Language Learners are born in the United States. Some of these students are just starting school in the primary grades; others are long-term English Language Learners, with underdeveloped academic skills. Some students come from their native countries with a strong educational foundation. The academic skills of these newly arrived students are well developed and parallel the skills of their native English-speaking peers. Other English Learners immigrate to the United States with little academic experience.

These English Learners are not "blank slates." Their oral language proficiency and literacy in their first languages can be used to facilitate literacy development in English. Systematic, explicit, and appropriately scaffolded instruction and sufficient time help English Learners attain English proficiency and meet high standards in core academic subjects.

Beginning

This level of language proficiency is often referred to as the "silent" stage, in which students' receptive skills are engaged. It is important that teachers and peers respect a language learner's initial silence or allow the student to respond in his or her native language. It is often difficult for teachers to identify the level of cognitive development at this stage, due to the limited proficiency in the second language. It is important to realize that these beginning students have a wide range of abilities in their first language. They are able to transfer knowledge and skills from their first language as they develop English and learn grade-level content. Beginning students include those with limited formal schooling: young students just starting school, as well as older students. Other beginning students have had schooling in their native language and are academically parallel to nativeEnglish-speaking peers.

The Beginning Student...

- recognizes English phonemes that correspond to phonemes produced in primary language;
- is able to apply transferable grammar concepts and skills from the primary language;
- initially demonstrates more receptive than productive English skills;
- produces English vocabulary to communicate basic needs in social and academic settings;
- responds by pointing to, nodding, gesturing, acting out, and manipulating objects/pictures;
- speaks in one-or two-word responses as language develops;
- draws pictures and writes letters and sounds being learned.

Early Intermediate

At this level, students are considered more advanced beginning English Learners. They are developing early production skills, but their receptive skills are much more advanced than their speaking ability. At this stage it is critical that the students continue to listen to model speakers.

The Early Intermediate Student...

- recognizes English phonemes that correspond to phonemes produced in primary language;
- is able to apply transferable grammar concepts and skills from the primary language;
- understands more spoken English than the beginning student;
- speaks in one- or two-word utterances;
- may respond with phrases or sentences;
- produces English vocabulary words and phrases to communicate basic needs in social and academic settings;
- begins to ask questions, role-play, and retell;
- begins to use routine expressions;
- demonstrates an internalization of English grammar and usage by recognizing and correcting some errors when speaking and reading aloud;
- increases correct usage of written and oral language conventions.

Intermediate

Students at this level begin to tailor their English language skills to meet communication and learning demands with increasing accuracy. They possess vocabulary and knowledge of grammatical structures that allow them to more fully participate in classroom activities and discussions. They are generally more comfortable producing both spoken and written language.

The Intermediate Student...

- pronounces most English phonemes correctly while reading aloud;
- can identify more details of information that has been presented orally or in writing;
- uses more complex vocabulary and sentences to communicate needs and express ideas;
- uses specific vocabulary learned, including academic language;
- participates more fully in discussions with peers and adults;
- reads and comprehends a wider range of reading materials;
- writes brief narratives and expository texts;
- demonstrates an internalization of English grammar and usage by recognizing and correcting errors when speaking and reading aloud.

Early Advanced

Students at this language proficiency level possess vocabulary and grammar structures that approach those of an English-proficient speaker. These students demonstrate consistent general comprehension of grade-level content that is presented.

The Early Advanced Student...

- applies knowledge of common English morphemes in oral and silent reading;
- understands increasingly more nonliteral social and academic language;
- responds using extensive vocabulary;
- participates in and initiates more extended social conversations with peers and adults;
- communicates orally and in writing with fewer grammatical errors;
- reads with good comprehension a wide range of narrative and expository texts;
- writes using more standard forms of English on various content-area topics;
- becomes more creative and analytical when writing.

Advanced

The student at this language proficiency level communicates effectively with peers and adults in both social and academic situations. Students can understand grade-level text but still need some English language development support, such as preteaching concepts and skills. While the English language proficiency of these students is advanced, some linguistic support for accessing content is still necessary.

The Advanced Student...

- understands increasingly more nonliteral social and academic language;
- responds using extensive vocabulary;
- communicates orally and in writing with infrequent errors;
- creates more complex narratives and expository writing in all content areas.

English Language Learner Profiles
Facilitating Language Growth

Beginning

Student's Behaviors	Teacher's Behaviors	Questioning Techniques
■ Points to or provides other nonverbal responses ■ Actively listens ■ Responds to commands ■ Understands more than he or she can produce	■ Gestures ■ Focuses on conveying meanings and vocabulary development ■ Does not force students to speak ■ Shows visuals and real objects ■ Writes words for students to see ■ Pairs students with more proficient learners ■ Provides speaking and writing frames and models	■ Point to the _____. ■ Find the _____. ■ Put the _____ next to the _____. ■ Do you have the _____? ■ Is this the _____? ■ Who wants the _____?

Early Intermediate

Student's Behaviors	Teacher's Behaviors	Questioning Techniques
■ Speaks in one- or two-word utterances ■ Uses short phrases and simple sentences ■ Listens with greater understanding	■ Asks questions that can be answered by yes/no ■ Asks either/or questions ■ Asks higher-order questions with one-word answers ■ Models correct responses ■ Ensures supportive, low-anxiety environment ■ Does not overtly call attention to grammar errors ■ Asks short "wh" questions	■ Yes/no (Did you like the story?) ■ Either/or (Is this a pencil or a crayon?) ■ One-word responses (Why did the dog hide?) ■ General questions that encourage lists of words (What did you see in the book bag?) ■ Two-word responses (Where did I put the pen?)

Intermediate

Student's Behaviors	Teacher's Behaviors	Questioning Techniques
■ Demonstrates comprehension in a variety of ways ■ Speaks in short phrases or sentences ■ Begins to use language more freely	■ Provides frequent comprehension checks ■ Asks open-ended questions that stimulate language production	■ Why? ■ How? ■ How is this like that? ■ Tell me about _____. ■ Talk about _____. ■ Describe _____. ■ What is in your book bag?

Early Advanced

Student's Behaviors	Teacher's Behaviors	Questioning Techniques
■ Participates in reading and writing activities to acquire information ■ Demonstrates increased levels of accuracy and correctness and is able to express thoughts and feelings ■ Produces language with varied grammatical structures and academic language ■ May experience difficulties in abstract, cognitively demanding subjects	■ Fosters conceptual development and expanded literacy through content ■ Continues to make lessons comprehensible and interactive ■ Teaches thinking and study skills ■ Continues to be alert to individual differences in language and culture	■ What would you recommend/why? ■ How do you think this story will end? ■ What is this story about? ■ What is your favorite part of the story? ■ Describe/compare _____. How are these similar/different? ■ What would happen if _____? ■ Why do you think that? Yes, tell me more about _____.

English Language Learners

Fostering Classroom Discussions

Strategies for English Language Learners

One of the most effective ways in which to increase the oral language proficiency of your English Language Learners is to give students many opportunities to do a lot of talking in the classroom. Providing the opportunities and welcoming all levels of participation will motivate students to take part in the class discussions. You can employ a few basic teaching strategies that will encourage the participation of all language proficiency levels of English Language Learners in whole class and small group discussions.

☑ WAIT/DIFFERENT RESPONSES

- Be sure to give students enough time to answer the question.

- Let students know that they can respond in different ways depending on their levels of proficiency. Students can
  - answer in their native language;
  - ask a more proficient ELL speaker to repeat the answer in English;
  - answer with nonverbal cues (pointing to related objects, drawing, or acting out).

> **Teacher:** Where is Charlotte?
>
> **ELL Response:** (Student points to the web in the corner of the barn.)
>
> **Teacher:** Yes. Charlotte is sitting in her web. Let's all point to Charlotte.

☑ REPEAT

- Give positive confirmation to the answers that each English Language Learner offers. If the response is correct, repeat what the student has said in a clear, loud voice and at a slower pace. This validation will motivate other ELLs to participate.

> **Teacher:** How would you describe the faces of the bobcats?
>
> **ELL Response:** They look scared.
>
> **Teacher:** That's right, Silvia. They are scared. Everyone show me your scared face.

☑ REVISE FOR FORM

- Repeating an answer allows you to model the proper form for a response. You can model how to answer in full sentences and use academic language.

- When you repeat the answer, correct any grammar or pronunciation errors.

> **Teacher:** Who are the main characters in the story *Zathura*?
>
> **ELL Response:** Danny and Walter is.
>
> **Teacher:** Yes. Danny and Walter <u>are</u> the main characters. Remember to use the verb <u>are</u> when you are telling about more than one person. Let's repeat the sentence.
>
> **All:** Danny and Walter <u>are</u> the main characters.

☑ REVISE FOR MEANING

- Repeating an answer offers an opportunity to clarify the meaning of a response.

> **Teacher:** Where did the golden feather come from?
>
> **ELL Response:** The bird.
>
> **Teacher:** That's right. The golden feather came from the Firebird.

☑ ELABORATE

- If students give a one-word answer or a nonverbal cue, elaborate on the answer to model fluent speaking and grammatical patterns.
- Provide more examples or repeat the answer using proper academic language.

> **Teacher:** Why is the girls' mother standing with her hands on her hips?
>
> **ELL Response:** She is mad.
>
> **Teacher:** Can you tell me more? Why is she mad?
>
> **ELL Response:** Because the girls are late.
>
> **Teacher:** Ok. What do you think the girls will do?
>
> **ELL Response:** They will promise not to be late again.
>
> **Teacher:** Anyone else have an idea?

☑ ELICIT

- Prompt students to give a more comprehensive response by asking additional questions or guiding them to get to an answer.

> **Teacher:** Listen as I read the caption under the photograph. What information does the caption tell us?
>
> **ELL Response:** It tells about the butterfly.
>
> **Teacher:** What did you find out about the butterfly?
>
> **ELL Response:** It drinks nectar.
>
> **Teacher:** Yes. The butterfly drinks nectar from the flower.

Making the Most of Classroom Conversations

Use all the speaking and listening opportunities in your classroom to observe students' oral language proficiency.

- Response to oral presentations
- Responding to text aloud
- Following directions
- Group projects
- Small Group work
- Informal, social peer discussions
- One-on-one conferences

The **English Language Learner Resource Book** provides Speaking and Listening Checklists to help you monitor students' oral language proficiency growth.

Support for Students with Dyslexia

Characteristics of Dyslexia

A student with dyslexia is a student who continually struggles with reading and spelling but displays an ability to learn when there are no print materials involved. Even though the student receives the same classroom instruction as most other students, he continues to have difficulties with reading and spelling.

Students identified with dyslexia often have difficulties in the following areas

- reading words in isolation
- decoding nonsense words accurately
- oral reading (slow and inaccurate)
- learning to spell

The difficulties in these areas are usually the result of student's struggles with:

- phonological awareness: segmenting, blending, and manipulating words
- naming letters and pronouncing their sounds.
- phonological memory
- rapid naming of the letters of the alphabet or familiar objects

Effective Instruction

To address the needs of a student with dyslexia, instruction should be delivered in small groups. The instruction should be explicit, intensive, employ multisensory methods, as needed, and be individualized. It should include instruction on:

- phonemic awareness that has students detect, segment, blend and manipulate sounds
- phonics, emphasizing the sound/symbol relationships for decoding and encoding words
- morphology, semantics and syntax
- fluency with patterns of language
- strategies for decoding, encoding, word recognition, fluency and comprehension

Resources:
The International Dyslexia Association Website: www.interdys.org
The Dyslexia Handbook: Procedures Concerning Dyslexia and Related Disorders (Revised 2007) Texas Education Agency, Austin, TX, Publication Number: GE8721001

ᴛreasures Reading and Language Arts Program

Treasures is a scientifically-based core program that offers sequential, explicit, and effective instruction in phonological awareness, phonics, morphology, fluency, vocabulary, and reading comprehension. Students are given many opportunities to practice and review these skills to help prevent reading difficulties before they begin.

 **INTERVENTION**

Weekly Small Group Lessons
Intervention Teacher's Editions

Tier 2 Instruction is provided in weekly small group lessons in the *Treasures* **Teacher's Editions**. These lessons provide targeted instruction in priority skills taught in the week. ***Tier 2 Intervention Teacher's Editions*** provide additional instruction for struggling students in the areas of phonemic awareness, phonics, vocabulary, fluency, and comprehension, grammar and writing.

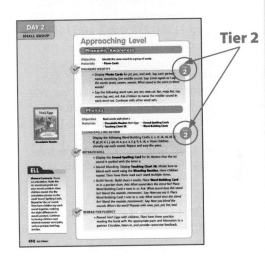

 **INTERVENTION**

Reading Triumphs
Intervention Program

Reading Triumphs provides intensive instruction. Explicit, sequential lessons delivered through clear instructional routines for all the key components of reading are embedded in the program. The "no assumption instruction" allows for both teacher and student success.

Index

A

Index

Key 1 = Unit 1

D

E

G

Genre

H

I

J

Key 1 = Unit 1

Index

M

Main idea and details, identifying. *See* **Comprehension strategies: main idea and details, identifying.**

Math, 8:1977

Media Literacy, 1:257, **2:**509, **3:**769, **4:**1029, **5:**1289, **6:**1549, **7:**1809, **9:**2329, **10:**2589

Mental images, creating. *See* **Comprehension skills: mental images, creating.**

Monitor Comprehension: reread. *See* **Comprehension skills: monitor comprehension: reread.**

Music, 1:S63, S81, S87

See also **Songs, rhymes, chants.**

N

National tests correlation charts. *See* **Assessment: unit assessment.**

O

On Level Options

comprehension, **1:**74, 80, 158, 164, 242, 248, **2:**326, 332, 410, 416, 494, 500, **3:**586, 592, 670, 676, 754, 760, **4:**846, 930, 1014, **5:**1106, 1190, 1274, **6:**1366, 1450, 1534, **7:**1626, 1710, 1794, **8:**1886, 1970, 2054, **9:**2146, 2230, 2314, **10:**2406, 2490, 2574

Decodable Reader, rereading the, **1:**74, 80, 158, 164, 242, 248, **2:**326, 332, 410, 416, 494, 500, **3:**586, 592, 670, 676, 754, 760, **4:**842, 926, 1010, **5:**1102, 1186, 1270, **6:**1362, 1446, 1530, **7:**1622, 1706, 1790, **8:**1966, 2050, **9:**2142, 2226, 2310, **10:**2402, 2486, 2570

high-frequency words, **1:**60, 74, 144, 158, 228, 242, **2:**312, 326, 396, 410, 480, 494, **3:**572, 586, 656, 670, 740, 754, **4:**832, 846, 916, 930, 1000, 1014, **5:**1092, 1106, 1176, 1190, 1260, 1274,

6:1352, 1366, 1436, 1450, 1520, 1534, **7:**1612, 1626, 1696, 1710, 1780, 1794, **8:**1872, 1886, 1956, 1970, 2040, 2054, **9:**2132, 2146, 2216, 2230, 2300, 2314, **10:**2392, 2406, 2476, 2490, 2560, 2574

Leveled Reader Lessons, **1:**74, 80, 158, 164, 242, 248, **2:**326, 332, 410, 416, 494, 500, **3:**586, 592, 670, 676, 754, 760, **4:**846, 852, 930, 936, 1014, 1020, **5:**1106, 1112, 1190, 1196, 1274, 1280, **6:**1366, 1372, 1450, 1456, 1534, 1540, **7:**1626, 1632, 1710, 1716, 1794, 1800, **8:**1886, 1892, 1970, 1976, 2054, 2060, **9:**2146, 2152, 2230, 2236, 2314, 2320, **10:**2406, 2412, 2490, 2496, 2574, 2580

phonemic awareness and phonics, **1:**60, 144, 228, **2:**312, 396, 480, **3:**572, 656, 740, **4:**832, 916, 1000, **5:**1092, 1176, 1260, **6:**1352, 1436, 1520, **7:**1612, 1696, 1780, **8:**1872, 1956, 2040, **9:**2132, 2216, 2300, **10:**2392, 2476, 2560

Pre-decodable Reader, rereading the, **1:**66, 150, 234, **2:**318, 402, 486, **3:**578, 662, 746

Online instruction. *See* **Digital learning.**

Oral grammar. *See* **Grammar.**

Oral language, 1:S7, S11, S21, S25, S31, S35, S39, S49, S53, S59, S63, S67, S77, S81, S87, 14, 22, 34, 44, 52, 58, 62, 98, 106, 118, 128, 136, 142, 146, 182, 190, 202, 212, 220, 226, 230, **2:**266, 274, 286, 296, 304, 310, 314, 350, 358, 370, 380, 388, 394, 398, 434, 442, 454, 464, 472, 478, 482, **3:**526, 534, 546, 556, 564, 570, 574, 610, 618, 630, 640, 648, 654, 658, 694, 702, 714, 724, 732, 738, 742, **4:**786, 794, 806, 816, 824, 830, 834, 836, 870, 878, 890, 900, 908, 914, 918, 920, 954, 962, 974, 984, 992, 998, 1002, 1004, **5:**1046, 1054, 1066, 1076, 1084, 1090, 1094, 1096, 1130, 1138, 1150, 1160, 1168, 1174, 1178, 1180, 1214, 1222, 1234, 1244, 1252, 1258, 1262, 1264, **6:**1306, 1314, 1336, 1344, 1350, 1354, 1356, 1390, 1398, 1420, 1428, 1434, 1438, 1440, 1474, 1482, 1504, 1512, 1518, 1522, 1524, **7:**1566, 1574, 1596, 1604, 1610, 1614, 1616, 1650, 1658, 1680, 1688, 1694, 1698, 1700, 1734, 1742, 1764, 1772, 1778, 1782, 1784, **8:**1826, 1834,

1864, 1870, 1874, 1876, 1910, 1918, 1930, 1940, 1948, 1954, 1958, 1960, 1994, 2002, 2014, 2024, 2032, 2038, 2042, 2044, **9:**2086, 2094, 2124, 2130, 2134, 2136, 2170, 2178, 2208, 2214, 2218, 2220, 2254, 2262, 2274, 2284, 2292, 2298, 2302, 2304, **10:**2346, 2354, 2376, 2384, 2390, 2394, 2396, 2430, 2438, 2450, 2460, 2468, 2474, 2478, 2480, 2522, 2544, 2552, 2558, 2562, 2564

See also **Vocabulary development: oral vocabulary.**

Oral Vocabulary. *See* **Vocabulary development: oral vocabulary.**

Oral Vocabulary Cards, 1:34, 118, 202, **2:**286, 370, 454, **3:**546, 630, 714, **4:**806, 890, 898, 974, 982, **5:**1066, 1150, 1234, 1242, **7:**1594, 1762, **8:**1854, 1930, 1938, 2014, **9:**2274, 2282, **10:**2450, 2458, 2542

P

Paired selections. *See* **Big Book of Explorations.**

Peer discussion starters. *See* **English Language Learners: grammar.**

Penmanship, 1:19, 103, 187, **2:**271, 355, 439, **3:**531, 615, 699, **4:**791, 875, 959, **5:**1051, 1135, 1219, **6:**1311, 1395, 1417, 1479, **7:**1571, 1655, 1677, 1739, **8:**1831, 1915, 1999, **9:**2091, 2113, 2175, 2197, 2259, **10:**2351, 2373, 2435, 2457

directionality (left-to-right, top-to-bottom), **1:**19, 103, 187, **2:**271, 355, 439, **3:**531, 615, 699, **4:**791, 875, 959, **5:**1051, 1135, 1219, **6:**1311, 1395, 1417, 1479, **7:**1571, 1655, 1677, 1739, **8:**1831, 1915, 1999, **9:**2091, 2113, 2175, 2197, 2259, **10:**2351, 2373, 2435, 2457

uppercase and lowercase letters, **1:**19, 103, 187, **2:**271, 355, 439, **3:**531, 615, 699, **4:**791, 875, 959, **5:**1051, 1135, 1219, **6:**1311, 1395, 1417, 1479, **7:**1571, 1655, 1677, 1739, **8:**1831, 1915, 1999, **9:**2091, 2113, 2175, 2197, 2259, **10:**2351, 2373, 2435, 2457

Personal response. *See* **Literary response; Talk/Sing About It.**

Key 1 = Unit 1

Q

Key 1 = Unit 1

Key 1 = Unit 1

"A Rainy Day" by Robin Nelson. Copyright © 2002 by Lerner Publications Company. Published by arrangement with Lerner Publishing Group, 241 First Avenue North, Minneapolis, MN 55401 U.S.A.

"Bear Snores On" by Karma Wilson, illustrated by Jane Chapman. Text copyright © 2002 by Karma Wilson. Illustrations copyright © 2002 by Jane Chapman. Published by arrangement with Margaret K. McElderry Books, an imprint of Simon & Schuster Children's Publishing Division.

"A Cloud," "Rain on the Rooftops," "Slip on Your Raincoat," "Window Watching," and "The Wind" from SING A SONG OF POETRY by Gay Su Pinnell and Irene C. Fountas. Copyright © 2004 by Gay Su Pinnell and Irene C. Fountas. Reprint by permission of FirstHand, an imprint of Heineman, a division of Reed Elsevier Inc.

"In The Yard" by Dana Meachen Rau, illustrated by Elizabeth Wolf.

Copyright © 2002 by Compass Point Books. Published by arrangement with Compass Point Books, a division of Coughlan Publishing.

"Little Dog" from MCGRAW-HILL BIG BOOK OF PHONICS RHYMES AND POEMS. Copyright © 2001. Published by The McGraw-Hill Companies, Inc. Used by permission. (Original Title: Little Pig)

"You'll Sing a Song and I'll Sing a Song" Words and Music by Ella Jenkins. Copyright ©1966 Ell-Bern Publishing Company.

Book Covers

A WINTER DAY. Reprinted by permission of HarperCollins Publishers.

ANIMALS IN WINTER. Reprinted by permission of HarperCollins Publishers.

CAPS, HATS, SOCKS AND MITTENS. Reprinted by permission of Scholastic, Inc.

LITTLE CLOUD. Reprinted by permission of Scholastic, Inc.

ONE HOT SUMMER DAY. Reprinted by permission of HarperCollins Publishers.

RAIN. Reprinted by permission of Random House, Inc.

SNOW ON SNOW ON SNOW. Reprinted by permission of Penguin Putnam Books for Young Readers.

THE WIND BLEW. Reprinted by permission of Simon & Schuster Children's Publishing Division.

TIME TO SLEEP. Reprinted by permission of Henry Holt and Company, LLC.

Photography Credits

All Photographs are by Ken Cavanagh or Ken Karp for Macmillan/McGraw-Hill (MMH) except as noted below:

xiii: Veer. 1561: Brad Perks Lightscapes/Alamy. 1645: Medioimages/PunchStock. 1729: Rich Reid/National Geographic/AGE Fotostock.

Acknowledgments

Use this page to record lessons that work well or need to be adapted for future reference.

Lessons that work well.

Lessons that need adjustments.

Use this page to record lessons that work well or need to be adapted for future reference.

Lessons that work well.

Lessons that need adjustments.

Teacher Notes

Use this page to record lessons that work well or need to be adapted for future reference.

Lessons that work well.

Lessons that need adjustments.